The Prosperity Paradox

Critical Frontiers of Theory, Research, and Policy in International Development Studies

Series Editors: Alfredo Saad Filho, Andrew Fischer, Giles Mohan, and Tanja R. Müller

Critical Frontiers of Theory, Research, and Policy in International Development Studies is the official book series of the Development Studies Association of the UK and Ireland (DSA).

The series profiles research monographs that will shape the theory, practice, and teaching of international development for a new generation of scholars, students, and practitioners. The objective is to set high quality standards within the field of development studies to nurture and advance the field, as is the central mandate of the DSA. Critical scholarship is especially encouraged, within the spirit of development studies as an interdisciplinary and applied field, with a classical focus on national and global processes of accumulation and structural transformation, and associated political, social, and cultural change. In this manner, the series seeks to promote a range of applied theory and empirics based on the analysis of historical development experiences, as was the methodological and epistemological strength of classical development studies.

Also in this series

The Aid Lab
Understanding Bangladesh's Unexpected Success
Naomi Hossain

Taken for a Ride
Grounding Neoliberalism, Precarious Labour, and Public Transport in an African Metropolis
Matteo Rizzo

Playing with Fire
Deepened Financial Integration and Changing Vulnerabilities of the Global South
Yilmaz Akyüz

Inclusive Dualism
Labour-intensive Development, Decent Work, and Surplus Labour in Southern Africa
Nicoli Nattrass and Jeremy Seekings

Developmentalism
The Normative and Transformative within Capitalism
Graham Harrison

Going Nowhere Fast
Mobile Inequality in the Age of Translocality
Sabina Lawreniuk and Laurie Parsons

Susceptibility in Development
Micropolitics of Local Development in India and Indonesia
Tanya Jakimow

The Prosperity Paradox

Fewer and More Vulnerable Farm Workers

PHILIP MARTIN

OXFORD
UNIVERSITY PRESS

OXFORD

UNIVERSITY PRESS

Great Clarendon Street, Oxford, OX2 6DP,
United Kingdom

Oxford University Press is a department of the University of Oxford.
It furthers the University's objective of excellence in research, scholarship,
and education by publishing worldwide. Oxford is a registered trade mark of
Oxford University Press in the UK and in certain other countries

© Philip Martin 2021

The moral rights of the author have been asserted

First Edition published in 2021
Impression: 1

Published in the United States of America by Oxford University Press
198 Madison Avenue, New York, NY 10016, United States of America

British Library Cataloguing in Publication Data
Data available

Library of Congress Control Number: 2020941708

ISBN 978-0-19-886784-5

Printed and bound in Great Britain by
Clays Ltd, Elcograf S.p.A.

Preface

This book examines a paradox: why do farm workers become more vulnerable as countries get richer? Around the world, the share of a country's workers employed in agriculture falls as per capita incomes increase, so that rising incomes and declining employment on farms are among the surest signs of economic development.

As agricultural employment shrinks, the most capable workers exit the farm workforce first. The "people left behind" to fill seasonal farm jobs are less capable of protecting themselves because they lack the skills and contacts needed to find nonfarm jobs, which usually offer higher wages and more opportunities for upward mobility than seasonal jobs on farms. In many countries, domestic workers are joined by legal and unauthorized migrants from poorer countries in the farm-labor market.

Agriculture was once the largest employer in almost every society, making agricultural history human history. The Industrial Revolution in the mid-eighteenth century accelerated outmigration from agriculture and prompted governments to regulate the wages and working conditions of workers employed in expanding nonfarm factories and services. Industrial and service workers eventually gained protections from workplace injuries, the right to form unions, and coverage under minimum-wage and related laws that regulate overtime pay, pensions, and other work-related benefits.

In a bid to protect and preserve family farms, agriculture was often partially or fully exempted from labor laws under the theory that agriculture was different from nonfarm industries. Many governments believed that small farmers could not cope with the labor laws that evolved to protect nonfarm workers, and that some hired farm workers wanted to become farmers, making them more interested in crop prices than in minimum wages. Even though few hired farm workers climb the agricultural ladder from hired hand to farmer, the notion that many hired workers are farmers-in-waiting continues to justify incomplete labor-law protections for farm workers.

This book is based on decades of research on farm employment, farm workers, and the farm-labor market. Its catalyst was a series of articles in the *Los Angeles Times* in December 2014 that documented poor conditions among the often indigenous workers employed on Mexican farms that export fresh fruits and vegetables to the US.[1] The *LA Times* series emphasized that many of the

---

[1] http://graphics.latimes.com/product-of-mexico-camps.

commodities produced by vulnerable farm workers in Mexico such as raspberries are purchased primarily by high-income Americans, suggesting that the desire of richer Americans for fresh berries contributes to farm-worker exploitation in Mexico.

Labor-market realities in Mexico's export-oriented agriculture are more complex than a simple story of berry exporters taking advantage of vulnerable workers. One major theme of the book is that when farmers run out of local workers, they turn to intermediaries such as labor contractors to recruit, transport, house, and often supervise migrant workers. Governments have found it difficult to protect the often vulnerable workers recruited by intermediaries.

Farm labor has long been a problem, but the hope of many reformers in the past was that the farm-labor problem would solve itself as mechanization eliminated farm jobs. There has been labor-saving mechanization in all agricultural systems, but expanded production of labor-intensive commodities such as berries means that, as fast as jobs are eliminated by mechanization in wine grapes, more farm jobs are created in another commodity, such as to pick strawberries and raspberries.

The prosperity paradox emphasizes the need for all stakeholders, employers, workers, buyers, and governments to understand that farm-labor problems will not wither away. Globally, a billion people, over a quarter of the world's 3.6 billion workers, are employed in agriculture, including 400 million who work for wages at least part of the year.[2] Many young people in rural areas realize that they will never get rich farming as their parents and grandparents did, prompting them to leave for urban areas. However, there are still enough people employed in agriculture to make farmer and farm worker the world's number-one occupation.

The US illustrates what is occurring in most rich countries. The average employment of hired farm workers, or the number of year-round equivalent jobs, has been stable at about 1.5 million over the past quarter century. There are more workers than jobs due to seasonality and turnover, and an estimated 2.5 million workers are employed for wages on US farms each year. The average educational level of all US workers rose from 12 to 14 years over the past quarter century, while the average educational level of US farm workers fell from 10 to 8 years as Mexican-born workers replaced US-born workers.

This paradox of more vulnerable farm workers in ever-richer countries justifies the call to do more to protect farm workers. Self-help farm-worker unions are usually ineffective because the most capable farm workers who could become union leaders are among the first to leave for nonfarm jobs. More labor law enforcement is needed, but labor inspectors often depend on complaints, and vulnerable workers rarely complain.

---

[2] Hired farm workers include workers who are hired for wages year-round and seasonally. Some may be small farmers themselves.

Buyer-imposed pressures on growers to protect workers may hold the most promise. Private labor-compliance programs that put pressure on buyers to require growers to abide by labor protocols, or fair-trade programs that create consumer demand for certified products that pay premiums to farmers that are used to support community projects, are too small to effectuate systemic change in agricultural labor systems. But all farmers share a desire to sell perishable commodities before they spoil, and buyers who refuse to purchase unsafe food or commodities produced in violation of labor laws could become effective agents to improve labor-law compliance.

The best protection for all workers at all times is the power to say no to bad jobs and exploitative labor because workers have alternative decent work options. Until there is decent work for all, the food-safety experience may offer the best model for improving protections for vulnerable farm workers. Buyers have been able to insist that farmers obey food-safety protocols in order to sell their produce, and they could also insist that farmers protect their employees if they want to sell perishable produce. The threat of not being able to sell fruits and vegetables may be the most powerful incentive for producers to obey protective labor laws.

This book reflects four decades of teaching and conducting research on farm-labor issues. My farm-labor work began in the optimistic 1970s, when Cesar Chavez and the United Farm Workers (UFW) were expected to negotiate contracts for most US farm workers and transform seasonal farm labor into a construction-style labor market of high wages when there was work and unemployment benefits during the off season. Instead, internal UFW struggles, a changing structure of agriculture, and rising unauthorized migration reduced the importance of unions in the 1980s. The new research questions involved who replaced US-born and legal Mexican-born workers, and whether unauthorized newcomers would remain farm workers or seek nonfarm jobs.

The 2008–9 recession marked a new era in US farm labor. Improved border controls made it more expensive to slip into the US illegally, and foreigners who eluded the Border Patrol wanted jobs that paid more than seasonal farm work. Farm-labor costs are rising, prompting a race in the fields between machines that replace workers, migrant guest workers, and imported fruits and vegetables. The "winning strategy" is likely to vary by commodity and to be shaped by trade and migration policies as well as technical progress and consumer acceptance of machine-handled produce.

Farm-labor systems are converging in rich countries under the influence of factors that range from concentration in supermarkets to fewer local workers available to fill seasonal farm jobs. The universal trend is ever more vulnerable workers. Details vary, but countries from Brazil to Spain are struggling to protect the ever more vulnerable workers who comprise the hired farm workforce.

I am indebted to many colleagues who enhanced and refined my understanding of farm labor, including Daniel Carroll, Agustin Escobar, Tom Hertz, Dan

Sumner, and Ed Taylor. Students, farm employers, farm workers, and others involved in hiring, supervising, and regulating the farm labor market were always a source of insight. The Giannini and Rosenberg Foundations have been longtime supporters of my farm-labor research, and this book benefitted greatly from the generous support of several other foundations that support the collection of reliable data and credible analysis for evidence-based policies. I am solely responsible for any errors and omissions.

My greatest thanks are to my family. My wife Cecily supported and sometimes accompanied me to visit farming systems from California to South Africa, my daughter Jessica harvested wine grapes in Moldova, and my son Ricky harvested strawberries in California. I am grateful for the wise counsel of my brother James.

Philip Martin
Davis, CA

Contents

III. MOVING FORWARD

List of Figures

List of Tables

List of Abbreviations

AEWR	Adverse Effect Wage Rate
AgJOBS	Agricultural Job Opportunity Benefits and Security Act
AHIFORES	Alianza Hortofrutícola Internacional para el Fomento de la Responsabilidad Social (International Fruit and Vegetable Alliance for the Promotion of Social Responsibility)
AJP	Agricultural Justice Project
ALP	Association of Labour Providers
ALRA	Agricultural Labor Relations Act
ALRB	Agricultural Labor Relations Board
AMHPAC	Mexican Association of Protected Horticulture
AMLO	Andrés Manuel López Obrador
ANC	African National Congress
ARMS	Agricultural Resource Management Survey
AWU	annual work unit
BEE	Black Economic Empowerment
BLS	Bureau of Labor Statistics
C&D	Canadian Occupations C and D
CAP	Common Agricultural Policy
CAW	Certified Agricultural Worker
CBA	collective bargaining agreement
CBSA	Canadian Border Services Agency
CFSAN	Center for Food Safety and Applied Nutrition
CIW	Coalition of Immokalee Workers
CNTE	Coordinadora Nacional de Trabajadores de la Educación
CONASUPO	National Company of Popular Subsistences
CONTAG	Brazil's National Confederation of Agricultural Workers
CROM	Regional Confederation of Mexican Workers
CRS	Catholic Relief Services
CSO	Community Service Organization
CTM	Confederation of Mexican Workers
DETRAE	Brazilian Division of Inspection for the Eradication of Slave Labor
DGI	Dirección General de Migraciones
DHS	Department of Homeland Security
DOL	Department of Labor
DOP	Protected Designation of Origin
EAA	Economic Accounts for Agriculture
EFI	Equitable Food Initiative
FARMS	Foreign Agricultural Resource Management Service
FDA	US Food and Drug Administration

FERME	Fondation des Entreprises en Recrutement de Main-d'œuvre Agricole Étrangère
FFP	Fair Food Program
FFSC	Fair Food Standards Council
FJC	Food Justice Certified
FLC	farm-labor contractor
FLO	Fair Trade Labeling Organization
FLOC	Farm Labor Organizing Committee
FLPG	Farm Labor Practices Group
FPAA	Fresh Produce Association of the Americas
FSMA	Food Safety Modernization Act of 2010
FSS	Farm Structure Survey
FTE	full-time equivalent
FWMA	Farm Workforce Modernization Act
FVH	fruits, berries, and nuts, vegetables and melons, and horticultural specialties from flowers to mushrooms
FWP	Fair World Project
FY	fiscal year
GAP	Good Agricultural Practice
HACCP	Hazard Analysis and Critical Control Point
HFWF	Hired Farm Working Force
HHS	US Department of Health and Human Services
HRDC	Human Resources Development Canada
ICE	Immigration and Customs Enforcement
ILO	International Labour Organization
IMF	International Monetary Fund
IMSS	Instituto Mexicano del Seguro Social/Mexican Social Security Institute
INEA	Italian National Institute of Agricultural Economics
INEGI	Mexican National Institute of Statistics and Geography
INPS	Italian National Institute of Social Security
IOM	International Organization for Migration
IRCA	Immigration Reform and Control Act
IRPP	Institute for Research on Public Policy
KNOMAD	Global Knowledge Partnership on Migration and Development
LAT	Los Angeles Times
LGMA	California Leafy Green Products Handler Marketing Agreement
LMIA	Labor Market Impact Assessment
MAPA	Brazilian Ministry of Agriculture
MOU	Memorandum of Understanding
MTE	Brazilian Ministry of Labor and Employment
NAFTA	North American Free Trade Agreement
NAICS	North American Industry Classification System
NAWS	National Agricultural Workers Survey
NEET	not in education, employment, or training
NGO	nongovernmental organization

NLRA	National Labor Relations Act
NLRB	National Labor Relations Board
NOC	National Occupational Classification
PICs	Pacific Island Countries
PMA	Produce Marketing Association
PRI	Mexican Institutional Revolutionary Party
QCEW	Quarterly Census of Employment and Wages
QCS	Quality Certification Services
RSE	Recognized Seasonal Employers scheme
SADER	Secretaría de Agricultura y Desarrollo Rural
SAGARPA	Secretariat of Agriculture, Livestock, Rural Development, Fishing, and Food
SAW	Special Agricultural Worker
SAWP	Seasonal Agricultural Workers Program
SAWS	Seasonal Agricultural Workers Scheme
SEDESOL	Mexican Secretariat of Social Development
SEGALMEX	Seguridad Alimentaria Mexicana
SNAP	Supplemental Nutrition Assistance Program
SNE	Mexican public employment service
SWP	Seasonal Worker Program
TIP	Trafficking in Persons
TVPA	Victims of Trafficking and Violence Protection Act
UF	United Fresh
UFCW	United Food and Commercial Workers
UFW	United Farm Workers
UNDP	United Nations Development Programme
USCIS	United States Citizenship and Immigration Services
USDA	United States Department of Agriculture
USMCA	United States–Mexico–Canada Agreement
WHM	working holiday maker
WIC	women, infants, and children

Prologue

Jose Martinez wakes up at 4 a.m. to ensure he is on time for a ride to the fields. After a quick breakfast, Jose meets his raitero, the driver of a van that carries seven workers to fields up to two hours away. Arriving at the orchard at 6:30 a.m., Jose will work four hours, take a break, work another two hours and, after a half-hour lunch and an afternoon break, quit at 3:30 p.m. and make the drive back to the mobile home he shares with his wife and three children. Jose earns California's 2019 minimum wage of $12 an hour or $96 for an eight-hour day, but was away from home thirteen hours. He paid $10 for the ride to and from work.

Juan Garcia used to pick fruit with Jose, but now works in a warehouse. Both Jose and Juan were born in Mexico, have seven years of schooling, and speak little English, but Juan's cousin finished high school and helped him to move from the fields to a warehouse job that pays the same $12 an hour as working in the fields but comes with benefits such as health insurance and a 401(k) savings plan. More important, Juan has a year-round job and has learned how to operate a fork lift, which means he will soon be earning $15 an hour. Juan's year-round job and higher wages encouraged him to move his family to a better neighborhood with better schools.

The experiences of Jose and Juan highlight a fundamental truth: the best way to help seasonal farm workers and their children to get ahead is to help them to find nonfarm jobs. Nonfarm workers earn more than farm workers, so moving out of farm work means higher incomes due to more hours of work and new opportunities for upward mobility, as when learning English and new skills leads to promotions. Picking peaches, on the other hand, offers few opportunities for upward mobility.

This is a book about farm workers, people employed for wages on farms. Farmers and their families are small businesses whose incomes are the difference between what they receive for the commodities they sell and the cost of producing them. Farm incomes fluctuate with weather, consumer demand, and many other factors, which is why many governments intervene in agricultural markets to bolster the incomes of farmers by setting minimum prices for the commodities they produce or providing direct payments to farmers.

Hired farm workers receive wages whether farm prices and incomes are high or low. Agriculture's biological production process means that most farm workers are employed seasonally, often less than the standard 2,000 hours a year that

The Prosperity Paradox: Fewer and More Vulnerable Farm Workers. Philip Martin, Oxford University Press (2021).
© Philip Martin.
DOI: 10.1093/oso/9780198867845.001.0001

reflects 40 hours a week for 50 weeks of work. Farm-worker wages are generally lower than nonfarm wages, and the combination of lower wages and fewer hours of work translates into lower incomes. In the US, the median hourly earnings of private-sector workers are $25 an hour, so a full-time worker earns $50,000 a year. Typical seasonal farm workers are employed 1,000 hours a year and earn $12,500, a quarter as much.

Most of the world's workers were employed in agriculture until the twentieth century, when economic development in industrial countries pushed and pulled farmers and farm workers into nonfarm jobs. Most small farmers and hired workers preferred the certainty and higher wages of nonfarm work to the uncertainties of seasonal farm work, explaining the rural–urban migration that occurred throughout the twentieth century in industrial countries and is occurring around the world in developing countries today. Many ex-farmers and their children prefer the grind of factory and assembly-line work to the vagaries of farming.[1]

Despite past and ongoing current rural–urban migration, agriculture remains the world's major employer, employing a quarter of the world's 3.6 billion workers in 2017 and two-thirds of all workers in low-income developing countries.[2] All countries with more than 50 percent of their workers employed in agriculture are poor,[3] and all countries with fewer than 5 percent of their workers employed in agriculture are rich.[4]

The share of a country's workers employed in agriculture declines as incomes rise, but the share of farm work done by hired workers increases as the number of people in agriculture declines and farm production becomes concentrated on fewer and larger farms. The total number of farms may remain stable, as with the roughly two million farms in the US over the past three decades, but an ever-smaller number of farms account for most farm output and employment. For example, the largest 10,000 US farms with expenses for farm labor in 2017

---

[1] China has developed the world's largest steel industry, producing over half of the world's steel in 2016 and offering ever more nonfarm jobs: "By 2016, China's steel industry employed about five million [workers]. That lifted workers from the brutal vagaries of farming to the security of state-owned mills that often provided free or subsidized housing, hospitals, and schools." Chuin-Wei Yap, 'How China Built a Steel Behemoth and Convulsed World Trade,' *Wall Street Journal*, December 24, 2018. http://www.wsj.com/articles/how-china-built-a-steel-behemoth-and-convulsed-world-trade-11545668295?mod=searchresults&page=1&pos=1.

[2] World Bank modeling of ILO data for 2017 reports that 26 percent of the world's workers were employed in agriculture, including 3 percent in high-income countries, 27 percent in middle income countries, and 68 percent in low-income countries. Five percent of workers in OECD countries, including Chile, Mexico, and Turkey, were employed in agriculture. https://data.worldbank.org/indi-cator/SL.AGR.EMPL.ZS?view=chart.

[3] The World Bank counted fifty countries with less than 5 percent or fewer workers employed in agriculture in 2017, led by Ireland and Korea with almost 5 percent and ending with the UK and Brunei with 1 percent.

[4] The World Bank counted fifty countries with 50 percent or more workers employed in agriculture in 2017, led by Burundi with 91 percent and ending with Myanmar with 50 percent.

accounted for over half of total farm labor expenditures.[5] Most of the two million US farms are small hobby and retirement operations, while the largest 10,000 farms account for over half of farm labor expenditures.[6]

The workers employed by these "factories in the fields" tend to be more vulnerable than the hired farm workers of the past for three reasons. First, the farm workers most capable of protecting themselves are the first to leave agriculture: their ambition, education, and contacts help them to find better nonfarm jobs. Second, as the domestic supply of farm workers decreases, farmers look further afield for workers, recruiting minorities left behind by economic growth, lawful guest workers, and unauthorized migrants. Hard-to-regulate contractors are often involved in the recruitment, transport, and housing of local minorities and foreign workers, increasing the vulnerability of the workers they bring to farms. Third, as a competitive industry with many small producers, agriculture is usually exempted from or treated differently from other sectors under labor laws and social-welfare programs. Children may be allowed to work on farms, there may be a separate and lower minimum wage for farm workers, and farm workers may not be eligible for or earn full access to employment-linked programs such as pensions, unemployment insurance, and workers' compensation for workplace injuries.

This combination of more vulnerable workers, intermediaries, and the incomplete farm-labor regulatory and social safety net coverage widens the gap between farm and nonfarm workers as per capita income rises. Take education. In 1979, the average US hired farm worker aged 25 and older had ten years of schooling, while the average American adult had twelve years, a two-year education gap (Whitener and Coltrane, 1981, p. 11). Today the NAWS reports that US crop workers average eight years of schooling, six years less than the average fourteen years of all US workers. The reason for this widening gap is straightforward: over the past four decades, Mexican-born workers have replaced US-born workers in the farm workforce.

When farm workers are found in poor housing, indebted to recruiters, or working under exploitative conditions, it may seem that agriculture has not

---

[5] The US has a stable 2.1 million farms, defined as places that sell $1,000 worth of farm commodities a year. The 2017 Census of Agriculture reported 513,100 US farms with a total $31.6 billion in farm-labor expenses for directly hired workers. The 10,000 US farms that each had farm-labor expenses of $500,000 or more collectively paid $16.5 billion or 52 percent of US farm-labor expenses. In 2015, the 65,300 farms that each had Gross Farm Cash Income of $1 million or more accounted for over half of cash farm income, while the half of farms that each had less than $10,000 in sales accounted for less than 1 percent of gross cash income. The median gross cash income of all US farms was $11,000, demonstrating that most farms have very low sales (McDonald et al. 2018).

[6] Some authors confuse the number of farms with their share of farm output. For example, Schmitt (1991) argues that the persistence of family farms in industrial countries suggests they must be efficient or they would have been replaced by larger farms with hired workers. Family farms can persist even if most farm output comes from larger farms that rely on hired workers.

broken links with a past that included slavery, serfdom, and other institutions that exploited farm workers.

Farmers often respond to reports of poor working conditions by emphasizing that they are offering jobs to workers who have no better job options, and that the "exploited workers" portrayed in media stories nonetheless return year after year to fill seasonal jobs. This may reflect a gap between college-educated reformers who have never done farm work and see all manual labor as exploitative and farmers producing essential food with the help of low-skilled workers who have few other options.

The best protection for all workers at all times is the power to say no to poor wages and exploitative working conditions. Workers can say no to exploitative farm jobs if they have better alternatives. However, empowering workers by ensuring they have alternatives leaves unanswered the question of what to do until more development offers options for farm workers. Chapter 7 and the Epilogue examine the most promising option, viz., enlist buyers of farm commodities to require farm employers to comply with farm-labor laws, just as they require producers to comply with food-safety laws and protocols.

PART I
AGRICULTURE AND
DEVELOPMENT

Part 1 analyzes the declining role of agriculture in developing economies with rising per capita incomes. Throughout human history, most people were employed in agriculture to produce food for themselves and a surplus for others, making access to land and the food produced on farm land a central concern of governments and the people they ruled. In many political systems, all land belonged to the king, the nobility, or the church, so land reforms that gave farmers secure rights to the land they farmed were a rallying cry of many peasant protests and some revolutions.

Chapter 1 shows how the share of workers employed in agriculture falls as per capita incomes rise. In almost all developing economies, the share of labor employed in agriculture is larger than the share of agriculture in GDP, which means that incomes are lower in agriculture than in the nonfarm economy. Lower farm incomes provide an incentive for farmers and farm workers to seek nonfarm jobs. Among those who remain in agriculture, the share of workers who are hired rises and the share who are farmers and family workers declines over time.

Chapter 2 explores the policy recommendations of economists who have grappled with the farm-labor prosperity paradox. Nobel Prize winner W. Arthur Lewis was born on the Caribbean island of St. Lucia, which had a traditional agricultural economy and a modern manufacturing sector. Lewis believed that the productivity of many farmers and farm workers in St. Lucia and other developing countries was close to zero, so that labor could move from farm to nonfarm jobs without reducing food output. Rural–urban migration, Lewis argued, would hold down manufacturing wages and generate the profits needed to expand the modern manufacturing sector, creating nonfarm jobs for ex-farmers and their children. The result would be a virtuous circle in which a shrinking agriculture meant upward mobility for individuals and economic development for the country.

The Lewis model led the neglect of agriculture in many developing countries. Governments focused on the nonfarm modern sector, offering incentives to attract foreign investment and using their limited resources to develop the infrastructure needed by foreign firms. Some governments subsidized food for urban workers so that manufacturers could hold down wages, and held down prices for farmers to reduce the cost of food subsidies. However, holding down prices for farmers discouraged investment in agriculture and hastened rural–urban migration.

Development advice has changed and now acknowledges the importance of improving agricultural productivity by providing credit, technical help, and other services to farmers. However, there is still a tendency for governments in rich countries to subsidize agriculture and governments in poor countries to tax agriculture. Developing country governments looking to the future see agriculture as a shrinking sector with a reservoir of low-skilled labor rather than a beacon pointing the way to a prosperous future.

1
Labor in Agriculture

Agriculture, the production of food and fiber on farms, is the keystone of the larger food system that includes industries such as the seed and fertilizer firms that supply production inputs to farmers and the farm-related output sector comprised of firms that process and distribute food and fiber to consumers. As the first and largest industry in most countries, agriculture's share of employment falls with economic development, which means that a country with a smaller share of workers who are farmers and farm workers has rising per capita incomes and is more urbanized.

Within agriculture, fewer and larger farms usually produce an ever greater share of food for growing populations at home and abroad. Most farming systems obey a version of the 80–20 rule: the smallest 80 percent of producers account for 20 percent of the value of farm output, while the largest 20 percent of producers account for 80 percent of farm output.

There are two major types of workers employed in agriculture: farmers and their (unpaid) family members, and hired workers. The incomes of farm families represent the difference between what they receive for the commodities they sell and the cost of producing them, while the earnings of farm workers reflect the wages they earn per hour, day, or week. The incomes of farm families, which often include members with nonfarm jobs, may be supplemented by government subsidies that set minimum prices for the commodities they produce or provide direct payments to farmers.

Farm incomes are higher than nonfarm incomes in most rich countries. In the US, for example, the median farm operator household income of $76,000 in 2017 was 24 percent higher than the median US household income of $61,400. Figure 1.1 shows that US farm incomes have been higher than nonfarm incomes since 1998.

Hired farm workers, on the other hand, have lower than average earnings. Figure 1.2 shows that the average hourly earnings of US hired farm workers have been 50 to 60 percent of the average hourly earnings of nonfarm workers over the past quarter-century. The fact that farm workers earn less per hour, and often work fewer than 2,000 hours a year, means that the *annual* earnings of seasonal farm workers may be only a quarter of those of nonfarm workers.

This pattern of higher-than-average incomes for farmers, and lower-than-average earnings for hired farm workers, is consistent across the richer industrial

The Prosperity Paradox: Fewer and More Vulnerable Farm Workers. Philip Martin, Oxford University Press (2021).
© Philip Martin.
DOI: 10.1093/oso/9780198867845.001.0001

Median farm operator household income compared with median
U.S. household income, inflation adjusted, 1991–2017

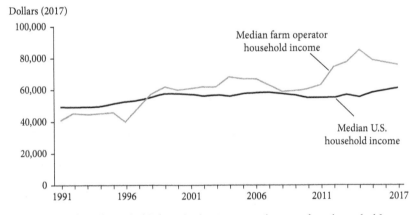

Figure 1.1 US farm households have higher incomes than nonfarm households.

Real wages for nonsuperviosry farm and nonfarm workers, 1990–2018

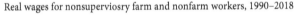

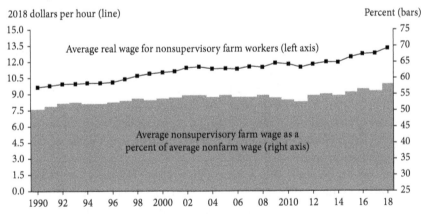

Figure 1.2 US hired farm workers have lower hourly earnings.

countries. The farm–nonfarm gap would be even wider if we considered wealth, the value of housing, land, and other assets owned by farm and nonfarm households. The average net worth of US farm households in 2016 was $1.6 million, far more than the average $97,000 for all US households.[1]

---

[1] Farm household net worth: https://www.ers.usda.gov/data-products/farm-household-income-and-characteristics/.

The Global Picture

A billion people around the world are employed in agriculture.[2] Most of the world's 600 million farmers produce food for their own families in developing countries or operate hobby and retirement farms in industrial countries. In developing countries, most family farms do not generate enough income to lift the family's income above the poverty line, while in industrial countries most hobby and retirement farms lose money farming but enjoy higher-than-average incomes due to earnings, pension payments, or savings.

Most of the world's 400 million hired farm workers are employed on the larger farms that account for most of the world's farm output.[3] The largest 10 to 20 percent of all farms account for two-thirds or more of the value of farm sales and a similar share of farm-worker employment. In all countries, hired farm workers are on the bottom rungs of the job ladder, earning less than nonfarm workers for reasons that range from low education and few skills to discrimination based on religion, ethnicity, and other grounds.

Figure 1.3 shows that the share of a country's workers employed in agriculture (orange line on y-axis), and the share of agriculture in GDP (green line on y-axis), decline as per capita GDP increases on the x-axis (World Bank Data, 2008). The figure highlights two important points. First, since the orange line is always above the green line, a higher share of a country's workers are employed in agriculture than the share of agriculture in that country's GDP, which means that farm incomes are lower than nonfarm incomes. For example, over 80 percent of Ethiopia's workers are employed in agriculture, but agriculture generates only 45 percent of Ethiopian GDP.

Second, the figure (1.3) shows that the share of workers employed in agriculture falls as per capita income increases, but at different rates in different countries. In China, the share of employment in agriculture declined gradually, from 80 to 65 percent between 1961 and 2003, as per capita GDP rose. The seemingly slow decline in the share of workers employed in Chinese agriculture may be misleading, since rural migrants who move to urban areas often maintain their household registration in rural areas despite having moved to cities.[4]

By contrast, the share of labor employed in agriculture in Nigeria fell from over 70 percent to less than 30 percent between 1961 and 2003 despite a stable

---

[2] The World Bank reported that 28 percent of the world's 3.6 billion workers were employed in agriculture in 2010.

[3] Pigot (2003) estimated that 35 percent of the then 1.3 billion people employed in agriculture were wage or hired workers, some 450 million. The hired labor share of people in agriculture has been climbing as the total number of people in agriculture declines.

[4] One reason for the slower decrease of labor in Chinese agriculture is the household registration system that ties many people to the place where they were born, so that many workers registered in agricultural villages may be working and living in urban areas.

Share of labor and GDP an agriculture

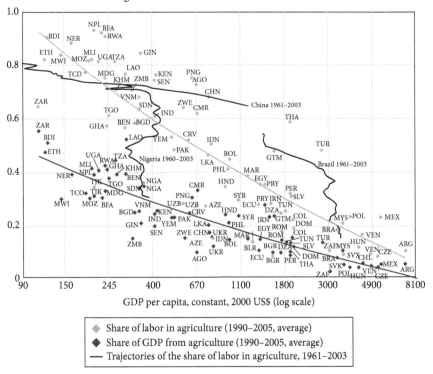

Figure 1.3 The share of labor in agriculture (y-axis) declines as per capita GDP rises (x-axis).

per capita GDP. In Brazil, there was a sharp drop from 55 percent of workers employed in agriculture in the 1960s to less than 40 percent by the 1980s as per capita GDP rose. However, the share of employment in Brazilian agriculture continued to decline even when GDP per capita stabilized in the 1990s.

The share of labor in agriculture is falling in most of the world's 200 countries. The International Labour Organization (ILO) estimates each country's share of employment in agriculture, industry, and services, and reported that agriculture's share of world employment fell from 43 percent in the early 1990s to 26 percent in 2017, down by 0.5 percent per year.[5] In Brazil, the share of labor in agriculture fell from 28 percent in the early 1990s to 10 percent by 2017, in China from over 50 percent to less than 20 percent, and in Nigeria from almost 60 percent to 35 percent.

As per capita income or GDP increases, more of those who are employed in agriculture are hired or wage workers. For example, the orange line in Figure 1.4 shows that there are very few hired workers in the poorest African countries,

[5] World Bank data: https://data.worldbank.org/indicator/SL.AGR.EMPL.ZS.

Share of wage workers in agricultural employment, %

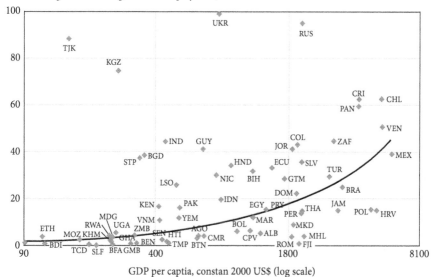

GDP per captia, constan 2000 US$ (log scale)

Figure 1.4 Share of hired farm workers (y-axis) rises with per capita GDP (x-axis).

where three-fourths or more of all workers are employed in agriculture. However, in Chile, Costa Rica, and Panama, 60 percent of those employed in agriculture are hired workers, reflecting the importance of large farms that export commodities from these countries.

The exception to the orange line showing a higher share of hired workers in countries with a higher per capita GDP is the ex-USSR. Poor countries such as Tajikistan and Kyrgyzstan as well as richer countries such as Ukraine and Russia have high shares of wage workers in agriculture, reflecting the privatization of previous collective farms that turned farmer-members of collectives into hired workers on private farms.

The panels in Figure 1.5 show different patterns across countries that reflect the importance of labor-intensive commodity exports. The left panel includes Malaysia, a major exporter of palm oil and rubber whose hired farm workforce includes many foreign guest workers. The number of farmers and family members is declining, raising the share of hired workers among those employed in Malaysian agriculture from 30 percent to 40 percent between 1990 and 2000. By contrast. Pakistan's four major crops—cotton, rice, wheat and sugar cane—are mostly consumed domestically. The share of hired workers in Pakistan's agricultural labor force remained at 10 percent between 1975 and 2000.

The middle panel of Figure 1.5 includes several Latin American countries that export fresh fruits and vegetables, such as Chile and Mexico. The share of wage workers in Chilean agriculture has been high for decades, and rose during the 1990s, while the share of wage workers in Mexican agriculture almost doubled

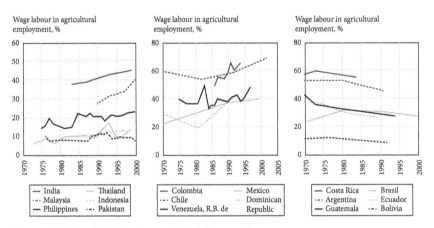

Figure 1.5 Trends in the share of hired farm workers are uneven.

between 1970 and 2000 from 20 to 40 percent. Chile is a major exporter of fresh fruit during the winter months in the northern hemisphere and wine and seafood year-round, while Mexico is the world's largest exporter of avocados and fresh tomatoes.

The third panel of Figure 1.5 includes several countries that have been major agricultural exporters for decades—Costa Rica, Argentina, Brazil,[6] and Ecuador. In these countries, the share of hired workers in agricultural employment fell after 1970, in some cases reflecting increased mechanization, as with Brazil's coffee and sugar sectors. Brazil is one of the few countries that is bringing new farm land into production, adding jobs for farmers and hired workers in the Amazon and midwestern cerrado areas.

Whither Farm Labor?

The world's labor force of 3.6 billion in 2017 increases by 40 million a year, but the share of workers employed in agriculture, a billion, is shrinking by about 5 million or half a percent a year. Within agriculture, the share of work done by farmers and members of their families is decreasing, while the share of farm work done by hired or wage workers is rising, reflecting the consolidation of farm production on larger farms that rely on hired labor.

There is no natural end in sight to the two dominant trends, viz., (1) a shrinking agricultural labor force that (2) includes a higher proportion of hired workers. Indeed, faster economic growth tends to speed exits from agriculture and raise the share of hired workers among those who remain employed in agriculture.

[6] Brazil's major agricultural exports are coffee, soybeans, beef, sugar cane, ethanol, and frozen chickens.

Higher nonfarm wages draw farmers and farm workers out of agriculture, promoting the consolidation of farming into fewer and larger units that rely on hired workers.

An agricultural system with relatively fewer farmers and more hired farm workers raises many challenges. As the number of farmers shrinks and incomes rise, governments often intervene to prop up farm incomes, so that over half of net farm income in Japan, Norway, and Switzerland represents government subsidies. The OECD reports the producer support estimate for each industrial country, which is the percentage of gross farm receipts that are provided by governments and consumers to farmers. In 2018, almost 47 percent of farm income in Japan was provided by the government and consumers, in Norway 62 percent, and in Switzerland 54 percent.[7]

In poorer countries, by contrast, governments often tax farmers by licensing only one buyer of commodities such as cotton or cocoa. This buyer may be a government agency or a private firm, and it often offers farmers a lower-than-world price for their commodities and then sells them for the higher world price, taxing farmers by keeping the difference. Farmers with no contacts or transportation to other buyers have no choice but to sell to the government-designated buyer.

Some governments allow monopolies on farm inputs as well, licensing only one firm or agency to import seed, fertilizers, and chemicals, or equipment, and permitting this importer to charge farmers higher-than-world prices. The OECD reported that the producer support estimate for India was minus 6 percent in 2018, meaning that farm incomes would have been 6 percent higher without government intervention, and minus 11 percent in Vietnam.

The net result of rich-country governments subsidizing farmers and poor-country governments taxing farmers is to encourage farmers in rich countries to remain in agriculture and to encourage farmers in poor countries to leave agriculture. Farmers in rich countries often announce that they are the third, fourth, or fifth generation to operate a particular farm, while youth who grow up on farms in developing countries are often the first in their families to seek nonfarm opportunities.

Farm workers have lower than average wages in both industrial and developing countries. The ILO (Pigot, 2003) emphasizes that farm work is often associated with violations of core labor standards, such as prohibitions on child labor. For example, the ILO estimated that 71 percent of the world's 152 million child laborers aged 5 to 17 are employed in agriculture.[8]

In industrial countries, farmers have long relied on workers who could not find nonfarm jobs to fill seasonal farm jobs, paying them only when they worked, and assuming there will always be a pool of such workers available. Some

[7] See OECD Agricultural Support: https://data.oecd.org/agrpolicy/agricultural-support.htm.
[8] https://www.ilo.org/global/topics/child-labour/lang--en/index.htm.

rich-country farmers hire guest workers from poorer countries who can earn more in several months abroad than they could earn in a year at home. Farmers dependent on seasonal guest workers often emphasize that richer countries must import workers from poorer countries to harvest food, or import food from poorer countries where wages are lower.

In developing countries, most hired farm workers are also employed only seasonally. Many are local workers who would otherwise be housewives or small farmers, but some are internal migrants from poorer areas of the country, as with Mexicans who have small farms in mountainous areas in southern states and migrate north to large farms to harvest crops for three to six months. As production and harvest seasons become longer, in part because many of Mexico's labor-intensive crops are produced with protected culture structures such as plastic-covered metal hoops, some workers settle near their workplaces, a process of internal migration that leads to population growth in richer farming areas and depopulation in poorer areas.

Some countries that were previously colonies have plantations, such as tea, rubber, or palm-oil enterprises, that employed and housed local or migrant workers. The British overseers of Malaysia's colonial-era rubber and palm-oil plantations imported Chinese and Indian workers who were housed on the plantations where they worked. Since independence in the 1960s, Malaysia's plantations rely more on Bangladeshi and Indonesian guest workers to fill plantation jobs, many of whom are supplied by contractors.

Plantation workers in "breakfast commodities" such as bananas, coffee, sugar, and tea are sometimes among their countries' working elite, receiving relatively high wages and provided with on-plantation housing, education, and medical services. Plantations that house families can also facilitate child labor. For example, Indian tea plantations typically allow children to work alongside their parents until age 12, after which they are allowed to work for five hours instead of eight hours for half the adult wage until age 16 (Pigot, 2003). Some 50,000 children were registered among the 670,000 workers employed on Assam tea plantations in India in 1991.

Some multinational marketers of breakfast commodities buy from growers who have replaced year-round workers who had housing, schools and other amenities on the plantation with men and women who are hired seasonally and offered few or no benefits. Pigot (2003) reported that the state of Maharashtra in southwestern India, which includes Mumbai (Bombay), had a million cane cutters to supply cane to 150 sugar mills. Sugar mills were privatized in the 1990s, and many sold or leased their plantations to "outgrowers" who stopped providing on-farm housing and services to hired cane cutters.

In some new export crops, such as flowers in Tanzania, Kenya, and Colombia, or Chile's export-oriented fruit industry, seasonal workers are often women. Some are hired directly by export farms, while others are organized into crews and brought to farms by farm-labor contractors. In countries that require employers to provide benefits to year-round workers, employers may make their employees seasonal via periodic layoffs, so that workers may be employed almost year-round but do not receive the benefits associated with year-round employment.

The International Union of Food, Agriculture, Hotel, Restaurant, Catering, Tobacco and Allied Workers' Associations (http://www.iuf.org/) aims to help unions that represent food-related workers to improve wages and working conditions. The IUF had only European affiliates until 1950, and claimed 430 member organizations in 130 countries in 2017. Many of the campaigns mounted by IUF member unions try to help workers employed in food processing firms and hotel chains. The IUF's farm-oriented unions may include both farmers and farm workers. For example, Brazil's National Confederation of Agricultural Workers (CONTAG) has 4,000 member unions that represent 20 million rural farmers and workers in a country where a million hired farm workers have formal sector jobs.[9]

---

[9] http://www.contag.org.br/.

2
Development and Rural–Urban Migration

Economic development is associated with higher per capita incomes, a declining share of workers employed in agriculture, and a higher share of workers employed in industry and services. In the world's 30-plus rich countries, the share of workers employed in agriculture is less than 5 percent of the workforce. In the world's 170 developing countries, the share of workers employed in agriculture averages 45 percent, and is over half in the 47 least-developed countries that range from Bangladesh to Zambia. There are no exceptions to the rule that a small share of workers in agriculture signifies a rich country, while a large share of workers in agriculture signifies a poor country.

Productivity and wages are lower in rural agriculture than in urban industry and services, providing a supply push that encourages farmers and their families to move from rural to urban areas. There may also be urban pull forces, including the availability of educational institutions that attract rural youth and more opportunities for upward mobility in cities. The question is whether governments should influence the movement of labor out of agriculture, and how they should deal with the changing structure of agriculture, the shift from mostly small and medium-sized farms to the fewer and larger farms that remain after large-scale rural–urban migration.

Lewis and Todaro

W. Arthur Lewis, winner of the 1979 Nobel Prize in economics, developed a dual-sector model of agriculture and industry that encouraged governments to accelerate the movement of labor out of traditional agriculture in order to generate the profits and capital needed to expand the modern nonfarm economy (Lewis, 1954). Lewis assumed there was unproductive labor in subsistence agriculture that could be attracted to industry, where wages are higher because urban workers have access to capital that increases their productivity.

Lewis believed that rural–urban migration could supply a continuing stream of workers to industry and hold down wages in manufacturing, allowing factories to make profits and reinvest them to create nonfarm jobs at a faster pace.[1] Lewis

---

[1] Lewis argued that the marginal product of labor in agriculture was zero or negative, that is, an additional farm worker led to no more farm output or less farm output, as when too many workers

The Prosperity Paradox: Fewer and More Vulnerable Farm Workers. Philip Martin, Oxford University Press (2021).
© Philip Martin.
DOI: 10.1093/oso/9780198867845.001.0001

expected food production to remain unchanged despite rural–urban migration because redundant farm workers would not be missed in agriculture, so farm labor could be transferred to the modern manufacturing sector with no loss of food output.

Lewis recognized that poor countries lacked the capital needed to raise worker productivity and wages (Gollin, 2014). Lewis believed that low farm wages could help to generate this missing capital by holding down factory wages via rural–urban migration, generating the factory profits needed to fuel industrial expansion and to create more nonfarm jobs. Lewis pictured a virtuous circle: the fewer farmers who remain in rural areas maintain the supply of food, rural–urban migration keeps manufacturing wages low, and manufacturers invest their profits to expand nonfarm production and employment.

Ever-fewer farmers also earn some profits and invest in machinery to raise farm productivity to feed the growing population, continuing the virtuous circle. Eventually, economies reach the Lewis turning point, when the productivity of labor and wages are equal in agriculture and manufacturing. Rural–urban migration stops because wages are the same in the farm and nonfarm sectors.

The Lewis model encouraged governments to favor industry over agriculture. This seemed natural to governments located in the growing capital cities associated with modernity.[2] One way to keep city residents satisfied was to ensure that they had plentiful and cheap food, which meant low prices for farmers and perhaps food subsidies to allow manufacturers and other urban employers to hold down wages. However, the low farm prices needed for food subsidies reduced the incentive for farmers to invest, slowing the equalization of productivity and wages between the farm and nonfarm sectors that was expected to end rural–urban migration.

Subsequent research found that Lewis's assumptions did not always hold. There was no surplus army of farm labor in many countries, many farm workers had trouble making a seamless transition from agriculture to industry, and government neglect of agriculture made it very hard to encourage the investment needed to improve agricultural productivity, increase food production, and raise farm income and wages. Within traditional or subsistence agriculture, there was considerable variation in incomes.

Michael Todaro (1969) tackled a problem that Lewis did not anticipate: rural–urban migration continued even though many rural–urban migrants could not find jobs in urban areas. Todaro noted that nonfarm wages were higher than

meant socializing rather than working. Workers survive even if they do not contribute to more farm production because of sharing within families and villages.

[2] Lewis recognized that there could be modern commercial agriculture that relied on capital alongside traditional subsistence agriculture that depended mostly on animal and human power. Commercial agriculture would be part of the modern sector in a Lewis model.

farm wages, and that rural–urban migrants knew that they had a chance, a probability, of finding a higher wage nonfarm job if they were physically in cities. The presence of foreign firms, unions, and minimum wages in cities made some nonfarm wages higher than the marginal product of labor of employed workers, that is, workers may be paid $20 a day when the value of what they contributed to the firm was $15.

Even with unemployment in cities, expected earnings for rural–urban migrants could be higher than if they remained in agriculture. For example, if the city wage was $20 a day and there was a 50-percent chance of getting a city job, expected earnings would be $10, higher than the $5 a day wage in agriculture. Under these conditions, people move to cities and hope to at least double their earnings, even if they suffer spells of unemployment.

Todaro's model explains why many cities in developing countries have slums of rural–urban migrants seeking jobs, and why government make-work schemes aimed at reducing unemployment in cities may instead increase the number of jobless workers due to more rural–urban migrants. For example, the Kenyan government in the 1960s tried to reduce unemployment in Nairobi by using government funds to add 15 percent more jobs. Instead of eliminating unemployment, the unemployment rate rose as more people arrived from rural areas seeking higher-wage urban jobs.

There have been many refinements of the Todaro model. Rural residents with friends and relatives who are employed in cities have a higher probability of getting an urban job than rural residents who move to cities without a network to help them navigate an unfamiliar urban labor market. Rural residents with more education have better prospects in cities, explaining why improving education in rural areas can speed outmigration. Young people with few assets in rural areas may treat movement to cities as an investment in potentially higher earnings, while older migrants who own a house or land in rural areas may stay put. Social networks, education, and age are some of the variables that affect who moves and how rural–urban migrants fare in cities.

Todaro's model also explains why the slums surrounding cities in developing countries continue to grow despite poor housing and widespread underemployment. So long as urban wages remain higher than rural wages, and there is some chance for rural–urban migrants to earn these higher wages, rural residents are drawn to the cities. Network and individual characteristics influence exactly who moves and where they go, leading to a universal rule: young and better-educated rural residents with friends or relatives in cities are most likely to become rural–urban migrants.

The Lewis and Todaro models assume that people move from rural to urban areas to earn higher wages. There are also other reasons to leave rural areas. These range from the personal, such as marriage or education, to youth wanting new experiences away from villages where everyone knows everything about their neighbors. There can be risk and insurance reasons to have some family members in cities and some in rural areas, so that, when crops fail, rural family members still have some income via remittances. When the urban job seeker loses his or her job, he or she can get support from home or return home.

What is the best policy to manage rural–urban migration? The year 2007 marked the first time in human history that more people lived in urban than in rural areas. Rural–urban migration is expected to continue, so that by 2030 two-thirds of the world's people are projected to live in cities.

Half of the residents of developing countries, and three-fourths of residents of industrial countries, lived in cities in 2013, up from 30 percent in 1980. The world has 47 megacities, each with more than 10 million people, led by Tokyo with 38 million. Most megacities are in developing countries, including Jakarta with 32 million residents, Delhi with 27 million, and Manila with 24 million. These megacities are surrounded by slums and shantytowns that include large numbers of recently arrived rural residents.[3]

Nobel Prize-winning economist Theodore Schultz considered the challenge of managing rural–urban migration in the context of both the US and developing countries. Instead of Lewis-style policies that encouraged rural–urban migration by prioritizing industry over agriculture, Schultz argued that the best policy was to promote education and good health in rural areas so that, when rural people move to cities, they can take advantage of opportunities there.[4]

Schultz criticized food aid to developing countries, noting that free food depressed prices for local farmers and did nothing to prepare ex-farmers and their families for life in cities. In this way, Schultz was the opposite of Lewis, emphasizing that farmers could raise their productivity and incomes with the correct incentives. Lewis, on the other hand, saw farmers and their families as a reserve army of workers for modern industry.

Agricultural Changes

Lewis, Todaro, Schultz, and others who sought to understand the role of farm labor in economic development stress the transition economies undergo as they change from having most people employed in agriculture to having most people

---

[3] Lagos, Nigeria, exemplifies the challenges of megacities in developing countries. A city of 300,000 in 1950 and over 18 million today, Lagos may be the world's largest city by 2050, when it is projected to have over 40 million residents. Nigeria's population is growing rapidly, and the country could surpass the US as the world's third most populous country, with 400 million residents by 2050.

[4] Schultz emphasized that the fast recovery of Germany and Japan was due to their well-educated populations being able to quickly adapt to postwar conditions. Schultz won the Nobel Prize in 1979, along with W. Arthur Lewis.

employed in nonfarm jobs. The process of industrialization and urbanization has attracted even more study.

The first phase of industrialization and urbanization typically features labor-intensive mass production in factories. As wages rise, machines replace workers in factories, and ex-factory workers find jobs in the service sector of the economy rather than return to agriculture. Urban societies often develop social safety nets to care for those who are laid off and cannot find new jobs.

As societies industrialize, government attention shifts from rural areas to the cities where most residents live. The sunrise industries and services powering the future are typically in cities, and sunset industries such as agriculture draw less research or policy attention. The farming sector changes as it shrinks in overall importance in several important ways, including size structure, capital intensity, and who does farm work.

Land is the fundamental input needed to produce food and fiber, and societies developed different mechanisms to allocate and control land. In most European countries, kings, nobles, and churches owned land, and laws and customs required peasants who lived on feudal manors to work and fight for their lord in exchange for protection and the right to farm their own plot. Many of the Europeans who migrated to the Americas and Australia in the 1700s and 1800s were attracted by free land, something few peasants could hope to obtain in Europe.

Customs varied across countries, but land was often inherited by the first-born son or subdivided between sons, so that plots could become ever smaller as populations grew. Farming ever-smaller plots with limited knowledge and capital to improve productivity meant ever-lower incomes and vulnerability to famine and starvation if crops failed. In many European countries, emigration and urbanization allowed land to be consolidated into fewer and larger farms whose operators could invest to increase productivity. Some of these larger farms became too large for farmers and their families to operate, necessitating the hiring of workers.

Other farms began as large operations, and have long depended on slaves or hired workers. Sugar plantations in Brazil and the Caribbean were begun because slaves were available to harvest sugar cane, and coffee, tea, palm-oil, rubber, and other plantation farms relied first on indentured servants and later on hired workers who lived on the farm where they worked. Codes were developed to regulate the treatment of indentured servants, workers who agreed to work for several years to repay the cost of their transportation to the plantation. After ex-colonies became independent countries, many governments enacted laws that required plantations to pay minimum wages and to provide schooling and health care to plantation employees and their families.

This tradition of regulating labor conditions in only parts of agriculture continues in many developing countries. Export-oriented agriculture is like plantation agriculture in the sense that there is often foreign capital involved in developing large farms, hired workers do most of the work, and there are worries that foreigners are once again taking advantage of poor people in poor countries. For these reasons, many developing countries have labor laws that apply to only some of their farming sectors, typically those that hire workers to produce commodities that are exported.

Family-operated farms have also changed as fewer and larger farms account for a rising share of output. Many farm families have both owned and rented land and use family labor to operate the machinery needed for large acreages of grain. Farm families in Midwestern US states plant large acreages of corn, soybeans, and wheat, and sometimes rely on custom harvesters who bring workers and equipment to their farms to harvest crops.

Some sectors of agriculture remain labor-intensive, including fresh fruits and vegetables and horticultural specialty crops such as flowers and mushrooms. These commodities generate a sixth of the $400 billion a year in US farm sales, but account for two-thirds of the wages paid to hired farm workers. Fruits, vegetables, and horticultural specialty (FVH) commodities are often both capital- and labor-intensive, as with California strawberries that cost $30,000 an acre,[5] about the size of a football field, to plant, and $20,000 an acre to harvest. However, strawberries generate gross revenue of $60,000 to $70,000 an acre, far more than the $500 to $1,000 an acre revenue from Midwestern corn and soybeans.

A bifurcated size structure, in which most farms are small but the large farms that produce most farm output require ever more capital to buy or rent land and invest in improved seeds and animals, accompanies the third major trend—a higher share of farm work done by hired workers. Many family grain farms operate with only family labor, supplemented by seasonal hired workers who are brought to the farm by custom operations that apply chemicals and fertilizers or harvest crops. However, large fresh fruit and vegetable and specialty crop farms rely on hired workers to do most or all of their farm work, since all workers are hired if the managers are paid employees. Large and capital-intensive FVH farms have workers at all rungs of the job ladder, from accountants to harvesters, but most are low-skilled manual workers engaged in pre-harvest and harvest work.

The farm structure in most industrial countries obeys 80–20 or 90–10 rules, viz., many small farms that account for a small share of farm output and a few large farms that account for almost all farm output and farm-worker employment. Most farms, defined in the US as places that normally sell at least $1,000 worth of farm commodities a year, are small hobby or retirement operations that lose money farming. Meanwhile, most farm commodities are from a relative handful of large commercial farms that are mechanized or hire workers.

---

[5] A US football field is 100 yards or 300 feet long and 160 feet wide, or 48,000 square feet. An acre is 43,560 square feet.

The fact that most farms are small and money-losing operations, while most farm output comes from a relative handful of large farms, distorts averages. Saying that the average US farm had 441 acres and sales of $190,000, as the US Census of Agriculture reported for 2017, obscures the fact that the 105,000 largest US farms, about 7 percent of the total, accounted for 75 percent of the market value of agricultural products sold in 2017.

Figure 2.1 highlights the fact that the 65,300 farms that each had gross farm cash income of $1 million or more in 2015 accounted for over half of US cash farm income,[6] while the half of US farms that each had less than $10,000 in sales accounted for less than 1 percent of gross cash income. Fewer than 5,000 farms had gross cash income of $10 million or more, including a third that were fruit and nut, vegetable and melon, or horticultural specialty (FVH) crop farms, a quarter that were dairies, and an eighth that were cattle-feed lots, that is, almost 70 percent of farms with gross cash income of $10 million or more were FVH farms, dairies, or feed lots.

This same trend of many small subsistence farms and a few large commercial farms is emerging in many developing countries. African countries whose agriculture is dominated by small subsistence farms also have large commercial farms that export fruits and vegetables, flowers, or other commodities. These export-oriented farms are very much like their counterparts in industrial countries, viz.,

U.S. farms and production by GCFI class, 2015
The distribution of farms and the value of production is skewed

Percent of farms of production

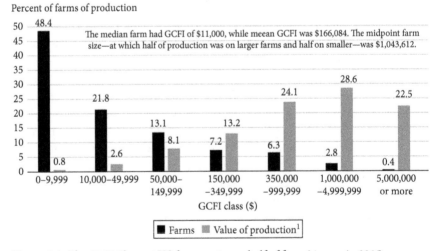

Figure 2.1 The 63,500 largest US farms got over half of farm income in 2015.

---

[6] The median gross cash income was $11,000 in 2015, demonstrating that most US farms have very low sales.

capital-intensive operations with hired managers and hired workers. A major difference is that the wages of hired workers on commercial farms and plantations in developing countries may be comparable to wages in nonfarm industries, while the wages of hired farm workers in industrial countries are typically lower than those of nonfarm workers.

Middle-income countries such as Brazil and Mexico have both factories in the fields and subsistence farms. Brazil is the world's leading exporter of many com-modities, from coffee to sugar, while Mexico has a modern agricultural sector that uses the same machinery, computers, and other inputs as US farms, in part because of US investment. Mexico's modern agricultural sector hires workers with a wide range of skills, from multilingual managers to farm workers with no schooling, to produce commodities that are often exported to the US.

Just as it can be misleading to examine averages in industrial country agricul-tural systems that have many small and a few large farms, it is hard to generalize about hired workers in export-oriented agriculture in Brazil and Mexico and other middle-income countries. Many of the hired workers are local residents employed seasonally or year-round. Workers employed in protected structures such as greenhouses or plastic-covered hoop structures may consider themselves akin to factory workers, since they enter and exit buildings at designated points and their hours and activities are recorded.

Mexico also has open-field fruit and vegetable farms that depend on subsist-ence farmers who migrate from the mountains and poorer southern Mexican states to work seasonally for wages. As we will see in Chapter 4, the wages and working conditions of these internal migrants, who often face discrimination at the hands of other Mexicans, vary widely.

Migration and Trade

Rich countries have a small share of workers employed in agriculture, while poor countries have a large share of workers employed in agriculture. The process of moving workers out of agriculture has never been easy, and government policies aimed at managing rural–urban migration have not been consistent.

During the enclosure movement in Britain in the 1700s and 1800s, rich land-lords enclosed or fenced their land so that smaller farmers could not use what had been common land to grow crops or graze livestock, sending many farm families into cities and providing a labor force for the factories that marked the beginning of the Industrial Revolution. At the same time, estates in Prussia and throughout Eastern Europe tightened laws that prevented peasants from leaving their masters to ensure there were enough workers for agriculture.

Rural–urban migration is the major type of migration occurring around the world today. Data on internal migration vary by country, but there are believed to be four migrants who crossed significant internal borders within their country, as when moving from rural to urban areas, for each migrant who crossed an international border, suggesting a billion internal migrants and 258 million international migrants in 2017.[7]

Most of the billion internal migrants are in developing countries, and most have left rural areas for cities. Lewis considered rural–urban migration a marker of economic development, since it moved people from less productive to more productive jobs. Schultz, on the other hand, cautioned that if rural–urban migrants do not have sufficient education, they may have trouble taking advantage of opportunities in cities.

The value of the world's farm output was $5 trillion or 6 percent of the world's $80 trillion GDP in 2017 (Beckman, 2017). About $1 trillion worth of farm goods are traded between countries, making the value of farm trade 5 percent of the $20 trillion of annual trade in goods. Figure 2.2 shows that the (nominal) value of world trade in farm goods tripled between 1995 and 2014 and doubled in real or inflation-adjusted terms, a period during which the world's population rose by 25 percent and world GDP rose by 75 percent.

Most trade in farm goods is between industrial or developed countries. Industrial countries accounted for an average 54 percent of farm exports between

Quantity and value of global agricultural trade, 1995–2014

Imports, value in U.S. dollars, quantity in deflated U.S. dollars, 2010 base
$ Billion

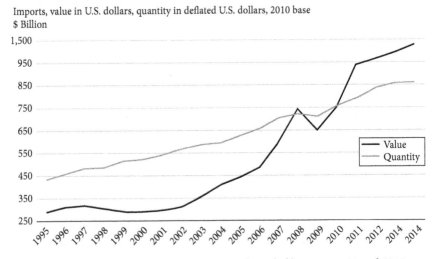

Figure 2.2 The value of world trade in farm goods tripled between 1995 and 2014.

---

[7] UNDP (2009) estimated that there were four internal migrants for each international migrant. The UNDP report urged a lowering of barriers to internal and international migration to allow people to take advantage of opportunities elsewhere and fulfill their human potential.

Average 2010–14

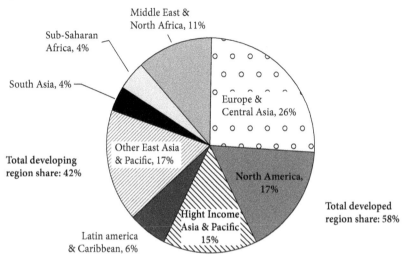

Figure 2.3 Industrial or developed countries accounted for 58 percent of farm imports, 2010–14.

2010 and 2014, led by Europe's 24 percent of farm exports and North America's 22 percent. Figure 2.3 shows that industrial countries received 58 percent of all farm imports, led by the Europe's 26 percent.

The top twenty farm-importing countries accounted for almost all of the world's imports of farm goods, led by the EU and China, which each accounted for 13 percent of global farm imports between 2012 and 2014; the US was next with 11 percent. The top twenty exporters of farm goods between 2012 and 2014 accounted for almost all farm exports. The EU and the US each exported farm goods worth $150 billion or 15 percent of global farm exports, followed by Brazil, $84 billion; China and Canada, $46 billion each; and Argentina and India, about $40 billion each. Mexico's farm exports of $23 billion were similar to the $23 billion worth of farm exports from New Zealand, but less than Australian exports of $37 billion, Indonesia's $30 billion, Malaysia's $26 billion, and Thailand's $25 billion.

Most farm-exporting countries rely on internal and international migrants to fill most of the farm jobs that pay wages. Farmers in richer countries in the EU, the US, Canada, Australia, and New Zealand often rely on migrant workers from poorer countries, while farmers in China, Brazil, and India rely on local workers employed seasonally and internal migrants from poorer areas of the country. Farmers in several middle-income countries, including Costa Rica, Malaysia, and Thailand, rely on migrants from poorer neighboring countries.

PART II
DEVELOPMENT AND FARM-WORKER VULNERABILITY

The farm-labor prosperity paradox is straightforward: farm workers become more vulnerable to exploitation as the share of workers employed in agriculture declines. The three chapters in Part II show this process at work in the US, Mexico, and other countries. In all of these countries, the number of farm operators and family members declined faster than the number of hired farm workers as per capita incomes rose and economies were dominated by industry and services.

Two-thirds of US farm work, as measured by average employment, is done by hired workers. Many are brought to farms by nonfarm support service providers, such as contractors and temporary staffing agencies. In California, more farm workers have been brought to farms by nonfarm support firms than were hired by farm employers for the past decade.

Mexico is experiencing the same prosperity paradox. The growth of modern farms that produce fresh fruits and vegetables for export has increased the employment of hired farm workers, including local workers and internal migrants from poorer mountainous areas in the Mexican states with export-oriented farms, and migrants from southern Mexican states such as Chiapas and Oaxaca. Managing this internal migration from poorer to richer areas of Mexico raises many of the same issues that arise in international labor migration, from keeping recruiters honest to providing decent housing and working conditions for migrants in the areas where they work.

Australia, Canada, and New Zealand are immigration countries that increasingly rely on foreign workers to fill seasonal farm jobs. Each has programs available to farmers who cannot find sufficient local workers to hire guest workers. The farm guest-worker programs of Australia, Canada, and New Zealand are sometimes considered models to be emulated even as critics point to limitations on guest workers that increase their vulnerability.

Most European countries have extensive labor-market regulation, expansive social safety nets, and fewer factories in the fields than in the US. Farmers in northern European countries often hire seasonal workers from poorer countries, as with British and German farms that hire Poles and Romanians under relatively well-regulated guest-worker programs. Farmers in southern European countries such as Italy also rely on migrants, many of whom are from non-EU countries and are irregular. Conditions for Africans and others employed in southern Italian agriculture can be very poor.

Brazil is a middle-income developing country and a major exporter of farm commodities. As in Mexico and most Latin American countries, Brazil is marked by inequalities, including a poor north and a richer south. Most labor-intensive agriculture is in the south, but Brazil is also adding farm land in the cerrado of the midwest and in the Amazon, which attracts poor Afro-Brazilians to remote areas where they may be exploited. The Brazilian government adopted a very broad definition of slavery by including long hours of work and poor housing alongside forced labor and debt bondage as indicators of slavery, and has struggled to prevent farmers from exploiting vulnerable workers.

3
US Farm Labor

The first US census of population in 1790 found that 95 percent of the four million Americans lived in rural areas, and almost all rural residents were involved in agriculture. The number of Americans and people employed in agriculture rose with the westward expansion, but the share of all US workers employed in agriculture fell with industrialization, from 70 percent in 1840 to 40 percent in 1900 and to less than 2 percent since the 1980s.

Families, Slaves, and Migrants

In the early 1800s, US farmers obtained seasonal labor in three major ways (Martin, 2003, ch. 2). Large farm families produced crops and livestock to satisfy their own needs and relied on family members to work during peak harvest seasons; children went to school or had leisure time when there was little farm work. There was no reason for family farms in the northeastern states to expand and produce a surplus to sell, since there were few cities and transport to them was very expensive. New York, the largest US city and the major market for farm commodities, had 60,000 residents in 1800.

Expanding US cities and infrastructure such as the Erie Canal, completed in 1825, linked the Great Lakes with the Atlantic Ocean and encouraged family farms to produce a surplus for growing US cities and Europe. Most farms remained family-sized, but agricultural innovations saved labor and raised productivity.

Some family farms had hired hands, usually a young man who lived and worked with the farm family and might marry the farmer's daughter and become a farmer in his own right. The notion that most hired farm workers were aspiring farmers with the same interests as their employers persisted long after it became almost impossible to climb the agricultural ladder from worker to farmer. The myth of the hired hand as apprentice farmer was one justification for excluding farm workers from protective labor laws in the mid-1930s.

Plantations in the south that produced cotton and tobacco for export to Europe needed more seasonal labor than even large farm families could provide. They relied on slaves. In a country that offered free land, free workers were unwilling to work for low wages on plantations, which needed workers for six to eight months.

The Prosperity Paradox: Fewer and More Vulnerable Farm Workers. Philip Martin, Oxford University Press (2021).
© Philip Martin.
DOI: 10.1093/oso/9780198867845.001.0001

Plantations could justify the provision of food and housing for slaves year-round to ensure that workers were available for planting and harvesting.

Before slavery ended with the Civil War in the 1860s, the price of land used to grow cotton and the price of slaves rose together with cotton prices. There was little fertilizer used on cotton fields in the pre-Civil War south, so areas with older and less productive cotton land such as Virginia specialized in producing slaves for areas where cotton acreage was increasing, as in Louisiana and Texas. Conrad and Meyer (1958) conclude that slavery was profitable, as some areas specialized in producing slave labor and others in producing cotton.

After slavery ended in the 1860s, plantations relied on ex-slaves to be share-croppers, tenant farmers who grew and harvested cotton in exchange for half of the revenue from the sale of the crop. Labor-saving mechanization in the 1930s dramatically reduced the labor needed to produce cotton, sending many black sharecroppers north to Chicago and other cities in search of nonfarm jobs. Cotton has been mechanized, but tobacco remains a labor-intensive crop, and is produced on fewer and larger farms in the middle South with the help of Mexican guest workers who are admitted under the H-2A program (Gale et al., 2000).

The third US farm-labor system had its roots in Spanish and later Mexican colonial policies. The Spanish and Mexican governments granted land to favored elites and the Catholic Church for missions, often 50,000 acres or more, to create ranchos that grazed cattle and produced wheat.[1] Many of these large ranchos were bought by Americans after California became a state in 1850, ushering in an era of cattle grazing for meat and hides and "bonanza" wheat farming. Just as finding gold was uncertain, large farms planted wheat in the fall and hoped for winter rains and a bonanza harvest in the spring.

Large ranchos were expected to be broken into family-sized units after the transcontinental railroad was completed May 10, 1869,[2] making it easier for small farmers to move west. Meanwhile. the development of irrigation systems and lower transportation costs made the production of fruit profitable. Fruit pro-duction was labor-intensive, and it was widely assumed that large wheat farms would have to be broken into family-sized parcels in order to obtain seasonal fruit pickers.

California agriculture was expected to evolve into a system of family farms that produced fruit for cooperatives and other associations of small farmers that handled sales and marketing. However, large farms did not need to be subdivided into family-sized units because workers with no other job options were available

---

[1] Wheat was planted in the fall and harvested in the spring. Many large wheat farms were known as bonanza farms, owned by absentee owners who reaped a harvest and a bonanza if winter rains pro-duced a crop.

[2] The Union Pacific and Central Pacific railroads met May 10, 1869, at Promontory Summit, Utah, reducing the trip across the US from months to days and integrating California into that of the other states.

to be seasonal farm workers. Over 15,000 Chinese workers were imported from Guangdong by the Central Pacific to help to build the railroad from west to east through the Sierra Nevada mountains for $1 a day.[3] When the railroad was completed, the Chinese were laid off, and most moved to Sacramento, San Francisco, and other cities rather than returning to China.

The railroad brought cheaper manufactured goods to California from other states, prompting layoffs of white workers as the factories that had supplied goods for California residents closed. The Chinese who had recently moved to California cities were blamed for the layoffs, and jobless white workers drove many of the Chinese out of California cities, accusing them of working for low wages. Farmers did not discriminate against the Chinese, but they also did not pay workers when there was no need for them. Many of the Chinese workers who had been laid off after the railroad was completed became seasonal farm workers. Contemporary observers described them as cheaper than slaves because they "came with the wind and went with the dust," that is, they were paid only when they worked (Fuller, 1991).

Waves of other immigrants without nonfarm job options followed the Chinese into the fields and preserved the system of large farms inherited from Spain and Mexico. The Japanese government legalized emigration in 1886, and newcomers from Japan soon replaced aging Chinese workers on California farms. The Japanese were unique among the waves of migrant farm workers because some agreed to work for a share of the crop rather than wages, which gave them experience selling fresh produce and allowed some to become farmers.

Some Japanese farm workers bought marginal farm land near cities and sold fruits and vegetables to local consumers. This competition angered white farmers, prompting a Gentlemen's Agreement between Japan and the US in 1907 that stopped more Japanese from arriving.[4] Farmers angry about competition from Japanese farmers went further, persuading the state legislature to enact laws in 1913 and 1920 that prohibited "aliens ineligible for citizenship" such as the Japanese from owning farm land or signing long-term leases for farm land. Japanese farmers evaded California's restrictive land laws by buying land in the names of their US-born and thus US-citizen children.

Large farmers turned to South Asia, a British colony, and the US territory of the Philippines to fill the ranks of the expanding seasonal farm workforce early in the twentieth century. Most immigration from Asia was halted by federal laws in

---

[3] Over 1,000 Chinese died, especially during the winter of 1868–9 in the Sierras. The Chinese were not included in the photo commemorating the completion of the railroad. The Union Pacific, which was building the railroad from east to west, relied on Irish workers, many of whom were Civil War veterans.

[4] The Gentlemen's Agreement of 1907 was an informal agreement between the US and Japan that involved Japan not allowing its citizens to leave for the US and the US not banning migration from Japan, as it had from China.

the 1920s that favored European immigrants who settled in the east and Midwest. California growers during World War I encouraged Mexicans to move north to become seasonal farm workers. Many Mexicans responded, but during the Depression of the early 1930s, some were "repatriated" to Mexico in order to open up jobs for US workers.

During the 150 years of labor-intensive agriculture in California that began in the 1870s, there was only one period when most seasonal farm workers were white US citizens. In the 1920s the western plains states such as Oklahoma were settled by small farmers who borrowed money to plow native grasses and plant wheat. Plowing virgin prairie set the stage for a Dust Bowl in the 1930s, when crops failed and drought whipped up dirt and dust storms. Millions of farmers were unable to repay their bank loans, and at least 1.5 million people from Arkansas, Oklahoma, and other states moved to California to begin anew, as exemplified by the Joad family portrayed in John Steinbeck's 1939 novel *The Grapes of Wrath*.

Farm workers had been excluded from protective labor laws in the mid-1930s under the theory that most were aspiring family farmers. Many Dust Bowl migrants who moved to California expected to be apprentices on fruit farms before becoming family fruit farmers. However, they soon learned that fruit pickers had little interaction with the owners of large California farms that relied on supervisors and contractors to assemble crews of farm workers who were hired and laid off as needed. There was little hope of upward mobility in this factory-farming system.

Dust Bowl migration, Steinbeck's novel, and congressional hearings that high-lighted the iron grip of large landowners on California's economy and justice system set the stage for reforms that could have extended labor-law protections at least to workers employed on large farms that received federal subsidies (Fuller, 1991). However, after the US declared war on Germany and Japan in December 1941, many Dust Bowl migrants were drafted or found jobs in nonfarm defense industries, reducing the drive for farm-labor reforms.

Farmers complained that the exit of Dust Bowl migrants created labor shortages and won a bracero program, a series of agreements that admitted almost 5 million Mexicans between 1942 and 1964 as legal guest workers. Many Mexican braceros returned year after year, but up to 2 million Mexicans gained experience working in US agriculture before the program ended in 1964 as a form of civil rights for Hispanics. President Kennedy hoped that, without braceros in the fields, Mexican-American farm workers would earn higher wages.

Agricultural economist Varden Fuller (1991) reviewed California's farm labor history and concluded that political decisions shaped the size, characteristics, and wages of hired farm workers. Lack of education and few nonfarm job opportunities encouraged US farm workers to adjust to seasonality, accepting seasonal farm jobs in order to have some earnings rather than be jobless and have no income. Poverty and low wages abroad made immigrants and guest workers eager to work in California agriculture.

Fuller concluded that there were several effects of the political decisions that created an excess supply of farm workers. First, with farm wages half of nonfarm levels, farm workers and their children learned that they had to get out of agriculture to climb the economic ladder, leading to treadmill-style labor market that relied on a continuous influx of new farm workers who had few other US job options. Second, low farm wages were capitalized into higher land prices, benefitting large landowners who could produce labor-intensive commodities in California, ship them long distances, and be competitive with local produce. Third, armies of seasonal farm workers discouraged family farmers who relied on their own labor from producing fruits and vegetables, since the value of the time that farm families spent doing work that was done on other farms by hired workers was the same as the low wages paid to these workers.

Cesar Chavez and the UFW

The end of the bracero program in 1964 ushered in a short-lived golden era for California farm workers. The demand for fresh fruits and vegetables was rising during the baby boom of the 1960s, when the interstate highway system made it faster and cheaper to ship fruits and vegetables from California to the eastern states where most Americans lived.

Cesar Chavez began to organize farm workers in California's San Joaquin Valley in 1962, helping Mexican-American farm workers to complete government forms in exchange for a small membership fee that also provided access to a credit union. Filipino grape harvesters in 1965 protested the decision of table-grape growers to reduce wages. At the time, braceros but not US farm workers were protected by minimum wages.

Chavez supported the Filipino strike and, without braceros to break the strike and with Chavez's charismatic leadership, the table-grape pickers' strike drew support from nonfarm unions, churches, students, and others for what became the La Causa, the effort of powerless farm workers to encourage agribusinesses to pay higher wages. By 1966, the fledgling United Farm Workers (UFW) union led by Chavez won a 40-percent wage increase for the grape harvesters who were employed by a subsidiary of liquor conglomerate Schenley Industries, raising the base wage of grape harvesters from $1.25 to $1.75 an hour.

Other grape growers refused to follow Schenley's lead and sign contracts with the UFW, prompting one of the most successful union-called boycotts in history, the table-grape boycott of the late 1960s. According to polls, up to 15 percent of Americans avoided eating table grapes. Students, clergy, and activists demonstrated outside supermarkets to urge stores not to sell grapes and consumers not to buy grapes. Cesar Chavez became a household name after *Time* magazine put him on the cover of the July 4, 1969 issue, extolling his advocacy of non-violent protests and the fasts that drew attention to the plight of farm workers. A combination of factors, including low grape prices due to the boycott, encouraged most table-grape growers to sign contracts with the UFW in 1970.

There were no government-supervised elections to determine if farm workers wanted to be represented by the UFW because farm workers were excluded from the National Labor Relations Act (NLRA) of 1935, the basic law that grants private-sector workers the right to form or join unions or to refrain from union activities, and compels employers to bargain with unions that the government has certified to represent their workers.[5] Organizing in the 1960s meant that the UFW sent contracts to growers saying that their workers wanted the UFW to represent them and asking growers to sign the contract or face a boycott of their commodity.

After winning contracts with table-grape growers, the UFW turned to lettuce growers, where the Teamsters union represented many nonfarm workers who packed and transported lettuce. Instead of signing UFW contracts, most lettuce growers extended their Teamster contracts to farm workers, or signed new contracts with the Teamsters covering farm workers. The Teamsters quickly became California's dominant farm-worker union, drawing demonstrations and protests from the UFW and its supporters.

The rivalry between the Teamsters and the UFW led many farmers to believe that their workers would be represented by a union, and the only question was which union. With police needed to break up disputes between growers and the UFW, and between the Teamsters and the UFW, state leaders agreed that farm-labor disputes should be moved from the streets into bargaining rooms and the courts. Jerry Brown was elected governor in November 1974, and the Agricultural Labor Relations Act (ALRA) was enacted in 1975, making California the first state to grant farm workers the right to organize and bargain with farm employers under state supervision.

California created a state agency, the Agricultural Labor Relations Board (ALRB), to supervise elections to determine if farm workers wanted to be represented by unions and to adjudicate charges that the rights granted to farm workers by the ALRA were violated by employers or unions. The ALRA and unions were widely expected to usher in a new era in farm labor, with most farm workers represented by unions and the occupation of farm worker becoming akin to that of construction worker, offering high hourly wages when there was work and unemployment insurance benefits during the off season.

---

[5] Farm workers remain the largest group of private-sector workers excluded from the NLRA.

During the late 1970s, a unionized agriculture took shape in California, as the UFW won hundreds of elections on farms around the state and negotiated over a hundred contracts with farms. The UFW reached a high-water mark in 1979, but has since declined into a union that represents the majority of workers in only one commodity, mushrooms.

The decline of the UFW has been the subject of countless books and articles. There are four major explanations for why Cesar Chavez and the UFW failed to transform seasonal farm work from a job into a career (Martin, 2003). The first explanation centers on Chavez's flaws, explaining that he wanted to lead a poor people's movement rather than a union and was dismayed to realize that most farm workers preferred a middle-class lifestyle to a perpetual struggle for a new society (Pawel, 2009). The UFW lost most of its lawyers when Chavez insisted that they move from Salinas, the US salad bowl, to the UFW's mountain head-quarters in Keene, southeast of Bakersfield.

The second explanation for the UFW's demise focuses on state politics. The ALRA is one of the most pro-worker and pro-union laws in the US, with detailed election procedures that permit quick elections before seasonal workers move to other farms and extra remedies if employers fail to bargain with a certified union in good faith. The ALRA was enacted under Democrats, who also made the first appointments to the ALRB, the agency that investigates charges that worker rights were violated and proposes remedies. When Republicans began to make appoint-ments to the ALRB in the 1980s, the UFW charged that the state agency was biased against farm workers and refused to cooperate with it.

The third explanation for the demise of the UFW involves the changing struc-ture of agriculture, that is, who owns farm land, who operates farms, and who hires workers. UFW boycotts were most effective against conglomerates with farming subsidiaries. For example, Schenley was a New York liquor firm based in the Empire State Building, one of the big four that also included Seagram, National Distillers, and Hiram Walker. UFW supporters picketed liquor stores selling Schenley whiskey during the Christmas buying season in 1965, reducing sales and prompting Schenley leadership to agree to a UFW table-grape contract over the objections of Schenley's California farm managers.

UFW boycotts and the agricultural crisis of the 1980s, when commodity and land prices fell, prompted many conglomerates with agricultural operations to sell their farm land. Oil firms such as Shell and Tenneco, Hawaii land developer Amfac, and other conglomerates that earned most of their profits from nonfarm businesses sold land to farmers who were not as susceptible to boycotts. These farmers, in turn, often relied on farm-labor contractors (FLCs) to obtain workers, and FLCs whose crews had pro-union leanings found few farmer clients.

Chavez anticipated that FLCs would make it harder to unionize farm workers, and insisted that the farm operator be considered the employer of workers brought to farms by FLCs for union purposes. The ALRA makes farmers rather than FLCs the employers of workers that FLCs bring to farms, so that an FLC employed on ten farms could be employed under ten different union contracts. However, Chavez did not anticipate that many FLCs would bring both equipment *and* workers to farms and thus be considered custom harvesters who were the sole employers of the workers they brought to farms under all laws, including tax, labor, and immigration.[6] Employees of custom harvesters may work on ten farms but have only one union contract if their employer was unionized.

The fourth explanation for the demise of the UFW was rising unauthorized Mexico–US migration. The UFW called a strike against lettuce growers in 1979 as its first contracts with vegetable growers that were signed under the ALRA were expiring to support a demand for a 40-percent wage increase, from $3.75 to $5.25 an hour. The late 1970s were a period of high inflation, and President Carter asked employers and unions not to increase wages more than 7 percent, the wage increase offered by farmers. The UFW feared that unauthorized Mexicans would enter the US and replace strikers in the fields, and mounted "wet patrols" along the border that involved UFW supporters using bats to deter unauthorized entries.

The UFW won a Pyrrhic victory. Sun-Harvest, the vegetable division of United Brands (that sold Chiquita bananas), and other large vegetable farmers agreed to the UFW's demand for a $5.25 minimum wage in new contracts, but then went out of business, leaving workers without a contract as new owners changed commodities and farming methods. Pawel (2014) suggests that Chavez called the strike because of the UFW's inept handling of its health insurance plan, which made lettuce workers angry with the UFW when their health care bills were not paid and doctors refused to accept UFW health insurance.

Chavez hoped that a large wage increase would stifle worker anger, but the strike boomeranged and helped growers who shipped lettuce. The demand for lettuce is inelastic, meaning that consumers buy about the same amount whether the price is high or low. The strike and disease reduced the supply of lettuce, as several thousand workers refused to work and, with less lettuce sent to market, the grower price tripled. Even though less lettuce was shipped, the winter lettuce crop in 1978–9 was worth twice as much as in normal years.

The demand for most fresh fruits and vegetables is inelastic, and farmers usually overproduce, so anything that reduces supply, from strikes to weather, can raise prices and revenue. Growers can redistribute the extra revenue from a smaller crop with strike insurance, while the workers on strike lose wages. A consumer boycott, on the other hand, reduces the demand for a commodity and thus

---

[6] FLCs bring only workers to farms and take direction from the farm operator about where and how to work. Custom harvesters, on the other hand, bring equipment and workers to farms and harvest according to the requirements of packers and processors, not the farm operator. Chavez feared that unionized FLCs could easily go out of business after negotiating a union contract, leaving workers with a hollow victory; he did not envision the rise of custom harvesters.

the grower price. As long as grower prices are above the cost of harvesting the commodity, growers will harvest and workers will keep their jobs while their nonfarm supporters picket supermarkets to discourage the buying of grapes and other commodities. Traditional union weapons such as strikes are less useful to farm-worker unions because of the inelastic demand for farm commodities, while boycotts that reduce consumer demand and prices can have significant impacts on growers (Martin, 2003; Taylor and Charlton, 2018).

By the mid-1980s, the UFW had stopped trying to organize farm workers and had a dwindling number of contracts. Unauthorized newcomers from Mexico replaced aging Mexican-Americans who marched with the UFW in the 1960s and 1970s. Mexican newcomers often associated Cesar Chavez with boxing rather than a protective union.[7]

The UFW has been the largest and best-known US farm-worker union, started by ex-farm workers and supported by nonfarm unions and churches. The UFW had contracts with about thirty California farms and claimed 8,700 members (including retirees) in 2018, including 1,500 at D'Arrigo, a Salinas vegetable grower.[8] The UFW charges 3 percent of gross wages in dues, and reported $4 million in dues and agency fees in 2018. With 7,852 members and dues payers (retired members do not pay dues), this suggests an average $500 in dues and average worker earnings of $16,667.

The UFW got its third president in 2018 after Cesar Chavez (1962–93) and Chavez's son-in-law Arturo Rodriguez (1994–2018). UFW President Teresa Romero, a Mexican immigrant who did not do farm work in the US, says the UFW's top priorities are legalizing unauthorized farm workers and protecting female farm workers from harassment. The UFW actively supports the Farm Workforce Modernization Act (HR 5038) approved by the House in December 2019. HR 5038 would legalize currently unauthorized farm workers, streamline the H-2A program, and require farm employers to use E-Verify to check the status of newly hired workers.

There are other California farm-worker unions, including the Teamsters and the United Food and Commercial Workers, that each have a local with contracts covering farm workers in the Salinas area; most of the workers represented by these unions are nonfarm packing and processing workers. The Teamsters have the longest-lasting farm-worker contract, dating from the early 1960s, while the UFCW is the leader in organizing cannabis workers since California legalized recreational marijuana with Proposition 64 in 2016.[9]

---

[7] Julio César Chávez is a Mexican boxer who competed between 1980 and 2005, winning 107 of 115 fights.
[8] The UFW reported about 5,000 members to DOL until 2013, 10,000 in 2013, and now fewer than 8,000.
[9] California's Proposition 64 in November 2016 legalized recreational marijuana beginning January 1, 2018. An estimated 13.5 million pounds of marijuana were produced in California in 2016,

The Ohio-based Farm Labor Organizing Committee (FLOC) used the UFW's boycott strategy in the 1980s to persuade food firms Campbell's and Heinz to require the Ohio growers who produced cucumbers for their pickles to recognize FLOC as the bargaining agent for their farm workers and abide by the terms of a contract signed by FLOC and Campbell's and Heinz. FLOC was founded in 1967 by Baldemar Velasquez, became a union in 1979, and uses top-down pressure and boycotts of buyers of farm commodities to achieve collective-bargaining agreements that cover farm workers on farms that sell to targeted buyers.

After a march from Ohio to Campbell's headquarters near Philadelphia in 1986, FLOC reached an agreement with Campbell's Vlasic pickle subsidiary with the help of ex-DOL (Department of Labor) Secretary John Dunlop, and Heinz soon signed as well. Under these agreements, farmers who want to grow cucumbers for Vlasic or Heinz must recognize the FLOC as the union for their farm workers. Vlasic and Heinz raised the prices they paid to farmers to cover the higher wage and benefit costs of what became a three-way FLOC–Vlasic–grower agreement, with grievances resolved by the Dunlop Agricultural Commission.[10] The FLOC–Vlasic–grower agreement served as a model for FLOC activities in North Carolina.

North Carolina has twice the cucumber acreage of Ohio, and FLOC boycotted Mount Olive pickles until Mount Olive in 2004 signed an agreement with FLOC that requires its growers to abide by the contract's provisions. Mount Olive initially resisted FLOC, arguing that it did not hire any farm workers, and urged FLOC to negotiate with the farmers who do.[11] FLOC countered that Mount Olive prepared the contracts that cucumber growers signed and had market power over the growers, so that Mount Olive ultimately set wages and benefits of farm workers. It was also far more efficient for FLOC to target Mount Olive and thus win the right to represent workers on all farms that grow for Mount Olive rather than organize workers farm by farm.[12]

The FLOC–Mount Olive agreement of 2004 became a four-way agreement that included cucumber growers as well as the North Carolina Growers Association,

including 11 million pounds or over 80 percent that is produced illegally and sold outside the state. Relatively little is known about the structure of the cannabis industry and those employed in it. Anecdotal reports suggest that most growers are small, with fewer than 5,000 plants, but can have gross revenues of $100,000 a year. Some growers work for others, but most of the trimming of the flowers to obtain their buds is done by local residents who reportedly earn $25 an hour at a piece rate of $150 per pound of trimmed buds.

[10] Pickling cucumbers are picked into buckets, with piece-rate pay ranging from $0.40 to $0.70; the smaller cucumbers bring the highest piece rates. FLOC's goal was to double piece-rate picking wages.

[11] Mount Olive in 1999 issued a statement: "Our company does not employ farm workers - farmers do -and it is unfair for our company to influence farmers or farm workers to sign labor contracts...We do not want to interfere in the relationship between employer and employee."

[12] FLOC in 2014 (LM2 066–762) reported 5,215 members at the end of 2014 and another 5,000 agency payers. Dues income for 2014 was $415,600; with dues at 2.5 percent of gross earnings, total earnings were $16.6 million and average earnings almost $1,600.

which recruits Mexican H-2A workers for farms growing cucumbers, tobacco, and other commodities. The agreement allowed FLOC to monitor the recruitment of H-2A workers in Mexico in an effort to avoid H-2A workers having to pay recruitment fees. In April 2007, a FLOC organizer seeking to educate migrants about their rights, especially their right not to pay fees to recruiters, was killed in FLOC's Monterrey, Mexico office, where many Mexican workers obtain their H-2A visas at the US consulate, demonstrating the difficulty of enforcing US laws that require US farm employers to pay all recruitment costs for the H-2A workers they recruit in other countries.[13]

FLOC's membership rose from 7,500 to a peak of over 14,000 in 2006, and was 10,437 in 2018. Half of FLOC's members were agency payers rather than members, including many H-2A guest workers brought into the US by the NC Growers Association. FLOC charges dues of 2.5 percent and reported $600,000 in dues income from 10,437 members and payers, suggesting average dues of $57 and $2,300 in earnings. Over half of FLOC-represented workers have H-2A visas.

FLOC has been using the same top-down supply-chain pressure since 2007 to encourage tobacco firms to establish labor standards on the North Carolina farms from which they buy tobacco and to recognize FLOC as bargaining agent for tobacco workers. The US is the world's fourth-largest tobacco grower,[14] after China, India, and Brazil. Reynolds American, Altria Group (Philip Morris), and Lorillard are the Big Three US tobacco firms that sell 85 percent of US cigarettes.

FLOC targeted Reynolds American, which responded in a manner similar to Mount Olive, saying: "If workers want to be represented by a union, they and their employer should negotiate with the union...the bottom line is that these workers are not R.J. Reynolds employees." Nonetheless, Reynolds American in May 2012 agreed to meet with FLOC, growers, and others to discuss wages and working conditions on the farms from which it buys tobacco.[15]

These discussions led the Farm Labor Practices Group (FLPG), which Reynolds American says "has achieved significant success in training and education programs for growers and their employees...[to deal with] education and training, farm labor contractor compliance, and grievance mechanisms." The FLPG invited DOL to hold training sessions for tobacco growers in North Carolina and Kentucky to review their responsibilities under labor laws and to highlight common violations.

---

[13] Before FLOC intervened, Texas Rural Legal Aid said that Mexicans often paid $600 for H-2A visas, and recruiters expected a tip from the workers when they returned at the end of the season to get higher on the recruitment list for the next season.

[14] North Carolina, Kentucky, and Georgia accounted for 85 percent of the 800 million pounds of US-grown tobacco in 2012.

[15] Between 1933 and 2004, the federal government allotted the right to grow tobacco in exchange for a government-set minimum support price. The allotment and price support system was phased out between 2004 and 2014, and growers now contract directly with tobacco buyers or sell their tobacco at auction markets.

There is a long history of self-help and union efforts to turn farm work from a job into a career, but there are few durable successes. Organizing viable unions in agriculture is difficult because the best workers, those most likely to lead the union, are the workers who are first to find nonfarm jobs. Farm-worker unions are often led by charismatic leaders who are able to obtain support from nonfarm sources in their David and Goliath struggle. However, their victories on behalf of farm workers have been fleeting rather than durable, and most farm-worker unions have become top-down institutions more attuned to politicians and non-farm supporters than farm workers.

US Farms and Employment

There were 2 million US farms in 2017, according to the Census of Agriculture. There were more farm producers, 3.4 million in 2017, than farms because the COA for the first time allowed respondents to designate more than one producer per farm. However, only 2 million of these producers were primary producers, and the average age of primary producers was 59.

Farm Structure

The story of US agriculture involves the persistence of small farms despite the consolidation of farm production on fewer and larger farms. One measure of changing farm size is midpoint acreage, the acreage at which half of the production of a commodity is from larger farms and half is from smaller farms.

Figure 3.1 shows that half of all cropland, and half of all harvested cropland, was on farms with 1,200 or more acres in 2012, up from a midpoint of 600 acres in 1982 and 800 acres in 1997. Some 30,200 farms had more than 2,000 acres of harvested cropland (MacDonald et al., 2018). The midpoint acreage of corn was 630 in 2012, up from 200 in 1987, and midpoint wheat acreage was 1,000 acres in 2012, up from 400 in 1987. The midpoint acreage of tobacco was 108 acres in 2012, up from 12 acres in 1987.

Most fruit and nut, vegetable and melon, or horticultural specialty (FVH) crops have lower acreage midpoints and less dramatic consolidation on larger farms. Oranges had the highest midpoint acreage among fruits and vegetables: half of orange acreage in 2012 was on farms with 960 or more acres, followed by pistachios, where half of acreage was on farms with 925 or more acres.

Lettuce, broccoli, carrots, and potatoes had midpoint acreages of 1,000 or more, meaning that over half of the total acreage of these commodities was on farms with 1,000 or more acres in 2012. Lettuce has long been produced on large farms, but broccoli and carrot acreage consolidated on large farms between 1987 and 2012, while the midpoint acreage for cantaloupes declined.

Increasing midpoint acreages for cropland, 1982–2012
Midpoint acreages for cropland and harvested cropland roughly doubled between 1982 and 2020

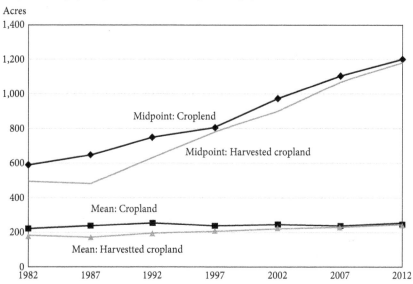

Figure 3.1 The midpoint acreage of US cropland per farm doubled in three decades.

Larger farms often specialize, producing only oranges or strawberries or let-tuce rather than a mix of crops. Larger farms invest in specialized machinery and need more acres to spread out machinery costs. Marketing factors also play a role in promoting specialization, since large farms can supply retailers year-round.

The consolidation of FVH production on large and specialized farms increases the demand for hired farm labor. Rising labor costs may become another factor encouraging the concentration of production on fewer and larger farms, since large farms can spread the fixed costs of guest workers over more acres or work-ers, lowering per unit costs.

Farm Employment

There are several measures of farm employment. The Bureau of Labor Statistics (BLS) estimates the average employment of self-employed and wage and salary workers in agriculture. Average employment is derived from monthly or quar-terly snapshots of employment, summed, and divided by twelve months or four quarters.

The most recent data in Table 3.1 show that there were an average 850,000 self-employed persons in US agriculture and an average 1.5 million wage and salary workers. The average self-employment of farmers and family members in agricul-ture declined by 5 percent between 2006 and 2016, and is projected to decline

Table 3.1 US agricultural employment, 2006–26

Sector	2006	2016	2026	Change 2006–16	Change 2016–26
Ag wage and salary	1,219	1,501	1,518	23%	1%
Ag self-employed	893	850	828	−5%	−3%
Total ag	2,112	2,351	2,346	11%	0%
Hired share	58%	64%	65%		

Source: US Bureau of Labor Statistics, Table 1; https://migration.ucdavis.edu/rmn/blog/post/?id=2098.

another 3 percent by 2026.[16] By contrast, there was significant growth in the average employment of hired workers between 2006 and 2016, up 23 percent, and BLS projects stable hired-worker employment through 2026.[17] This means that hired workers should continue to account for two-thirds of average employment in US agriculture.

An alternative measure of self-employed and hired-worker employment that is based on hours worked can be derived from the United States Department of Agriculture (USDA)'s Agricultural Resource Management Survey (ARMS), where employers report their own hours worked and the hours worked on their farms by family members and hired workers. ARMS finds more hours worked by principal farm operators, spouses, and other unpaid workers than by hired workers: 60 percent of on-farm hours worked in 2016 were contributed by operators and other unpaid workers, and 40 percent by wage and salary workers. This 60–40 split between the hours of operators and hired workers was 75-25 percent in 2003, indicating the same trend of fewer hours contributed by farmers and their families and more hours worked by wage and salary workers.[18]

Crop agriculture employs three-fourths of hired workers and offers many seasonal jobs, so there are peaks and troughs in hired-worker employment. The total number of workers employed in agriculture over a year exceeds average employment, making the number of farm workers a multiple of average employment. In California, there are about two farm workers employed sometime during the year for each year-round equivalent job, a two-to-one worker to job ratio (Martin, Hooker, and Stockton, 2018).

---

[16] The US labor force is projected to expand by a million a year, from 159 million in 2016 to 170 million in 2026. GDP is expected to grow 2 percent a year over the next decade, up from 1.4 percent a year over the 2006–16 decade. Employment in 2026 is projected to be 168 million, up from 157 million in 2016. There are expected to be 136 million workers employed in services, 20 million in goods-producing industries, and 2.3 million in agriculture.

[17] Agricultural employment includes forestry, fishing, and logging, which collectively account for less than 5 percent of agricultural employment.

[18] See http://www.ers.usda.gov/topics/farm-economy/farm-labor/.

Agriculture is similar to fast-food restaurants and other sectors that experience seasonality and have high worker turnover. For example, a McDonald's restaurant with 20 job slots may hire 40 workers sometime during the year to fill them, just as a farm with 100 year-round equivalent jobs may hire 200 or more workers sometime during the year to fill these jobs. The farm differs from the restaurant in the sense that there may be 150 jobs during the harvest peak and 25 jobs during the winter trough, while the restaurant has 20 jobs year-round.

Hired Farm Workers

Self-employed US farmers tend to be older than the average worker, white, and US citizens, while hired farm workers are younger than the average American worker, more Hispanic, and include mostly non-citizens. A familiar adage captures the contrast between farmers and farm workers: it is hard to find a farmer under 40 because of the capital required to operate a significant farm, and it is hard to find a farm worker over 40 because of the physical demands of farm work. Many farmers are the third, fourth, or fifth generation in farming, while few children of farm workers educated in the US follow their parents into seasonal farm jobs.

HFWF and QCEW

Between the 1950s and 1980s, USDA commissioned the Bureau of the Census to attach questions to the December Current Population Survey that asked if anyone in the household did farm work for wages sometime during the year. The result was the annual or biennial (after 1977) Hired Farm Working Force (HFWF) report that portrayed a largely casual hired farm workforce.

For example, the 1975 HFWF report found that 45 percent of wage earners did less than 25 days of farm work that year, while a seventh were employed 250 days or more in farm work. Average farm earnings were $2,000 for 111 days of farm work in 1975, but this average is misleading. The relatively few workers who did many days of farm work had most of total farm earnings, while the many workers who did very little farm work had a small share of total farm earnings.

The HFWF data found mostly young, male, and casual hired farm workers, with almost half reporting that they were in the labor force only while doing farm work. Almost 40 percent of hired workers said they were primarily students, and fewer than 10 percent were migrants, defined as crossing a county line and staying away from a usual home at least one night to do farm work. Almost 85 percent of farm workers lived away from the farm where they worked, and 40 percent were in the southern states. In the 1970s, whites were three-fourths of hired farm

Table 3.2 US average family, hired, and total farm workers, 1910–80

| | Average Annual Farm Employment | | | | | |
	Family	Hired	Total	Hired share	Hired workers	Ratio
1910	10,174	3,381	13,555	25%		
1920	10,041	3,391	13,432	25%		
1930	8,307	3,190	11,497	28%		
1940	8,300	2,679	10,979	24%		
1950	7,597	2,329	9,926	23%	4,342	1.9
1960	5,172	1,885	7,057	27%	3,693	2.0
1970	3,348	1,175	4,523	26%	2,488	2.1
1980	2,402	1,303	3,705	35%	2,652	2.0
1910–80	76%	61%	73%			
1950–80	68%	44%	63%		39%	

Average annual farm employment is average of quarterly estimates. 1980 hired workers is 1979 estimate.

Source: Whitener and Coltrane, 1981.

workers, and there were more black farm workers, 13 percent of the total, than Hispanics, 12 percent.

The HFWF and other farm-labor data in Table 3.2 suggest that average family farm employment fell 76 percent over seven decades, while average hired-worker employment fell 61 percent, based on quarterly estimates of employment on US farms. The decline in the average employment of family workers continued at the same pace between 1950 and 1980, while the decline in hired-worker employment slowed. The share of hired workers among those employed on farms rose from about 25 percent to 35 percent in the 1970s.

Average employment is a snapshot. There was also interest in the total number of workers employed for wages on farms sometime during the year, prompting USDA to pay the Census Bureau to attach a supplement to the December Current Population survey that ask if anyone in the household did farm work for wages during the year. Someone who did even one day of wage work on a farm was considered a hired farm worker, and his/her family was considered a farm-worker family. The number of farm workers fell almost 40 percent between 1950 and 1980, about the same as the 44 percent drop in the average employment of hired workers. The ratio of workers to average jobs was about two to one.

The HFWF's two-to-one ratio of workers to full-time equivalent jobs persists in California today, a state that requires all employers who pay $100 or more in quarterly wages to register with the unemployment insurance system and pay UI taxes so that laid-off workers can collect UI benefits. Federal law has since 1978 required farms employing ten or more workers for twenty or more weeks in a year, or who pay at least $20,000 in farm wages in a quarter, to register and pay UI taxes on their employees' wages. BLS estimated that average hired-worker employment in US agriculture (NAICS 11) was 1.6 million in 2016, including 81 percent of farm employment that was covered by the UI system.

Some 16,150 California agricultural establishments (NAICS 11) hired an average 425,500 workers and paid them $13.7 billion in 2016. Average employment of 425,500 reflects hired-worker employment on each farm for the payroll period that includes the 12th of the month; the monthly data are summed and divided by twelve months to estimate average employment. Average employment misses workers who were employed sometime during the month, but not during the payroll period that includes the 12th. However, total wages of $13.7 billion were the wages paid to all workers, including those who were employed at other times of the month but not during the payroll period that includes the 12th (Martin, Hooker, and Stockton, 2019).

All Social Security numbers reported by agricultural employers when paying unemployment insurance taxes are considered to be farm workers.[19] The California jobs of these farm workers can be tabulated, so that workers with several employers can be assigned to the commodity or NAICS in which they had their highest earnings. This procedure identified 804,200 primary farm workers, and those with their highest wages from an agricultural employer were 81 percent of the total 989,500 SSNs with at least one farm job. Primary farm workers had their highest earnings from an agricultural rather than a nonfarm employer, while primary vegetable workers had their highest earning job with a vegetable farmer.

Analysis of the UI or Quarterly Census of Employment and Wages (QCEW) data highlights three major items. First, the total farm workforce exceeds average employment in agriculture by at least two to one in California, which means that seasonal agriculture depends on a pool of workers who are employed only part of the year. There are many industries that offer seasonal jobs and assume workers will be available to fill them, from teaching to sports, and there are many occupations in which workers are employed full-time but perform their job for only part time, from firefighting to the military. Agriculture is almost unique in assuming workers will be available when needed at roughly the minimum wage, which is why economist Varden Fuller (1991) asserted that crop agriculture depends on "poverty at home and misery abroad" to assure itself a seasonal workforce.

Second, there is a gap between what a full-time worker would earn in a particular commodity and the average earnings of workers who were employed in that commodity. Table 3.3 shows that the average pay of full-time equivalent workers whose maximum earnings were from California agricultural employers in 2016 would have been $32,300. However, the actual average earnings of such primary farm workers were $16,100, half as much. A full-time worker is

---

[19] Some of those employed for wages on California farms are paid managers of corporate farms, office workers on such farms, and professionals including disease specialists.

Table 3.3 Full-time and actual average pay of California farm workers, 2016

		Share of FTE Employ	Full-time equivalent Pay($)	Primary Pay($)	Primary Share FTE	Hourly($) for 2080 hours
NAICS 11	All ag	100%	32,316	16,142	50%	15.54
NAICS 111	Crops	41%	34,411	20,540	60%	16.54
NAICS1112	Vegetables	8%	39,809	26,092	66%	19.14
NAICS1113	Fruits	23%	31,846	16,900	53%	15.31
NAICS1114	Nursery	6%	35,250	27,124	77%	16.95
NAICS 112	Animals	7%	37,372	30,989	83%	17.97
NAICS 112120	Dairy	4%	36,864	31,433	85%	17.72
NAICS 1151	Crop support	51%	29,956	12,297	41%	14.4
NAICS 115113	Machine harvesting	2%	35,457	17,571	50%	17.05
NAICS 115114	Other postharvest	10%	40,846	23,485	57%	19.64
NAICS 115115	FLCs	34%	24,589	9,026	37%	11.82

Source: Martin et al., 2019.

employed 40 hours a week for 52 weeks or 2,080 hours, so the implied hourly wage of a full-time worker in California agriculture was $15.54. However, most workers are employed fewer hours and/or at lower hourly earnings, which explains why they earn half as much or $16,100 (employers do not provide hours-worked data).

Third, the gap between full-time equivalent and actual average earnings varies by commodity. Hired workers in animal agriculture earn over 80 percent as much as full-time workers would earn because most are employed for long hours on one farm. Many large California vegetable farms operate in several areas to supply lettuce and other leafy green vegetables year-round. Some of the workers hired by vegetable farms that operate year-round move with the harvest, explaining why the average directly hired vegetable worker earns two-thirds as much as a full-time vegetable worker would earn.

The largest sector of farm employment, farm-labor contractors, had the largest gap between full-time and actual average earnings. FLCs employed a third of all primary farm workers in California in 2016. A full-time worker hired by an FLC would have earned $24,600 in 2016, equivalent to $12 an hour. However, workers whose maximum earnings were with FLCs earned an average $9,000, or 37 percent as much, equivalent to 900 hours of work at the then minimum wage of $10 an hour or 750 hours at $12 an hour.[20] This gap between full-time equivalent and average actual pay reflects some combination of fewer hours and lower hourly earnings.

NAWS

Researchers during the 1980s became increasingly dissatisfied with the HFWF. Farm workers played a prominent role in the debate over illegal immigration in the early 1980s that led to the Immigration Reform and Control Act (IRCA) of 1986. Farmers feared that newly legalized farm workers would leave for nonfarm jobs, leading to farm-labor shortages. Over 40 percent of the 2.7 million unauthorized foreigners who were legalized under IRCA, some 1.1 million, said they had done farm work in 1985–6, prompting the federal government to provide funding to determine whether IRCA's combination of legalization of unauthorized foreigners and sanctions on employers who knowingly hired unauthorized workers led to farm-labor shortages.

This research did not find labor shortages, but did create the National Agricultural Workers Survey or NAWS, the most frequently cited source of data

---

[20] The full-time versus actual earnings gap widened between 2015 and 2016. In 2015, FLC employees earned an average 44 percent of what a full-time FLC employee would have earned; by 2016, this was 37 percent (Martin et al., 2018).

on the characteristics, employment, and earnings of US crop workers. Unlike the HFWF, which was based on a sample of households, the NAWS is an employment-based survey, meaning that the NAWS relies on employer reports of how many workers each employer hired in order to select a sample of workers to interview. The NAWS interviews workers at the workplace rather than in their homes.

The NAWS interviews 1,500 to 3,000 workers a year who are employed on US crop farms, including a third in California, but does not interview H-2A guest workers and livestock workers. About two-thirds of the employers who are approached by interviewers agree to allow their workers to be interviewed. Sample workers are paid $20 to answer detailed questions about themselves and their families, their current and past jobs, and their health and access to welfare services in interviews that typically last forty-five minutes.

The NAWS began to interview crop workers in 1989; several years of data are usually combined in order to improve the reliability of the data. Many worker trends have a V-shape, beginning high, falling to a nadir around 2000 when unauthorized Mexico–US migration peaked, and rising since, especially after the 2008–9 recession reduced unauthorized migration (Table 3.4).

For example, the share of crop workers born in Mexico rose from 54 percent in 1990 to almost 80 percent a decade later, and has since stabilized at about 70 percent. The share of unauthorized workers rose from a seventh to over half in the 1990s, but has since stabilized at about half.

There are several definitions of migrant farm worker. The NAWS considers a worker to be a migrant if he moved at least 75 miles for a farm job, including moving from Mexico to the US within the past year. Under this definition, the share of migrants peaked in 2000 at 55 percent, when unauthorized migration was at its peak, and has since fallen to less than 20 percent. Half of the migrants in 2015–16 were shuttle migrants, meaning they had a usual home in Mexico and migrated each year to the US; most shuttle migrants are legal US immigrants. Only 6 percent of all crop workers are follow-the-crop migrants who have at least two farm jobs at least 75 miles apart.

Table 3.4 NAWS crop workers, 1989–91, 1998–2000, and 2015–16

Mexican-born %	54	79	69
Unauthorized %	14	54	49
Average age, years	33	31	38
Years US farm work	10	8	14
High school or more %	26	14	31
Migrant %	41	55	19
Follow the crop %	14	10	6
Farms below poverty income %		55	33
Farms receiving public assistance %	19	22	54

Source: NAWS, http://www.doleta.gov/naws/.

The crop workforce is aging. Between 1990 and 2000, the average age of crop workers fell as young rural Mexicans moved to the US. The slowdown in unauthorized Mexico–US migration means that the crop workforce is aging, approaching the average age of 42 for all US workers.

Crop workers have relatively little education and most do not speak English well. Crop workers across the US averaged eight years of schooling in 1990, seven in 2000, and eight today. About 60 percent of US crop workers have nine or fewer years of schooling, while a third completed high school.

Almost 60 percent of US and California crop workers are married parents, compared with 40 percent in 2000, when the crop workforce included many new-comers who had just arrived from Mexico. Median personal income is $15,000–$20,000 for US and California crop workers; a seventh of workers earned less than $10,000 in 2015–16, and a seventh earned more than $30,000. Median family income was $20,000–$25,000 in 2015–16, so that a third of crop-worker families had incomes below the poverty line.

One major change is the rising share of crop-worker families that include a member who received means-tested public assistance within the past year. Until 2000, when there were more solo male farm workers and fewer farm worker families with US-born children, about 20 percent of families reported that some-one in the household received means-tested federal benefits, such as Medicaid, Supplemental Nutrition Assistance Program (SNAP, and previously Food Stamps), and Special Supplemental Nutrition Program for Women, Infants, and Children (WIC) benefits for mothers and infants. In the 2015–16 data, over half of families had a member receiving such benefits.

The NAWS portrays an aging male and generally married crop workforce that is settling in the US with families.[21] The slowdown in unauthorized entries of young workers from Mexico means fewer migrants and more crop-worker fam-ilies receiving public assistance benefits, often for US-born children.

Employment data also follows a V-shaped trajectory, starting high, dipping in 2000, and rebounding since. For example, about 85 percent of US crop workers were hired directly in 1990, 73 percent in 2000, and 80 percent today. The California direct-hire shares were 73, 55, and 66 percent; that is, the California direct-hire share has not yet returned to 1990 levels.

Most NAWS crop workers are employed in fruits and vegetables, about 60 percent of US crop workers and almost 90 percent of California crop workers. In 1990, the NAWS found that 35 percent of US crop workers were in vegetables and 28 percent were in fruits and nuts. By 2000, it was 25 percent in vegetables and 37 percent in fruits and nuts, and today 35 percent of NAWS workers are in veget-ables and 30 percent are in fruits and nuts. In California, the 1990 vegetable

---

[21] More details on NAWS 2015–16 Crop Farm Workers are at https://migration.ucdavis.edu/rmn/blog/post/?id=2266.

share was 27 percent and the fruit and nut share 55 percent; these shares were 19 and 70 percent in 2000, and 26 and 63 percent today; that is, almost 90 percent of California workers are in fruits and vegetables.

The share of US and California crop workers in harvesting jobs has been falling. For the US, harvesting was the primary task of 40 percent of US workers when interviewed in 1990, 30 percent in 2000, and less than 20 percent today. For California, the harvesting share fell from almost half in 1990 to 30 percent in 2000 and 25 percent today. The most common current job is semi-skilled, such as equipment operator: a third of US workers, and 37 percent of California workers, had semi-skilled jobs when interviewed.

The NAWS data do not conform to stereotypes. For example, fruits and nuts are worth twice as much as vegetables, and hire large numbers of piece-rate harvesting workers. The NAWS interviews more non-harvest than harvest workers, and more vegetable than fruit workers, which may help to explain why almost 90 percent of workers interviewed by the NAWS reported being paid an hourly wage.[22]

The fact that NAWS has relatively few harvest workers who are paid piece rates may explain why NAWS reports that average hours worked were forty-six a week for men and forty for women; these would be more hours than usual for piece-rate workers. The relatively few piece-rate workers in the NAWS earned an average 2 percent more per hour than hourly paid workers.[23] The NAWS finds a higher share of workers who were hired by FLCs employed in vegetables, 60 percent, than in fruits, 35 percent, even though FLCs are often associated with seasonal fruit harvesting.

Helping Farm Workers

Agriculture employs large numbers of low-wage workers, and could be considered a target for unionization. Crop farmers are vulnerable to harvest-time strikes, so the threat of workers refusing to pick perishable crops should give unions leverage to win wage increases and working condition improvements. A major debate before California granted farm workers union organizing rights in 1975 was whether harvest-time strikes should be banned. They were not, and there have been very few strikes in California, including at harvest time (Martin, 2003).

Farm-worker unions such as the United Farm Workers union begun by Cesar Chavez have not been able to negotiate long-lasting contracts that raise wages for

---

[22] Piece-rate workers are guaranteed a minimum hourly wage, but their hourly earnings are typically higher to provide them with an incentive to work.
[23] Some studies suggest that piece-rate workers must earn at least 10 percent more per hour than hourly paid workers to give them an incentive to work fast without supervision.

three major reasons.[24] First, the farm workers most capable of being effective local union leaders are those who are first to leave for better nonfarm jobs, so that unions must constantly organize and educate new replacement farm workers about the benefits of unions.[25] Second, farm-worker unions do not have federal collective bargaining rights; only California has a state agency to organize elections to determine if farm workers want to be represented by a union and to compel farmers to bargain with the union certified to represent their workers.[26] Unauthorized migration for most of the period since the Agricultural Labor Relations Act (ALRA) was enacted in 1975 made it very difficult for the UFW and other unions to win wage increases, explaining why there are fewer than a hundred contracts in California agriculture after forty-five years, and fewer than a dozen contracts that have lasted for more than two decades.

Third, the structure of farm employment has changed to make it harder for unions to organize farm workers. Many farmers rely on intermediaries, including farm-labor contractors, custom harvesters, and similar nonfarm employers, to bring crews of workers to their farms. In the eyes of workers, the FLC or custom harvester is the employer, not the operator of the farm where they are employed temporarily.

The ALRA tried to strengthen the hand of unions by stipulating that the farm where workers are employed can be their employer for union purposes, even if the FLC is the employer for labor law and tax purposes. However, this effort to make farmers rather than FLCs be employers for union purposes was frustrated after most FLCs became custom harvesters who bring both equipment and labor to farms and thus are the sole employers of farm workers for all purposes, including collective bargaining.[27] FLCs are close to the workers they hire, and quick to learn of any union organizing efforts.

---

[24] Unions are organizations of workers whose purpose is to raise wages and improve conditions for members who pay the dues that support the union. Unions put pressure on employers with: (1) strikes that reduce the supply of a good or commodity, (2) activities that reduce the supply of labor, such as clauses in CBAs that limit mechanization, (3) political activities to obtain favorable laws and their interpretation, and (4) consumer boycotts to reduce demand for particular commodities. Employers counter these union weapons by replacing workers who strike or by shutting down production and locking out employees in a waiting game to see which side buckles first. Employers also engage in political activities and favor immigration and other policies that increase the supply of labor.

[25] The UFW largely stopped trying to organize new farm workers in the 1980s, when there was an influx of Mexican workers who thought Cesar Chavez referred to the Mexican boxer rather than the US leader of the UFW.

[26] New York's Farm Laborers Fair Labor Practices Act (S 6578) gives farm workers the right to organize into unions without employer interference and requires overtime pay after sixty hours of work a week after January 1, 2020. A provision of the state Employment Relations Act excluding farm workers from union protections was ruled unconstitutional by a state appellate court May 23, 2019. S 6578 includes a no-strike provision and card check, meaning that a union can be recognized as the bargaining representative for workers without a secret ballot election. S 6578, which also gives union organizers the right to enter farms to talk to workers about their union rights, will be administered by the state Public Employment Relations Board (https://perb.ny.gov/).

[27] The ALRB looks at several factors to determine whether a nonfarm entity bringing workers to a farm is an FLC (labor only) or custom harvester (equipment, supervision, and labor).

The failure of self-help unions to organize farm workers prompted other private efforts to improve wages and working conditions. The Coalition of Immokalee Workers (CIW) is a workers' center that negotiates Fair Food agreements with the buyers of tomatoes and other commodities produced in Florida (Martin, 2016). These Fair Food agreements require farmers who sell tomatoes to Taco Bell or Whole Foods to educate workers about their rights and to establish grievance systems where workers can report violations of labor laws. Buyers pay a premium price for commodities purchased from Fair Food-certified farms that is returned to the workers. Fair Food agreements are top-down; neither farmers nor workers vote for CIW agreements.

The Equitable Food Initiative (EFI) and Fair Trade USA involve similar top-down private efforts to improve conditions for farm workers by persuading buyers to require their farmer suppliers to implement a code of conduct that protects workers. EFI-certified farms have management-worker teams that educate workers and highlight worker concerns, while Fair Trade focuses on buyer-paid premiums that are returned to workers to improve their communities (Martin, 2016). Farmers pay for EFI or Fair Trade certification to become preferred suppliers. Some buyers require farmers to be certified in order to supply them with produce, as with Mexican farms that export commodities to the US. Workers do not vote for EFI or Fair Trade certification, but they may gravitate to certified farms because of the premiums paid or better working conditions.

Federal government policies toward farm workers have taken two major forms—inclusion and help for families. Farm workers were often excluded from labor laws when they were first enacted because of agricultural exceptionalism, the notion that agriculture was a unique and competitive industry comprised of family farmers. The hired hands on family farms were presumed to be farmers in waiting who had the same interests as their farm employers in high commodity prices, not labor law protections. Proponents of agricultural exceptionalism imagined a job ladder that involved workers learning how to farm while working for wages and making the transition to farmer, perhaps with the help of their farm employer.

The belief that hired workers and farmers had similar interests was a justification to exclude farm workers from minimum-wage, social-security, unionization, and unemployment insurance laws when they were first enacted. Coverage under federal protective labor laws has since been extended to most hired farm workers, but the pattern of labor-law exemptions and special laws persists, as with exceptions that permit some child labor on farms and the Migrant and Seasonal Workers Protection Act of 1983 that regulates farm-worker recruitment, transportation, and housing.[28]

---

[28] http://www.dol.gov/whd/mspa.

During the 1960s War on Poverty, farm workers were among the rural poor who were "left behind" by general prosperity. The conventional wisdom at the time was that labor-saving mechanization would eliminate most remaining hired farm workers in a decade or two. Most federal assistance programs that focused on reducing poverty concentrated on helping the poor in cities.

There was recognition that some poor farm workers would find it hard to escape from migrant and seasonal farm work, prompting the federal government to create education and health-assistance programs to help the children of farm workers obtain the education needed to find nonfarm jobs. These programs were successful in the sense that few children of farm workers who are educated in the US follow their parents into the fields, but they did not anticipate that a new and even needier workforce would replace farm workers who left agriculture (Martin and Martin, 1994). Today, a dozen federal programs provide over $1 billion a year in grants to public agencies and NGOs to assist migrant and seasonal farm workers and their children, with a third of the funds devoted to education of farm worker children.

4-S Responses to Fewer Newcomers

The two decades between the mid-1980s and 2005–7 were marked by large numbers of newly arrived and unauthorized rural Mexicans seeking jobs in the US, including in US agriculture. Mexico–US migration peaked in 2000, when a quarter of the hired workers employed on US crop farms were newcomers, defined as persons who were outside the US during the year before they were interviewed. Unauthorized Mexico–US migration declined after the 2008–9 recession, so that fewer than 2 percent of crop workers today are unauthorized newcomers.

The combination of fewer unauthorized newcomers, rising minimum wages, and health-care insurance mandates forced farmers to realize that labor costs are likely to continue to increase. Farmers are adjusting to the prospect of higher labor costs with 4-S strategies, viz., *satisfy* current workers to retain them longer, *stretch* current workers with mechanical aids that increase their productivity, *substitute* machines for workers where possible and switch to less labor-intensive crops, and *supplement* current workforces with H-2A guest workers. Satisfying and stretching are short-term responses that involve current workers, while mechanization, crop switching, guest workers, and imports are longer-term responses to rising labor costs.

Satisfy and Stretch Current Workers

Most farmers believe that the supply of farm labor inside US borders is fixed or inelastic, so that higher wages simply shuffle workers between farms rather than attract more US workers into farm work. This belief encourages farmers to avoid competing with each other for workers by raising wages, and prompts them to instead offer benefits and bonuses to *satisfy* their current workers to retain them. Bonuses can be paid in some years and not others, which many farmers see as better than raising wages, since it can be difficult to reduce wages in the future.

Many workers resent being seen as interchangeable members of crews that range in size from twenty to sixty. The crew leaders responsible for recruiting and supervising one or more crews may favor some workers over others and harass women. Training first-level supervisors, and developing mechanisms to reduce favoritism and harassment, can help to satisfy current workers and keep them on a particular farm longer.

Stretching workers means increasing their productivity. Most fruits and vegetables are over 90 percent water. Harvest workers spend much of their time carrying harvested produce down ladders to bins or to the end of rows to receive credit for their work, so that a third of their time may involve carrying rather than harvesting produce. Management changes and harvest aids help to make workers more productive.

Three major changes can increase worker productivity. First, better scheduling and coordination between sales and production teams can reduce worker waiting time and maximize the time available for productive work. Instead of having workers report early and wait for work to begin because crops are too wet to pick, or there are not sufficient bins to hold harvested produce, work schedules can be optimized so that workers do not have to wait. Second, repicking fields once instead of two or three times so there is more produce to pick can raise piece-rate earnings. Other management changes include dwarf trees and trellises that allow more picking of fruit from the ground, which is faster and safer for workers.

Third, slow-moving conveyor belts that travel in front of workers reduce the need for hand harvesters to carry bags or trays of harvested produce to a collection station, enabling workers to pick more produce. The machine sets the pace of work, so workers harvesting lettuce, broccoli, and other vegetables behind a conveyor belt are often paid hourly wages and offered a group bonus rather than individual piece-rate wages. Strawberry pickers who work for individual or group piece rates behind conveyor belts develop more homogeneous crews, as slower and faster pickers sort themselves into compatible crews.

Substitute Machines for Workers and Supplement with Guest Workers

Agriculture is the story of machines replacing workers, and the *substitution* of machines for hand workers continues in all farming systems. Many fresh fruits and vegetables are fragile, and human hands are gentler than mechanical fingers on table grapes or peaches. Machines are fixed costs and workers are variable costs, explaining why farmers facing an uncertain future may be reluctant to invest in machines. For example, should smaller California raisin-grape growers invest to restructure their vineyards to machine harvest their grapes even though raisins can be imported more cheaply from Turkey? When there are profitable alternatives to labor-intensive crops, some farmers *switch* from hand-harvested to more mechanized crops, as from raisin grapes to almonds in the San Joaquin Valley.

There are numerous efforts to develop machines to replace workers in labor-intensive fruit and vegetable commodities. The most common are precision planting machines that facilitate the use of mechanical rather than hand weeders (Charlton et al. 2019). GPS devices inform weeding machines where plants are located, which enables the machine to remove any weeds between rows and plants. Similarly, "see and spray" machines apply fertilizers and protective sprays only to useful plants, reducing fertilizer and chemical costs.

Weeding affects many acres of crops, enlarging the market for machines, while harvesting machines are often crop-specific, increasing technical difficulties and reducing the market for machine manufacturers (Calvin and Martin, 2010). Machine harvesting often requires farm management changes, such as planting new orchards and vineyards to facilitate the pruning and harvesting of trees and vines mechanically. Machine-mounted cameras have difficulty "seeing" fruit hidden by branches and leaves, raising the cost of developing machines that can harvest fruits such as apples as efficiently as people. Pruning trees to create walls that expose apples facilitates machine harvesting, but technical issues continue to bedevil cameras that try to detect ripe fruit through a canopy of leaves (Zhang et al., 2016).

Soft fruits such as strawberries pose tougher challenges for machines. Instead of planting two rows in raised beds that are picked by workers wheeling carts between the rows, machines with guide wheels need firm edges to travel down rows and to pick berries that have been trained to grow over the side. Tabletop berry production is best for machine picking, but requires up-front costs of $80,000 an acre, versus $30,000 an acre to plant conventional strawberries. Estimates of when strawberry harvesters will be viable commercially range from five to fifteen years, with diffusion depending on how fast engineers solve technical problems and the cost and availability of hand workers (Mohan, 2017; Strong and Hernandez, 2018).

These examples demonstrate that machine harvesting is feasible but expensive. Committing to machine-harvesting systems often means investment and specialization. Growers must think about how to plant trees, vines, and plants to facilitate machine harvesting. The potential size of the market for machines also plays a role. The US has about 380,000 acres of apples and 14,000 acres of apricots, so there is far more interest in developing an apple harvester than an apricot harvester.

Farmers anticipating too few seasonal workers have been able to *supplement* their workforces with legal guest workers under Mexico–US bracero programs from 1917 to 1921 and again between 1942 and 1964, and under the H-2 and H-2A programs since 1952 (Martin, 2009). Receiving DOL certification to employ H-2A guest workers requires employers to satisfy three major obligations: (1) trying and failing to recruit US workers, (2) providing free and approved housing to guest workers, and (3) paying the state or regional Adverse Effect Wage Rate (AEWR) that ranges from $11 to $16 hour in 2020.

The H-2(A) program evolved from a World War II program that imported mostly Jamaicans to cut sugar cane in Florida and to pick apples along the eastern seaboard. The Immigration Reform and Control Act (IRCA) of 1986, the law that imposed sanctions on US employers who knowingly hire unauthorized workers, was expected to curb illegal immigration and lead to the expansion of the H-2A program (Martin, 2014). Instead, IRCA legalized over 1.1 million unauthorized farm workers, and taught rural Mexicans how to use false documents to satisfy the I-9 worker documentation requirements that were key to effective employer sanctions, increasing rather than decreasing illegal migration and reducing grower interest in legal guest workers.

IRCA helped to spread first newly legalized and later unauthorized Mexican-born workers throughout US agriculture (CAW, 1992). Meanwhile, the Florida sugar-cane harvest was mechanized in response to worker suits alleging under-payment of wages to H-2A workers, so that only 15,100 farm jobs were certified to be filled with H-2A guest workers in 1995, including a quarter in tobacco (Martin, 2009, ch. 4).

The H-2A program remained small and concentrated on the eastern seaboard until the 2008–9 recession, when the slowdown in unauthorized Mexico–US migration prompted California and Washington farmers to request more H-2A workers. Table 3.5 shows that almost 258,000 farm jobs were certified to be filled with H-2A workers in FY19, double the number in FY14. The number of visas per job certified has been falling, suggesting that more H-2A workers are staying longer and filling just one US farm job.

Most H-2A workers are in the US less than the usual ten-month maximum stay permitted. If H-2A workers average six-month stays, then 200,000 H-2A visas means 100,000 full-time equivalent workers, suggesting that 10 percent of the million full-time equivalent jobs in US crop agriculture are filled by H-2A workers. In the mid-1950s, when the employment of hired farm workers averaged two million, a peak 450,000 braceros filled 20 percent of crop jobs.

H-2A workers are brought into the US in several ways. Most common is direct employment, when a farmer turns to a US lawyer or agent to recruit guest workers abroad and transport them to the US, making the farmer responsible for ensuring that program regulations are followed by recruiters abroad and supervisors in the US. The second system involves employer associations such as the North Carolina Growers Association or the Washington Farm Labor Association. These associations recruit and transport H-2A workers and sometimes move

Table 3.5 H-2A jobs certified and visas issued, 2005-19

	Jobs Certified	Visas Issued	Jobs/Visa
2005	48,336	31,892	1.5
2006	59,110	37,149	1.6
2007	76,814	50,791	1.5
2008	82,099	64,404	1.3
2009	86,014	60,112	1.4
2010	79,011	55,921	1.4
2011	77,246	55,384	1.4
2012	85,248	65,345	1.3
2013	98,821	74,192	1.3
2014	116,689	89,274	1.3
2015	139,832	108,144	1.3
2016	165,741	134,368	1.2
2017	200,049	161,583	1.2
2018	242,762	196,409	1.2
2019	257,666		
2005-11	60%	74%	-8%
2012-18	185%	201%	-5%

Source: US Department of Labor, https://www.foreignlaborcert.doleta.gov/h-2a.cfm; US Department of State, https://travel.state.gov/content/travel/en/legal/visa-law0/visa-statistics/nonimmigrant-visa-statistics.html.

them from one farm to another, helping to ensure that H-2A workers are fully employed. Associations can deploy workers so that they are fully employed, but the association becomes jointly liable with individual farmers for violations of program rules.

The third mechanism for admitting H-2A workers involves farm-labor contractors who recruit, house, and move H-2A workers from one farm to another. These FLCs list the farms to which they are supplying workers on their applications for certification, and take responsibility for ensuring that H-2A regulations are followed. FLC employment of H-2A workers has expanded rapidly, and FLCs in 2019 accounted for almost half of the jobs certified to be filled with H-2A workers. As with associations, FLCs should improve efficiencies in the farm-labor market, employing the minimum number of workers needed to get the work done.

One factor slowing the expansion of the H-2A program is litigation. Employers seeking certification to hire H-2A workers create job orders that specify in detail the job to be done, wages and benefits, and work-related benefits such as housing and transportation to and from the fields.[29] California Rural Legal Assistance sued several labor contractors who bussed H-2A workers from employer-provided housing to fields, alleging that the workers should be paid for the time they ride

---

[29] H-2A job orders are posted at https://seasonaljobs.dol.gov/.

to and from the fields because they do not know where to report for work and because the workers have no alternative to company buses to get to work.

California labor law is clear: if employers require workers to ride on company buses to fields, workers must be paid for their travel time. The California Supreme Court in the 2000 decision in Morillion v. Royal Packing ruled that Royal's requirement that its workers ride Royal's buses to and from the fields meant that Royal workers must be paid for this travel time. However, the court said that "employers may provide optional free transportation to employees without having to pay them for their travel time, as long as employers do not require employees to use this transportation."

CRLA alleged that H-2A farm workers have no choice but to use employer-provided transportation, so that employer-provided transportation for H-2A and other workers who are housed by employers is effectively mandatory rather than optional. Fresh Express settled the CRLA travel-time suit for $1 million in 2018, but will not have to pay for the travel time of H-2A workers in future (Rural Migration News, 2018).

HR 5038: IRCA Redux?

All three mechanisms to bring H-2A guest workers into the US—direct hiring, associations, and labor contractors—are expanding as Congress debates whether to revise the H-2A program to make it easier for farmers to hire guest workers (Martin, 2019). After the share of unauthorized workers in crop agriculture reached 50 percent in the mid-1990s, farm employers worried that immigration enforcement might lead to labor shortages, and urged the enactment of a new agricultural guest-worker program that would reduce requirements on employers.

Several bills were introduced in Congress that would have allowed farmers to hire free-agent guest workers who would have been required to work in agriculture in order to remain in the US legally. Employers would not have had to provide such free-agent guest workers with housing, and could have hired guest workers without first searching for US workers. However, President Clinton in June 1995 issued a statement: "I oppose efforts in the Congress to institute a new guest worker or 'bracero' program that seeks to bring thousands of foreign workers into the United States to provide temporary farm labor." Clinton predicted that a free-agent guest-worker program would increase illegal immigration, displace US farm workers, and depress wages and working conditions (Migration News, 1995).

Clinton's threat to veto any new farm guest-worker program blocked action in Congress during the 1990s. After the election of Mexican President Vicente Fox and US President George W. Bush in 2000, farm-worker advocates who feared that Fox and Bush would agree on a new guest-worker program negotiated the

IRCA-style Agricultural Job Opportunity Benefits and Security Act (AgJOBS), which would have legalized unauthorized farm workers and given farm employers easier access to guest workers. Then-Rep. Howard Berman (D-CA), a strong farm-worker advocate, urged a legalization program for currently unauthorized farm workers: "There are probably hundreds of thousands of undocumented agricultural workers who the growers already depend on to bring in the crops...Why not allow these undocumented workers to establish legal status?" (Rural Migration News, 1999).

AgJOBS would have repeated IRCA with several differences. Since unauthorized farm workers who were legalized under the Special Agricultural Worker (SAW) program in 1987-8 quickly left farm work for nonfarm jobs, AgJOBS would have given previously unauthorized farm workers only a temporary legal status that they could turn into an immigrant status if they continued to do farm work for the next several years. Farmers would no longer have to try to recruit US workers before hiring guest workers, could pay guest workers a housing allowance rather than provide them with housing, and the Adverse Effect Wage Rate, the minimum wage that must be paid to guest workers to avoid adversely affecting US workers, would be reduced.

AgJOBS was caught up in a broader debate over how to reform US immigration policy. Migrant advocates who wanted comprehensive immigration reforms, meaning a package of legalization, enforcement, and new guest-worker programs that would deal with all unauthorized foreigners in the US, not just farm workers, blocked efforts to deal with the two issues that had majority support in Congress—legalizing farm workers and legalizing unauthorized foreigners brought to the US as children, the so-called Dreamers. AgJOBS was included in the comprehensive immigration reform bills approved by the Senate in 2006 and 2013, but these comprehensive bills were not enacted despite the support of Presidents Bush and Obama due to opposition to "amnesty" for unauthorized foreigners.

The election of President Trump in 2016 dimmed prospects for any legislation that would put currently unauthorized foreigners on a path to legal immigrant status. Nonetheless, the House in December 2019 approved HR 5038, the Farm Workforce Modernization Act (FWMA), an AgJOBS-type bill to legalize currently unauthorized farm workers, streamline the H-2A program, and require farm employers to use E-Verify to check newly hired workers. Almost all House Democrats supported the FWMA, while three-fourths of Republicans opposed the bill.

HR 5038 would allow unauthorized farm workers who did at least 180 days or 1,045 hours of farm work during the previous 24 months to apply for Certified Agricultural Worker (CAW) status or H-2A visas. Applying for CAW status would grant the farm worker and his/her dependents renewable 5.5-year work permits that would be valid for employment in any industry. Unauthorized workers would be encouraged to apply because CAW application data are not to be used for immigration enforcement.

CAW work permits would be renewable indefinitely as long as workers per-form 100 days or 575 hours of farm work a year. CAW workers who were in the US at least 10 years could apply for immigrant visas after 4 years if they continued to perform 100 days or 575 hours of farm work a year, and those in the US less than 10 years could apply for immigrant visas after 8 more years of farm work. After the CAW legalization program is implemented, farm employers must use E-Verify to check the status of new hires.

There are currently 5,000 immigrant visas a year available for foreigners without college degrees who are sponsored by their employers. The FWMA would create 40,000 immigrant visas for farm workers who are sponsored by US employers or H-2A workers who worked at least 10 years in the US. H-2A workers who apply for immigrant visas, and who must wait in a backlog, would be allowed to stay in the US indefinitely while their applications for immigrant visas are pending.

The H-2A program would be modified to allow three-year visas rather than the current maximum ten-month visas, although there is an exemption from the ten-month limit for sheepherders who may generally remain in the US for three years. H-2A workers who complete a contract with one farmer, but have time remaining on their three-year visas, could stay in the US up to forty-five days to find a new employer who has been certified to hire H-2A workers.

Under HR 5038, employers would attest to their need for H-2A workers and begin to recruit US workers, hiring any who apply until a third of the work con-tract is completed; labor contractors would continue hiring US workers who apply for jobs until half of the contract is completed. Employers would not have to hire CAW workers if the H-2A worker they want to hire was employed by the employer three of the past four years. Recruiters of H-2A workers abroad would have to register with US embassies in the country of recruitment and promise not to charge any fees to the H-2A workers they recruit, to provide honest informa-tion about the US job, and to post a bond.

Employers of H-2A workers must offer and pay the higher of the federal or state minimum wage, the prevailing wage, or the Adverse Effect Wage Rate, which ranged from $11 to $16 an hour in 2020 based on employer responses to USDA's Agriucltural Labor Survey that obtains data on the average hourly earnings of non-supervisory crop and livestock workers.[30] Until 2018, the data came from about 11,000 farms, but the sample was expanded to 36,000 farms in 2019. About half of the farms in the survey provided employment and earnings data for the hired workers they hire directly, that is, the suvey does not collect data on workers brought to farms by contractors and other nonfarm employers.

HR 5038 would incorporate changes to the AEWR proposed by DOL in July 2019 that allow employers to shift from one AEWR for all types of farm workers

---

[30] The Agricultural Labor Survey is at https://usda.library.cornell.edu/concern/publications/x920fw89s?locale=en.

to giving each type of H-2A worker a job title and paying the AEWR associated with that job title. This means that the AEWRs for supervisors and equipment operators would rise, and the AEWRs for crop workers, who are currently over 90 percent of H-2A workers, would decline slightly.

AEWRs for 2020 are based on the 2019 USDA Farm Labor Survey. HR 5038 would freeze 2020 AEWRs and allow maximum increases of 3.25 percent a year, or 4.25 percent if the AEWR is less than 110 percent of the federal or state minimum wage. USDA and DOL would study the impact and need for AEWRs, and recommend how to proceed after 2030; that is, they could decide that AEWRs are not needed.

Up to 20,000 year-round farm jobs could be filled by H-2A workers, with 10,000 reserved for dairy farms, so that after three years there could be 60,000 H-2A workers in year-round farm jobs and 30,000 on dairy farms.[31] The cap on H-2A visas for year-round farm jobs could rise if USDA and DOL agree there is a need for more H-2A workers in year-round jobs, and the two agencies would make a determination after ten years about whether a cap on the number of H-2A workers in year-round jobs is needed. Employers of year-round H-2A workers would have to provide family housing for their H-2A employees and a paid trip home for each worker once a year.

A new pilot program would make 10,000 portable H-2A visas available to foreigners who could move from one farm employer to another. Portable H-2A workers would register with an online government platform and seek jobs posted by US employers seeking free-agent H-2A workers. After six years, DOL, Department of Homeland Security (DHS), and USDA must issue a report recommending what to do about portable H-2A visas.

As with previous AgJOBS proposals, there is little prospect that HR 5038 will become law. The top priority of the farm-worker advocates working with Democrats is to legalize unauthorized farm workers, while the top priority of farm employers working with Republicans is to reduce the cost of hiring legal guest workers. These priorities clash with those interested in broader immigration issues, including restrictionist groups that oppose the legalization of unauthorized foreigners and admissionist or pro-immigrant groups that oppose guest workers or "indentured servants" who are tied to a particular employer.

Trade versus Migration

An alternative to producing labor-intensive commodities in the US with foreign-born workers is to import commodities from lower-wage countries. Over half of

---

[31] There were an average 106,000 workers employed on US dairy farms in 2018 (NAICS 112120).

the fresh fruit consumed in the US, and a third of the fresh vegetables, are imported. Mexico accounts for half of US fruit imports and two-thirds of US fresh vegetable imports.

The US has had an agricultural trade deficit with Mexico since 2014.[32] The leading US imports from Mexico in 2016 were fresh and frozen fruits and vegetables worth $11 billion, representing almost half of the $23 billion of US agricultural imports from Mexico that year.

Mexico's export-oriented vegetable agriculture has been transformed over the past two decades, in part with US capital and expertise. Many Mexican growers of berries, tomatoes, and other vegetables erect protected structures, metal hoops covered with plastic that protect plants and reduce pests and diseases. These protected structures have controlled entry and exit points to reinforce worker adherence to food-safety protocols. Yields are up to three times higher for crops grown under protected structures than those grown in open fields, reducing the uncertainty inherent in agricultural production (Taylor and Charlton, 2018, Ch. 2).

The North American Free Trade Agreement (NAFTA) accelerated the adoption of science-based standards to evaluate the risk of transmitting pests and diseases across the Mexico–US border and facilitated the rapid transborder shipments of perishable commodities, encouraging some US growers and packers to form partnerships with Mexican growers to produce for US supermarkets. The North American fresh-produce supply chain is integrated in the sense that a US grower-packer may sign a contract to supply produce year-round to a US fast-food restaurant or supermarket chain, and grow the requisite produce in both the US and Mexico.

Candidate Donald Trump called the North American Free Trade Agreement "the worst trade deal ever negotiated by the US government," and President Trump threatened to withdraw the US from NAFTA if Canada and Mexico unless NAFTA was renegotiated. The US–Mexico–Canada USMCA that replaced NAFTA July 1, 2020 is expected to support rising cross-border trade in fruits and vegetables. However, Florida growers of tomatoes, who have long complained that Mexican growers "dump" fresh tomatoes in the US at below their cost of production, sued to block Mexican tomato imports in 1996, leading to a suspension agreement between Mexico and the US that suspends Florida growers' suit as long as Mexican producers sell their tomatoes in the US for at least the minimum or reference price stipulated in the agreement. The suspension agreement was negotiated in 1996, and updated in 2002, 2008, 2013, and 2018. It sets two reference prices: a higher price between October 22 and June 30, when Mexican imports are higher, and a lower price between July 1 and October 22; tomatoes cannot be imported from Mexico when the US price falls below the reference price.

---

[32] These commodities were a third of the $18 billion of US agricultural exports to Mexico in 2016.

Most farmers want a revised guest-worker program that could reshape the farm-labor and trade landscape. The Trump administration stepped up border enforcement, which reduced apprehensions of solo Mexican men just inside the US border and dried up the supply of new unauthorized workers seeking farm jobs. Instead of unauthorized Mexican men crossing the Mexico–US border surreptitiously and seeking farm jobs, most unauthorized border crossers since 2016 have been Central American families seeking asylum in the US. The Central Americans may enter the US illegally, but once inside the US they often seek out Border Patrol agents to surrender and apply for asylum.

The Trump administration took several steps to discourage Central American asylum seeking, including requiring asylum seekers to apply in the countries they transit en route to the US and requiring them to wait in Mexico until a US immigration judge hears their case.[33] After the outbreak of Covid-19 in spring 2020, the US government went further, closing US borders with Canada and Mexico to non-essential travel and allowing asylum officers rather than judges to decide that foreigners seeking asylum in the US because they have a well-founded fear of persecution there due to their race, religion, nationality, membership of a particular social group or political opinion are not likely to be recognized as refugees in need of protection and returning them to Mexico. These expedited removal procedures are used to deal with foreigners during the Covid-19 pandemic who illegally enter the US and are found within 100 miles of Mexican or Canadian borders.

Efforts to detect and remove unauthorized foreigners convicted of US crimes mean that searches for criminals in immigrant neighborhoods may detect other unauthorized foreigners who are detained and put into deportation proceedings. Immigration and Customs Enforcement (ICE) agency activities spread fear in immigrant neighborhoods, especially when state and local police agencies cooperate with ICE. Farmers say that many of their unauthorized workers stay home after ICE searches or news of police activity that could lead to their detection and detention.

A new guest-worker program that lowers labor costs could favor the expansion of fruit and vegetable production in the US rather than in Mexico. There have been many proposals in Congress for an employer-friendly guest-worker program for farm workers. Ex-Rep. Bob Goodlatte (R-VA) proposed a new H-2C program in 2018 that would have allowed all farm employers, including those offering year-round livestock and dairy jobs, to attest that they need guest

---

[33] Asylum seekers ask to be recognized as refugees fleeing persecution in their countries of citizenship. Over 80 percent of asylum applications from Central Americans are rejected, but the backlog of cases in the immigration system was over a million in 2019.

workers and to pay them at least 115 percent of the applicable federal or state minimum wage (Rural Migration News, 2018b).[34]

Under Goodlatte's proposal, farm employers would have to enroll in E-Verify to check the legal status of new hires, but would not have to provide housing to H-2C guest workers, who would pay their own way from their countries of origin to US farm jobs. H-2C workers could change employers in the US, and could remain in the US to do farm work for up to three years, after which they would have to return to their home countries for at least sixty days.[35]

Goodlatte's bill faced widespread opposition. Farm-worker advocates decried its provisions that would have reduced protections for US and foreign workers, while farm employers were divided. The American Farm Bureau Federation and most dairy associations supported the Goodlatte bill because it allowed guest workers to be employed in year-round jobs such as those on dairies, but the National Council of Agricultural Employers and the Western Growers Association opposed it, primarily because the number of H-2C visas was limited to 450,000 a year, including 40,000 for workers employed in meat and poultry processing. The Goodlatte bill was not enacted.[36]

President Trump's Virginia vineyard employs H-2A farm guest workers, and his hotels employ H-2B seasonal nonfarm guest workers, so many farm and non-farm employers expected Trump to make it easier for US employers to employ low-skilled guest workers. However, there were no major changes to the H-2A and H-2B guest-worker programs during Trump's first three years despite a promise in April 2018 that, "For the farmers, OK, it's going to get good. We're going to let your guest workers come in…they're going to work on your farms…but then they have to go out."[37]

What's Next

The US farm labor market is marked by three major features: stable average employment of 1.3 million jobs, 2.5 million aging and mostly unauthorized workers to fill these farm jobs, and ever more intermediaries or layers in the

[34] Goodlatte's bill, the Agricultural Guestworker and Legal Workforce Act (HR 6417), would have required farmers, as well as all other US employers, to participate in E-Verify, the online service that allows employers to submit documentation provided by newly hired workers to United States Citizenship and Immigration Services (USCIS) so that employers know immediately whether the new hire is authorized to work in the US.

[35] Details of Goodlatte's HR 4092 are at https://migration.ucdavis.edu/rmn/blog/post/?id=2172.

[36] H-2A workers returning to their previous employers would not count against the cap, and the cap could rise if employers requested all 450,000 visas. Since H-2C visas would be valid for up to three years, there could be over 1.3 million H-2C guest workers in the US after three years if employers requested all available visas.

[37] Quoted in Rural Migration News, 2018a. At Trump's request, the US Departments of State, Agriculture, Labor, and Homeland Security in May 2018 announced that they were "streamlining, simplifying, and improving the H-2A temporary agricultural visa program."

farm-labor market. Each of these factors—stable demand, uncertain supply, and intermediaries—affects who does farm work and how well farm workers are protected.

There have been predictions since the 1960s that the era of low-skilled hand workers in US agriculture is drawing to a close as machines replace workers. This has not occurred, largely because the expansion of one commodity has offset the loss of jobs that accompanies the mechanization of another. For example, the wine-grape harvest is largely mechanized, but almost all strawberries and rasp-berries are picked by hand, so the expansion of berry crops has helped to keep average US farm employment stable.

A review of the status of mechanization in 2000 distinguished between *labor aids* that make work easier for hand harvesters, such as conveyor belts that move slowly in front of workers as they pick strawberries or vegetables, and *labor-saving machines* that typically harvest a crop in a once-over fashion, as when shakers grasp the trunk or limb of a tree and shake the ripe fruit to the ground or into a catching frame, and *robotic systems* that selectively harvest marketable fruits and vegetables (Sarig et al., 2000). The major factors determining progress in the quest to replace farm workers with machines include the cost of machinery relative to the cost of hand labor, the need to compete with producers abroad, and food-safety concerns, with machine harvesting sometimes preferred to hand harvest-ing to minimize contamination.

The most typical US farm worker today is an unauthorized 40-year-old Mexican man with less than nine years of schooling who has been doing US farm work for over a decade. Most unauthorized farm workers have US-born children who anchor them to the US, making it unlikely they will return to Mexico volun-tarily. The fresh blood in the farm workforce are younger and legal Mexican-born men with H-2A visas who are in the US up ten months. These 30-year-old guest workers are selected for their ability to work fast. Their higher productivity helps to offset their higher costs, including the cost of recruitment in Mexico, transpor-tation to the US, and housing while employed in the US.

There have been many proposals to streamline the current H-2A program or replace it with another program that would make it easier for farmers to employ guest workers. The Goodlatte and similar proposals would reduce employer obli-gations and worker protections; similar H-2A streamlining proposals in the past, such as the Agricultural Job Opportunity Benefits and Security Act (AgJOBS) negotiated between worker and employer advocates in 2000, were accompanied by proposals to legalize currently unauthorized farm workers. AgJOBS was included in the comprehensive immigration reforms approved by the Senate in 2006 and 2013, but was not enacted into law, and HR 5038, approved by the House in December 2019, is also unlikely to become law.[38]

---

[38] The provisions of the 2013 Senate bill, S 744, are summarized at https://migration.ucdavis.edu/rmn/more.php?id=1769.

The farm-labor market is increasingly layered, with workers often unaware of who operates the farm where they work. The old stereotype of agricultural employment imagined a farmer who hired and worked alongside his employees. Today, many farm workers are assembled into crews of twenty to forty by contractors and other intermediaries and moved from farm to farm, with their paychecks coming from the contractor rather than the farm where they work. Workers consider the contractor whose name is on their check to be their employer, not the farm where they work.

Governments have struggled to regulate recruiters or merchants of labor effectively (Martin, 2017a). One of the founding principles of the International Labor Organization in 1919 was that workers should not pay to find jobs. Instead, governments should operate no-fee employment services where employers post job openings and workers seek jobs, prompting some governments to ban fee-charging job matchers, especially for low-skilled workers. Over the past half-century, the share of job placements made by no-fee public employment services has declined, while the share of workers employed by staffing agencies, labor contractors, and temp firms has risen. Temp agencies and labor contractors may not charge workers an up-front fee for jobs, but they make a profit by paying workers lower wages than they would earn if they were hired directly.

How can the mix of unauthorized workers, guest workers, and US citizens who are employed in agriculture be protected? Self-help unions generally fail because the workers who would be the most capable local union leaders are the first to leave for nonfarm jobs, and most remaining farm workers are more interested in moving out of agriculture than moving up in agriculture. Tougher labor laws and their enforcement can help to ensure compliance by making it more costly to violate rules and regulations that set minimum wages and working conditions. However, most labor-law enforcement depends on complaints, and fearful farm workers rarely complain.

As we will see in Chapter 7, the most effective protections for farm workers may lie with the buyers of perishable fruits and vegetables. Buyers set standards that producers must meet in areas ranging from how products are packed to the food-safety protocols that must be followed to grow and handle commodities. Many buyers require their suppliers to sign contracts that pledge adherence to all laws governing production, including food-safety and labor laws, and reserve the right to refuse to buy from noncompliant farms.

When should buyers invoke these refuse-to-buy provisions? Farmers point out that not all charges of labor law or food safety violations are sustained after further investigation, and experience shows that labor-law enforcement agencies often reduce or suspend penalties if farm employers remedy the violation. The overarching question is whether more of the same, viz., laws, enforcement, and detection of violations and corrections, is sufficient.

4

Mexican Farm Labor

Mexico was a Spanish colony for over three centuries. Spanish encomienda (from "to entrust") colonial policies granted farm land to conquering soldiers and white settlers, and obliged local indigenous residents to live on these latifundia (estates) and work for their Spanish owners, who were responsible for providing their workers with housing and food and converting them to Catholicism. The result was a system of haciendas, large estates devoted to crop and livestock farming that hired and housed millions of peasant families.

The Lerdo Law of 1856 broke up large corporate landholdings, including land owned by local governments and the Catholic Church. The intent of Mexico's Liberal government that came to power in 1855 was to create a middle class of farmers who owned their land, but flawed implementation and contradictions between federal and local laws and practices allowed a relative handful of individuals to acquire ever more land (Galindo, 2019). Peasants who lived on communal and church land were displaced, and landownership become concentrated among a few families. By 1910, about 2,000 families owned 87 percent of Mexico's rural land, and peasants were worse off than they were in 1855 (Hufbauer and Schott, 2005, 334). There were smaller farms as well, but land for the peasants became a rallying cry for change.

Revolution and Ejidos

The Mexican Revolution of 1910–17 was fought in part to ensure that peasants had their "own" land.[1] Article 27 of the Mexican Constitution of 1917 allowed Mexico's agrarian reform ministry to redistribute large private landholdings to ejido communal farms. Ejidatario members had the right to farm their plots as long as they actively worked and lived on the ejido, and their heirs inherited their land. The government did not want peasants to lose their ejido land, so ejidatario

[1] The proximate cause of fighting was the failure of the thirty-one-year-long regime of Porfirio Díaz to manage the presidential succession. Francisco Madero challenged Díaz in the 1910 presidential election. Diaz rigged the results, Madero and Pancho Villa led a revolt that toppled Diaz, and Madero was elected president in 1911. Madero was soon attacked by conservatives who saw him as too liberal, and by revolutionaries who saw him as too conservative, and he was forced out in 1913. Civil war that led to the deaths of 10 percent of the 15 million Mexicans followed, until the new constitution of 1917.

The Prosperity Paradox: Fewer and More Vulnerable Farm Workers. Philip Martin, Oxford University Press (2021).
© Philip Martin.
DOI: 10.1093/oso/9780198867845.001.0001

farmers could not sell or rent their land, nor could they borrow money using their land as collateral.[2]

Most of the 32,000 ejidos in 1990 included about 100 farmers and their families, giving Mexico 3.5 million ejidatarios who each farmed 5 hectares or less (Hufbauer and Schott, 2005, 334).[3] Most ejidatario farmers produced corn and beans without irrigation, often on several small and noncontiguous plots. Few ejidatario farmers produced a surplus to sell to the government at the higher-than-world price for corn that was the government's major anti-poverty policy in rural areas for most of the twentieth century. Instead, large farmers using irrigation and modern technology, and obtaining high yields, gained most of the benefits from the government's high-corn-price policy.

President Carlos Salinas, who proposed what became NAFTA in 1990, persuaded Mexico's Congress to amend Article 27 of the constitution in 1992 to permit ejido land to be sold, rented, and used as collateral for loans. In the quarter-century since, relatively little ejido land has been privatized, in part because a two-thirds majority of the ejidatario farmers must approve a sale during a meeting with at least 75 percent of members participating.

Many ejidatarios live in the US or in Mexican cities, making the participation requirement difficult to satisfy and explaining why less than 5 percent of the 10 million hectares of ejido land was sold between 1992 and 2015. The ejido land that has been sold often went to urban developers rather than staying in agriculture.

Mexico changed its agricultural policies in the 1990s, switching from subsidizing the price of corn to providing direct income support to poor farmers.[4] The theory behind this policy change was that large private farmers would switch from corn to fruits and vegetables, while poor farmers would get direct payments from the government.

Since NAFTA went into effect in 1994, economic growth in Mexico has averaged 2.6 percent a year. Mexico consistently runs a trade deficit, some $13 billion in 2016, reflecting imports of $387 billion and exports of $374 billion. Remittances of $27 billion, foreign direct investment of $27 billion, and foreign tourism receipts of $20 billion help to offset the trade deficit.

---

[2] Few private banks serve rural areas, in part because some past Mexican presidents won elections by promising to cancel farmers' debts. President Pena Nieto won the national election in 2012 by 3 million votes, but won by a margin of 5.4 million votes among farmers.

[3] Hufbauer and Schott (2005) report 3.5 million ejidatarios and 103 million hectares of ejido land in 2005.

[4] Subsistence farmers and landless workers can be hurt by high corn prices if they (1) do not produce a surplus of corn to sell and (2) do not have access to the subsidized tortillas made from government-bought corn.

Agriculture: NAFTA and USMCA

NAFTA transformed many sectors of the Mexican economy, especially auto manufacturing, which boomed as foreign investment and peso devaluations made Mexico an attractive place to produce auto parts and assemble cars and trucks for Americans, Canadians, and Mexicans.[5] By 2019, Mexico was the world's seventh-largest producer of autos and light trucks, producing over four million vehicles a year, and the fourth largest exporter, exporting over 80 percent of them.

Mexico's auto industry employs 800,000 workers, a fifth of the four million workers in Mexico's manufacturing sector. Mexico had 22 auto assembly plants in 2019 and 2,500 auto-parts factories. The largest auto cluster is in Aguascalientes, host to eight auto makers that assemble 1.5 million vehicles a year.

The keys to the growth of the Mexican auto industry include free-trade agreements and skilled and low wage labor. Over 80 percent of Mexican exports go to the US, but Mexico has free-trade agreements with forty-six countries, including most Latin American countries and the EU and Japan. One benefit of Mexican FTAs is that it can be cheaper to export cars from Mexico to the EU than from the US to the EU.

The fourth of Mexican auto workers employed in assembly plants have the highest wages, an average $2.30 an hour in 2016–17. Payroll taxes add 30 percent, making labor costs $3 an hour. Three-fourths of auto workers are employed in auto-parts plants and earn half as much or $1.20 a hour, with labor costs of $1.60 an hour. Labor costs in Mexico are at least $700 per car than in Canada or the US, and these labor-cost savings help to the offset additional costs of Mexico's lagging infrastructure.

The United States–Mexico–Canada Agreement (USMCA) aims to slow the exodus of US auto jobs to Mexico by raising the North American content requirement from 62.5 percent to 75 percent; that is, 75 percent of the parts must be made in North America for cars and light trucks to trade freely between Canada, Mexico, and the US. Furthermore, 40 to 45 percent of the auto's components must be made by workers earning at least $16 an hour. The USMCA required the Mexican government to modify its labor laws to allow more independent unions by creating a new Federal Center of Conciliation and Labor Registry to register unions and new Labor Courts that are part of the judiciary to resolve disputes.

Mexican agriculture also changed with NAFTA. Imports of less costly US yellow corn, soybeans, and wheat, as well as cheaper meat and dairy products,

[5] Mexico had an import-substitution policy until the 1980s that encouraged US and other manufacturers to establish auto-assembly plants in Mexico to avoid high tariffs. NAFTA expanded these assembly plants and led to the creation of an auto-parts industry.

encouraged a flight from the land as Mexican farmers with small plots realized they could not compete with lower-cost commodities imported from the US. Mexico's agricultural workforce shrank as farmers and their children left rural areas for Mexican cities and the US.

Then-President Salinas memorably suggested in 1990 that the US should support NAFTA because freer trade would allow Mexico to export more tomatoes and fewer tomato pickers to the US; that is, Salinas wanted to substitute trade in goods for the migration of workers. Salinas proved prescient, but he did not anticipate that more than a decade would be needed to create a globally competitive agricultural export industry in Mexico.

Mexico has become the world's largest exporter of fresh tomatoes and avocados, supplying over 85 percent of US consumption. The value of Mexico's agricultural output rose by an average 3.2 percent between 1994 and 2018, and rose faster after the 2008–9 recession, with the value of some fresh fruits and vegetables that are exported rising over 10 percent a year.

As Mexico's export-oriented fruit and vegetable agriculture expanded, an influx of avocados, berries, tomatoes, and other fresh fruits and vegetables into the US turned what had been a US agricultural trade surplus with Mexico into a deficit since 2014. Nonetheless, most assessments of NAFTA's effects on agricultural trade after a quarter-century echo the conclusions of Gantz (2019, 26); Mexico imports the products of mechanized US farms—grain and meat—and exports labor-intensive fruits and vegetables to the US, exactly what economic theory predicts.

Few of Mexico's 3.6 million farms export fruits and vegetables to the US, for several reasons. First, most Mexican farms are small. Over 70 percent of Mexican farms have less than 5 hectares, and half have less than 2 hectares or 5 acres, while the 25,000 Mexican farmers with more than 100 hectares of farm land have 30 percent of all Mexican crop land. Second, fresh fruit and vegetable farming for export requires capital, management ability, and infrastructure that most small farmers lack. Banks are reluctant to lend to small farmers because of historically high default rates and frequent government intervention to forgive farm debts (Hufbauer and Schott, 2005, 336).

Some 6.6 million of Mexico's 54 million workers were employed in agriculture in 2017, including 3 million or 45 percent who worked for wages on Mexican farms. Mexico has many agricultural sub-systems, from large and modern farms in the north and central states to subsistence farms in mountainous areas and southern states. Many modern farms in the north and center of Mexico rely on machinery rather than hired workers to produce corn and grains for the Mexican market, but an important subsector produces fresh fruits and vegetables to export to the US. Farms in southern Mexico are smaller, rely on rainfall to provide water for plants and animals, and produce mostly corn and grains for home consumption. There are exceptions to these generalizations in both northern and southern Mexico.

Corn occupies a special place in Mexico, with tortillas a staple of the Mexican diet. In 2015, some 8.2 million hectares of land were devoted to corn, 37 percent of Mexico's 22 million hectares of crop land. Corn farming involved 3.2 million farmers, family and hired workers, including 92 percent who worked on farms with less than 5 hectares of corn; over 80 percent of Mexican corn acreage is rain-fed rather than irrigated (Gonzalez and Macias, 2017, citing SAGARPA-CIAP). Almost 93 percent of Mexican corn acreage was white corn, and most of the 25 million tons of white corn produced in 2015 was used for tortillas. The remaining 7 percent of corn acreage yielded 14 million tons of yellow corn used mostly for animal feed.

Mexico produces about 80 percent of the corn consumed in the country. Mexican corn yields averaged 5 tons a hectare in 2014 (only 3.2 tons for white corn), versus 11 tons a hectare in the US. Corn yields in the north are similar to US yields, 12 to 15 tons per hectare, while yields in the south are 1 to 2 tons per hectare.[6] Another 20 percent of Mexican farm land is devoted to grains, but the 70 percent of Mexican farm land used for corn and grains accounts for only 35 percent of farm sales.

Fruits and vegetables occupy 10 percent of Mexico's crop land but generate 40 percent of Mexican farm sales. Fruit and vegetable exports to the US of $11 billion in 2016 were almost half of Mexico's $23 billion in farm exports, making Mexico's farm exports comparable in value to remittances and tourism receipts. Mexico's $18 billion in farm imports from the US were dominated by corn and soybeans, meat, and dairy products. Mexico has an overall trade surplus with the US, and has had a surplus in agricultural trade with the US since 2014.

Mexico has become a world leader in protected agriculture—greenhouses and hooped structures covered by plastic that fully or partially protect the plant during its growth period. AMHPAC, the Mexican Association of Protected Horticulture, reported that Mexico's protected agriculture area expanded from 330 acres in 2003 to 106,000 acres (42,500 hectares) in 2018, including 27 percent greenhouses, 29 percent hoop or macro tunnels, and 45 percent shade houses.[7] About 70 percent of Mexico's protected agriculture hectares in 2015 were devoted to tomatoes, 16 percent to bell peppers, and 10 percent to cucumbers, and over 80 percent of the vegetables produced under protective structures were exported to the US (Pratt and Ortega, 2019, 4).

There are several reasons why growers invest in protected agriculture structures, including the need for less water and fewer pesticides, higher yields, and more attractive working conditions.[8] Yield gains in protected agriculture are

---

[6] The result of these yield differences is that most of Mexico's corn and grain is produced in the north, although most of the land devoted to corn and grain is in the south.
[7] http://www.amhpac.org/es/index.php/descripcion.
[8] Some researchers say that workers in protected culture structures complain of hot working conditions during some times of the year and the presence of cameras and other control devices that require them to strictly observe food safety and other protocols.

striking. Open field production of tomatoes on irrigated land yields 40 tons per hectare, while high-tech greenhouses that use substrate instead of soil can have yields per hectare ten to thirty times higher. Low-tech hoop structures and shade houses raise tomato yields by three to ten times.

Many high-tech greenhouses produce year-round, which stabilizes the workforce and results in a higher share of female workers. High-tech greenhouses use fewer workers per hectare, ten compared with twenty or more in open fields and low-tech greenhouses, and almost always enroll their workers in Mexico's IMSS (Mexican Social Security Institute) program and pay taxes on worker wages that cover the cost of health and child care as well as pensions (Pratt and Ortega, 2019). Exposure to toxic chemicals is often less in high-tech greenhouses than in open-field agriculture or lower-tech protected structures, and safety and labor compliance protocols are more likely to be followed in high-tech greenhouses that involve significant investments and US buyers.

The Secretariat of Agriculture, Livestock, Rural Development, Fishing, and Food (SAGARPA, Secretaría de Agricultura, Ganadería, Desarrollo Rural, Pesca y Alimentación, now SADER, Secretaría de Agricultura y Desarrollo Rural), had a budget of 72 billion pesos ($3.8 billion) in 2018. Three-fourths of SAGARPA's budget supports three programs. The Program of Promotion for Agriculture (Programa de Fomento a la Agricultura) absorbs 23 percent of SAGARPA's budget and aims to increase farm-level productivity via support services and direct payments under the PROAGRO Productivo program.[9] The Program of Supports for Small Producers (Programa de Apoyos a Pequeños Productores) absorbs 22 percent of the budget and helps small farmers to increase their productivity via a variety of programs, including some that target beginning farmers. The Program of Supports for Marketing (Programa de Apoyos a la Comercialización) uses 13 percent of the budget to improve marketing efficiency and to promote exports.

The direct-payment PROAGRO Productivo program, previously PROCAMPO (Programa de Apoyos Directos para el Campo), began in 1994 as a way to provide transitional assistance to farmers and to compensate for the elimination of guaranteed prices for basic staples such as corn and beans. In 2018, PROAGRO Productivo payments ranged from 180 to 1,800 pesos ($10 to $85) per hectare, depending on farm size and access to irrigation. The OECD says that, despite changes to Mexico's farm policies, government support continues to be regressive, favoring the best-off farmers who produce corn, milk, and sugar.[10]

---

[9] https://www.ers.usda.gov/topics/international-markets-us-trade/countries-regions/nafta-canada-mexico/mexico-policy/.

[10] Until the 1980s, the Mexican government supported agriculture and consumers by having government agency CONASUPO (National Company of Popular Subsistences) pay farmers a high price for staples such as corn, and then CONASUPO sold staples and tortillas at subsidized prices to consumers. The OECD and others pointed out that this system benefitted the largest farmers, who had

MEXICAN FARM LABOR 73

Farm Workers

Mexico's population rose from 26 million in 1950 to 38 million in 1960 and doubled to 76 million in 1984. Since the mid-1980s, Mexico's population has increased by almost 70 percent to 128 million in 2016 (World Bank, 2017). The rural share of the population fell steadily, from 49 percent of residents in 1960 to 20 percent in 2016, but the number of rural residents rose from 19 million in 1960 to 26 million in 2016.

There are several sources of data on Mexico's total and agricultural labor force. World Bank data find that the share of Mexican workers employed in agriculture fell from 26 percent in 1991 to 13 percent in 2017, with an unexplained drop to 10 percent in 2014 followed by a rebound, as shown in Table 4.1. The share of all Mexican male workers who were employed in agriculture fell from 32 percent in 1991 to 19 percent in 2017, down 40 percent, while the share of all female workers who were employed in agriculture fell from 10 percent in 1991 to 4 percent in 2017, down 60 percent.

Table 4.2 shows that Mexico's labor force was 52.3 million in 2017, including 32.4 million men (62 percent), and 19.9 million women. Mexico's labor force increased by 800,000 a year over the last decade, adding an average 680,000 men and 120,000 women a year. Employment in agriculture rose from 6.2 million to

Table 4.1 Employment in Mexico, 2005–17

	Agriculture	Industry	Services
2005	6,219	10,761	25,100
2006	6,127	11,191	26,060
2007	6,045	11,418	26,769
2008	6,114	11,297	27,532
2009	6,217	10,859	28,359
2010	6,366	11,055	28,701
2011	6,394	11,237	29,507
2012	6,623	11,489	30,595
2013	6,666	11,744	30,818
2014	6,751	12,026	30,639
2015	6,744	12,504	31,364
2016	6,710	13,057	31,828
2017	6,811	13,377	32,152
2005–17	10%	24%	28%
2005–11	3%	4%	18%
2011–17	7%	19%	9%

Source: OECD Labor Force Statistics.

surplus corn to sell, rather than subsistence farmers, who did not have a surplus to sell or access to subsidized tortillas. This grower and consumer support system began to be dismantled in the 1980s, and CONASUPO was abolished in 1999.

Table 4.2   Mexico labor force, 2015

	Millions	Share %
Civilian Labor Force	52.6	
growth 2010–15	0.7	
Men	32.7	62%
Employed	50.3	96%
Unemployed	2.9	
Sector: all employed		**Share %**
Agriculture	6.8	14%
Industry	12.5	25%
Services	31	62%
Sector: employees		**Share %**
Agriculture	2.9	43%
Industry	9.7	78%
Services	21.6	70%

Source: OECD Labor Force Statistics, 2017.

6.8 million between 2005 and 2017, up 10 percent. Agriculture has the lowest share of employees or wage workers, 43 percent, compared to 78 percent wage workers in industry and 70 percent in services.

Of the 50.3 million employed persons in Mexico in 2017, 34.2 million were wage and salary employees, 13.4 million were self-employed (own-account), and 2.7 million were unpaid family workers.[11] Some 2.9 million workers were unemployed.

By sector, 6.8 million of the 50.3 million employed persons in Mexico in 2016 were in agriculture (14 percent), 12.5 million or 25 percent were in industry (including 8 million in manufacturing), and 31 million or 62 percent were in services. Among the 34.2 million employees, 2.9 million were in agriculture (43 percent of those employed in agriculture were employees), 9.7 million in industry (including 6.4 million in manufacturing), and 21.6 million in services. The share of self-employed persons is much higher in agriculture than in industry and services.

A major issue in Mexico is informality, defined by the Mexican National Institute of Statistics and Geography (INEGI) as workers employed by nonfarm informal firms, self-employed workers in agriculture, unpaid workers in family businesses, and workers not covered by Mexican Social Security Institute (IMSS) health and social security benefit programs (IMF, 2018). About 56 percent of Mexicans had informal jobs in 2017; most were employed in nonfarm informal

---

[11] Using the same definitions, the OECD reported that the US labor force was 157.1 million in 2015, including 83.6 million men and 73.5 million women; some 8.3 million of these US workers were unemployed. Of the 148.8 million employed persons, 139.2 million were employees and 9.5 million were self-employed (own-account). Mexico has relatively fewer women in its labor force and a much higher share of self-employed and unpaid family workers.

Formality by sector
(Perrcentage of emplyoed)

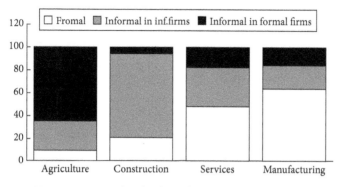

Figure 4.1 Formal and informal workers by sector, 2017.

firms that did not register their employees with IMSS and pay required payroll taxes.

Figure 4.1 shows that fewer than 10 percent of persons employed in agriculture in 2017 had formal jobs covered by IMSS, compared with 20 percent of persons employed in construction. Formal-sector workers have more education and higher productivity than informal workers, which helps to offset the cost of payroll taxes that formal-sector employers pay to IMSS. Formal workers can sue for unfair dismissal, adding a risk that may discourage small firms from becoming formal. Informality may beget more informality, as young and less educated workers have few opportunities and incentives to acquire new skills that could increase their productivity.

OECD data show that the number of self-employed and unpaid family workers in Mexican agriculture fell over the past decade, while the number of wage workers rose by over 40 percent. There are more self-employed than wage workers in Mexican agriculture, but the gap has narrowed significantly. Gonzalez and Macias, 2017, citing INEGI data, reported 6.7 million workers employed in Mexican agriculture in 2015.

Some 24 million people, 18 percent of Mexican residents, lived in rural areas in 2015. SEDESOL, the government's Secretariat of Social Development responsible for reducing poverty, released a Diagnóstico report in 2010 on hired farm workers that emphasized that most are poor people with few local options for decent work. Some migrants are recruited to work in agriculture far from their homes, including on farms that export produce to the US.

Mexican government agencies paint different pictures of agriculture and farm-worker employment. INEGI's report on farm workers to celebrate farm worker day May 15, 2016 (INEGI, 2016) reported 5.5 million people employed in agriculture at the end of 2015, 11 percent of the 51-million-strong workforce, including

56 percent or 3.1 million farmers and 44 percent or 2.4 million support workers. Of these support workers, two-thirds were hired workers and a third were unpaid family members, suggesting 1.6 million hired wage workers in Mexican agriculture, which was just over half of the 2.9 million agricultural employees reported by OECD.

INEGI's report included demographic characteristics. The average age of all persons employed in agriculture was 42 in 2015, average years of schooling were 5.9, and average earnings were 18.5 pesos or $1 an hour. Chiapas, Oaxaca, and Guerrero had the highest share of the state's workers employed in agriculture, 30 to 35 percent, followed by 20 to 25 percent in Puebla, Veracruz, Michoacán, and Zacatecas.

Migration to farming areas peaks in November–December. Workers are recruited by contractors and transported by bus or truck to farms, where they often move into farm-employer-provided housing in anticipation of the peak harvesting season between January and April. The major destination for migrant farm workers, many of whom are indigenous, is Sinaloa.

The minimum wage in Mexico in 2017 was 80 pesos or $4 a day, equivalent to $0.50 per hour for an eight-hour day. Large farms producing fruits and vegetables for export typically pay more, 90 to 130 pesos a day, especially in areas that produce high-value commodities in high-cost areas, such as berries in Baja California. Workers who hand-cut sugar cane earn the most, 150 to 200 pesos a day, to perform a very difficult job.

The Mexican public employment service SNE, begun in 1978, is decentralized, meaning that the federal government transfers funds to state governments to operate job centers to match workers with jobs. The SNE had programs to help farm workers move from poorer southern Mexican states such as Chiapas and Oaxaca to richer states with export-oriented farms in Sinaloa, Sonora, and Baja California, using liaison officers in migrant-sending communities to recruit workers and in destination areas to solicit job offers. Workers moving between states received $150, and those moving within states received $80 (ILO, 2018b); these migration subsidies ended in 2019.

Employers cover the transportation costs of solo migrant workers, but the government pays transportation costs for migrant families, and SNE liaison officers ensure that migrants arrive at the correct farm. The seasonal agricultural worker program can place a worker with three different employers in one year, providing three to eight months of employment. The program for migrant families provides food assistance, school uniforms, and support for health care to reduce child labor. The ILO (2018b, 14) reported that 1.6 million farm workers were eligible for the seasonal agricultural worker program in 2016, and that these eligible migrant workers had almost 5 million dependents. The SNE placed 110,180 farm workers via the seasonal agricultural-worker program in 2016, and served 200,700 farm workers and their families.

Several southern Mexican states employ legal and irregular workers from Central America, typically on large coffee and other farms. The often indigenous Mexicans who used to fill seasonal jobs on these farms now migrate north for higher wages, and Central Americans have replaced them. A World Bank survey in 2016 found that Guatemalans employed on southern Mexican farms had migration costs that averaged $60, and they earned an average $240 a month in Mexico. Hondurans and Salvadorans paid more for jobs in southern Mexico, an average $160, and earned similar wages, so that migration costs were less than a month's earnings for these mostly legal guest workers.

Berry Exports and Workers 2018

The berry industry is one of the fastest growing sectors of Mexico's export agriculture. Since berries are consumed disproportionately by richer consumers outside Mexico, the expansion of Mexico's berry industry is sometimes criticized as a case of poor workers in one country producing luxury commodities for affluent consumers in another.

Berries include two major subsectors: strawberries that are usually planted each year and perennial blueberries, raspberries, and blackberries that can produce fruit for decades, although most farmers replant these perennials after three or four harvests. Demand for fresh berries has been rising because of their perceived health benefits as well as year-round availability and convenient packaging, making berries the highest-revenue fresh produce item in US supermarkets.

Table 4.3 shows that strawberries represented 47 percent of the $6.4 billion in US retail fresh berry sales in 2017, followed by blueberries at 26 percent, raspberries at 14 percent, and blackberries at 9 percent (Cook 2017). Americans consumed 1.7 million metric tons of berries worth $6.4 billion in 2017, an average 12 pounds per person. Retail berry sales were 20 percent of the $31 billion in US

Table 4.3 US retail berry volume and sales, 2017

	Volume	Spending
Strawberries	65%	47%
Blueberries	21%	27%
Raspberries	7%	14%
Blackberries	5%	9%
Total	98%	97%
Total	1.8	$6.40

Volume is billion pounds; spending is $ billion.
Source: Cook (2017).

fresh fruit sales.[12] Berries are high-value commodities; they were only 8 percent of the quantity of fresh fruit sold in US supermarkets, but 20 percent of the value of fresh fruit sold.

US strawberry consumption per person doubled from 4 to 8 pounds between 2001 and 2016, while blueberry consumption quadrupled from 0.5 pounds to 2 pounds per person. Raspberry and blackberry consumption are each less than 1 pound per person per year, but their rate of increase is much faster, up eightfold since 2001 (Cook 2017).

Most of the strawberries available to US consumers are produced in the US, while most blackberries, blueberries, and raspberries are imported. The share of imports in US strawberry consumption is 14 percent, compared to 53 percent for blueberries[13] and 55 percent for raspberries (there are no data on blackberries, but almost all US blackberry imports are from Mexico). Mexico's strawberry exports peak between December and March,[14] and Mexico exports raspberries between October and May.[15] Most blackberry imports are from Mexico, except during the summer months when California is producing.

Four firms market most fresh strawberries in the US, led by market leader Driscoll's, which is also the dominant marketer of raspberries, accounting for 90 percent of US raspberry sales from farms in California and Mexico. Naturipe Farms is the leading marketer of blueberries in the US, and also markets other berries. Both Driscoll's and Naturipe market blackberries from Mexico, especially via Costco.

Growing berries is different from farming most other crops. Marketers such as Driscoll's develop and patent particular plant varieties, grow seedlings in cold climates away from where strawberries are planted,[16] and lease the plants to farmers under conditions that include a requirement that growers market the berries produced via Driscoll's, which sells the berries and deducts plant and marketing costs of 20 to 30 percent before sending the balance to the grower. Growers are responsible for growing the berries and delivering them to the marketer's cooling facility; that is, growers rather than Driscoll's hire farm workers (Baum, 2005).

US strawberry acreage is shrinking, while Mexican strawberry acreage is expanding. Most California strawberry acreage is in the coastal areas around

---

[12] Total retail fruit sales are not fully counted, but are at least $31 billion.

[13] Chile is the leading supplier of blueberries, followed by Canada, Mexico, Peru, and Argentina.

[14] Mexico exports a third of the strawberries that it produces, almost all to the US. Chile exported 103,000 metric tons of blueberries in 2016–17, two-thirds to the US, while Peru exported 40,000 metric tons, 55 percent to the US. Peru's blueberry exports are rising fast, often due to investments by Chilean firms and shipments by sea to the US. The La Libertad region of northwestern Peru is ideal for growing blueberries, but housing for workers is scarce.

[15] The US produced about 80,000 metric tons of raspberries in 2016, and imported 60,000 metric tons, almost all from Mexico.

[16] Many of California's strawberry-plant nurseries are in northeastern California, which has cold nights. When planted in warmer areas, the plants immediately begin to grow.

Salinas and Oxnard, where land and housing costs are high. Strawberries have been planted in these areas for decades, which means that nematodes and soil-borne pathogens can build up over time. Farmers were able to sterilize the soil with methyl bromide, covering fields with plastic and injecting the fumigant into the soil,[17] until 2016, when the use of methyl bromide was ended because it damages the ozone layer. The loss of methyl bromide, and the government's failure to approve methyl iodide after protests, increased disease issues (Guthman, 2019), prompting some marketers to turn to Mexico, where new land with fewer pests can be brought into production.

Mexico's export-oriented berry industry is expanding with the help of US and Chilean partners. Mexico produced about 850,000 metric tons of berries in 2016, including 55 percent strawberries, 29 percent blackberries, and 13 percent raspberries (Cook, 2017). A third of Mexican strawberries are exported to the US, and almost all of the raspberries and blackberries produced in Mexico are exported to the US.

Mexico's major berry production areas are Irapuato, Guanajuato (strawberries), Michoacán (strawberries and blackberries[18]) and Jalisco (blueberries and raspberries); Baja California also produces organic strawberries and raspberries on sandy soils using desalinated water—the high value of these berries justifies desalination. Mexican blueberry exports are expanding rapidly, especially during the March–April early spring period (Cook, 2017).[19] Mexico is the world's largest producer of blackberries.

Mexico had 28,000 acres of strawberries in 2018, and produced 468,000 tons of strawberries in 2016, including 73 percent in Michoacán, 15 percent in Baja California, and 8 percent in Guanajuato (SIAP, 2017). Many of the Guanajuato berries are frozen or used for jams and jellies.

There are several measures of Mexican berry exports. Table 4.4 shows that SAGARPA reports rapid growth in berry exports, especially of blackberries, blueberries, and raspberries. The value of other berry exports rose from $7 million in 2002 to $300 million in 2010, and exceeded $1 billion by 2017. The value of

---

[17] Methyl bromide mixed with a small amount of chloropicrin (a tear gas) sterilizes the soil, killing bacteria, nematodes, and weeds. It is especially effective against verticillium or wilt, a soil-borne fungus that transforms vigorous green leaves into dry brown litter. Guthman (2019, 200) argues that fumigation is key to understanding the development of the industry, encouraging on-the-ground production that required pickers to bend over to work.
[18] The major blackberry production area is Los Reyes in Michoacán.
[19] Chile is the world's second-largest blueberry producer, after the US, and the largest exporter of blueberries, exporting $647 million worth of blueberries in 2018 (global blueberry exports were worth $3.1 billion in 2018). Chilean farmers are partnering with Peruvian farmers to expand blueberry production in the La Libertad region of northwestern Peru, where 4,000 hectares of blueberries generated $548 million worth of blueberry exports in 2018. In northern Peru, blueberry plants can be pruned to produce berries almost any time of the year, and Peruvian blueberries can be shipped by boat to the US, reducing transport costs. See http://www.freshplaza.com/article/9162047/peru-could-replace-chile-as-world-s-leading-blueberry-exporter-in-2020/.

Table 4.4 Mexican strawberry and other berry exports, 2002–17

	Strawberries $ millions	Other Berries $ millions
2002	6	7
2003	14	17
2004	29	27
2005	45	68
2006	64	115
2007	94	174
2008	102	202
2009	147	247
2010	179	302
2011	224	224
2012	292	477
2013	275	512
2014	328	638
2015	339	826
2016	519	888
2017	557	1036

Other berries are blackberries, blueberries, and raspberries.
Source: Cook, 2017.

Mexican strawberry exports rose from $6 million in 2002 to $180 million in 2010, and topped $555 million in 2017. Cook (2017) believes that SARGARPA data underreport the value of Mexican berry exports.

Mexico produced 29,000 tons of blueberries in 2016, including 45 percent in Jalisco, 22 percent in Michoacán, and 15 percent in Sinaloa. Mexican blueberry exports were worth $188 million in 2016, up from $7.5 million in 2010. Mexico produced 112,700 tons of raspberries, 77 percent in Jalisco and 15 percent in Michoacán. Raspberry exports were $530 million in 2016, up from $145 million in 2010. Mexico produced 248,000 tons of blackberries in 2016, and blackberry exports were worth $335 million. Mexican blueberry exports are rising quickly.

All types of berry producers complain of too few workers. Growers are responding to higher labor costs with mechanical aids to increase labor productivity as well as changes in how berries are produced, such as tabletop production of strawberries to reduce stooping during harvest. Longer canes in raspberries and blackberries can facilitate both hand and machine harvesting. Many blueberries are harvested by machine, especially those destined for processing.

A survey in February–March 2018 of 4,489 workers who were employed by 205 berry farms[20] in Jalisco (100 farms) and Michoacán (105 farms) had five major findings. First, most berry workers are young: two-thirds were 18 to 35,

---

[20] These farms were operated by 130 owners or growers.

and 90 percent were under 50. Second, there were more men than women berry workers in Jalisco, and more women than men in Michoacán. Almost 60 percent of the men and women were married, and married workers had an average 2.8 children. Third, about 20 percent of berry workers were indigenous, and 70 percent of these indigenous workers were Purépecha speakers from Michoacán. Fourth, more workers were employed year-round, 55 percent, than seasonally, 45 percent. There was little variance by sex in who was employed year-round, but only 40 percent of those speaking an indigenous language were year-round workers, suggesting that many of the indigenous workers were hired to fill seasonal jobs. Fifth, large berry farms hire more indigenous workers, who have less education and experience, to fill seasonal jobs.

The employers of these workers were near six cities: Jocotepec (60 growers), Zapotlán el Grande (33), and Tapalpa (7) in Jalisco; and Jacona (51), Los Reyes (350), and Huiramba (19) in Michoacán. Smaller growers with less than 23 acres of berries hired more local workers, and these local workers are better educated, more experienced, and more satisfied with their wages and working conditions than migrants. The largest growers with over 90 acres of berries hired a higher share of migrants and indigenous workers, and these workers expressed more concerns about low wages and poor working conditions.

Some 1,871 workers were interviewed in Jalisco and 2,698 in Michoacán. The number of worker interviews varied by city: Jocotepec (693 worker interviews), Zapotlán el Grande (868), and Tapalpa (310) in Jalisco; and Jacona (1,409 worker interviews), Los Reyes (578), Huiramba (633), and 80 worker interviews elsewhere in Michoacán. Some 57 percent of the workers interviewed in Jalisco and 46 percent of the workers interviewed in Michoacán were men.

The largest group of workers were aged 18 to 25 (38 percent), followed by 29 percent who were 26 to 35 and 22 percent who were 36 to 49; 10 percent were 50 and older. There were slight differences between Jalisco and Michoacán, with 72 percent of workers in Jalisco aged 18 to 35, versus 63 percent in Michoacán. There are few differences in age between men and women.

Some 57 percent of the workers were married and 37 percent single; others were divorced or widowed. By sex, 65 percent of the men and 50 percent of the women were married, and 63 and 68 percent, respectively, had children, an average 2.8 each, with few differences between men and women or indigenous and non-indigenous workers.

The typical level of education was primary school, completed by 41 percent of workers (37 percent in Jalisco and 43 percent in Michoacán), followed by 35 percent of workers who completed secondary school. There were more workers with some college education, 19 percent, than with no schooling, 6 percent, and few differences in education between men and women. Over 93 percent of the workers could read and write in Spanish, and 99 percent could speak Spanish.

Almost 900 or 20 percent of the workers were indigenous, defined as speaking an indigenous language. There was a marked difference by state: 10 percent of workers were indigenous in Jalisco and 26 percent in Michoacán. By sex, 22 percent of men and 17 percent of women were indigenous. The most common indigenous language was Purépecha, spoken by 70 percent of the indigenous workers and common in Michoacán. The next largest group of 129 workers spoke Chiapas languages—Tzotzil, Tzeltal, Ch'ol, and Zoque—followed by 51 who spoke Nahuatl, Mexico's most common indigenous language, and 40 who spoke the Oaxacan languages of Mixtec, Mazatec, and Zapotec. About 61 percent of the indigenous workers were literate: 82 percent in Jalisco, and 56 percent in Michoacán.

Over half of the workers, 55 percent, were local workers employed year-round. There was little variance by sex. For example, 57 percent of men and 46 percent of women were employed year-round. There was a significant difference by indigenous status: 59 percent of non-indigenous and 41 percent of indigenous workers were employed year-round.

Almost 2,000 workers were employed seasonally in berries, including three-fourths of the local workers. The survey did not distinguish between local and migrant workers among those employed seasonally, so we do not know how many of the seasonal or temporary workers were migrants living away from their usual homes. Seasonal workers in berries had households with an average 5.4 members. Indigenous workers had on average 6-member households, while non-indigenous households averaged 4.8 members.

A sixth of seasonal workers migrated to the berry farm where they were employed in Jalisco or Michoacán from elsewhere in Mexico; the rest were local, which could mean commutes of an hour or more from home to work. Most seasonal workers did housework or worked on their own farms when they were not employed seasonally in berries.

There are three major berries in these states, and many workers were employed in only one type: 27 percent of the workers were employed on farms that grew only strawberries, 26 percent on farms that grew only blackberries, and 25 percent on farms that grew only raspberries. In Jalisco, blackberry and raspberry workers were concentrated in Jocotepec and Zapotlán el Grande, while in Michoacán 60 percent of the workers who were interviewed were employed on farms that produced only strawberries, many in Huriamba, while blackberry and raspberry workers were concentrated in Los Reyes. Michoacán produced 60 percent of Mexico's 392,000 tons of strawberries in 2016, followed by Baja California with 21 percent and Guanajuato with 8 percent.

Growers were considered small if they had less than 23 acres (70 growers), medium-sized with 23 to 92 acres (69 growers), and large if they had 93 acres or more (66 growers). The small berry growers employed a median 13 workers and a total of 794, the medium-sized growers a median 45 workers and a total of 1,316, and the large growers a median 597 workers and a total of 2,380.

Large berry growers hire more indigenous workers who have lower levels of education, and include a higher share of workers who are in their first year of picking berries. Small berry producers, on the other hand, tend to hire more local workers who have more education and more experience picking berries. Some local workers live an hour or more from the farms where they work, and 85 percent of employers paid for the transportation needed to get workers from their homes to the workplace.

Instead of being asked about the wages they earned, workers were asked whether their wages covered their basic needs for housing, food, health care, clothing, transportation, education costs, and recreational services. Workers answered yes or no, and the yes responses were divided into the seven areas. Most workers (61 percent) said that four of their seven basic needs were covered by their wages. Workers employed by smaller producers, who have more education and experience picking berries, reported that more of their needs were covered by their wages than workers who were employed by larger growers.

Over 80 percent of berry workers were enrolled in the Mexican social security system IMSS (Instituto Mexicano del Seguro Social), with a range of 77 percent of workers employed by large farms to 85 percent for small and medium-sized producers. Larger producers expanded after most available local workers already had jobs, prompting them to recruit indigenous workers who have less education and experience and less familiarity with IMSS benefits, which include health care and child care, disability insurance, pensions, and housing benefits via the National Housing Fund (Infonavit).

Workers reported on conditions in the fields. Some 83 percent reported always having drinking water available, and half reported that their bathrooms and dining rooms were good or very good, with a higher share of workers on smaller farms reporting good conditions. Over half of the workers wanted more education on their rights, and a third wanted more training on health and safety. Food safety is a major concern of growers and buyers, and over 80 percent of workers reported that they were concerned about food safety.

Two-thirds of workers signed contracts, and 80 percent fully understood their contracts. About 30 percent of workers reported that they were required to work additional hours, including 40 percent of those employed on large farms.

Over 80 percent of workers are satisfied or very satisfied with their work, with a higher share of workers on small farms satisfied or very satisfied, 91 percent, than workers on large farms, 75 percent. Over 95 percent of workers believe that the farm where they are working is the same or better than other berry farms. When asked what they most wanted to change on the berry farm where they were employed, over half mentioned higher wages, followed by 17 percent who said more and better-quality fruit to pick.

The winter 2018 berry survey found general satisfaction among berry workers in Jalisco and Michoacán: over 80 percent were satisfied with berry work, and

95 percent plan to return to seasonal berry jobs next year. Over half of the workers lived near the farm where they worked and were employed year-round. These local and year-round workers had more education and experience in berry work, and a higher share were employed on smaller farms.

Larger berry farms hired a higher share of seasonal and migrant workers, some of whom spoke indigenous languages. Migrant workers employed seasonally were less satisfied with their work. One reason may be that large berry farms expanded or started operations after available local workers had already developed stable employment relationships with smaller berry farms, explaining why larger growers recruited less educated migrants from other regions.

Visits to berry farms around Jocotepec, an hour south of Guadalajara on the western shore of Lake Chapala, highlight the opportunities and challenges in Mexico's export-oriented berry sector. There are hundreds of 20- to 50-acre raspberry and blackberry farms that use plastic-covered metal hoops to protect berries from birds and excessive sun.

Raspberries are picked every two to three days, and most farmers hire six to eight workers per hectare. Workers with shopping baskets containing the plastic clamshells in which blackberries and raspberries are sold and a bucket for rejects walk down rows of plants and place the berries into the retail clamshells; most work without gloves. Runners collect the full clamshells from pickers and take them to a checking and repacking area, where they are sorted and placed in boxes or flats, taken to coolers, and transported to markets. Rejects are 10 to 20 percent of berries, including what pickers and inspectors and repackers sort out, and are sold at low prices for processing.

Workers in Jocotepec earned 10 to 15 pesos ($0.70) a flat (twelve 6-ounce clamshells) for picking raspberries, with a guarantee of 200 pesos for an eight-hour day ($10.60); the 200-peso-a-day wage is paid while in training and doing nonharvest work. The higher piece rates are for workers who report to work each day and are careful pickers, minimizing the need to repack fruit. Daily earnings range from 200 to 400 pesos per day: a 300-peso-per-day worker would earn $16 a day or $2 an hour. With six-day weeks, weekly earnings are $96, and earnings over a 16-week season are $1,500.[21] A worker earning 12 pesos a flat and 300 pesos in an eight-hour day could pick 25 flats a day or three an hour. The best pickers average five to six flats an hour when yields are high, earning 60–80 pesos an hour or 500 pesos ($26) a day.

---

[21] (Stupková, 2016, 31) reported that the mostly female blackberry pickers in Los Reyes, Michoacán, earned 140 pesos per six-hour day in 2015, which is $7 a day or $1.15 an hour when the minimum wage was 66 pesos for an eight-hour day. Stupková reported that women picked ten boxes a day, much lower productivity than in Jalisco in 2018, but acknowledged that average productivity could be twenty-five trays a day during the peak of the harvest. Stupková in 2018 reported that strawberry pickers earned 1,200 pesos a week for six seven-hour workdays (7–2) with breaks and a half-hour lunch. Workers were paid 16 pesos per 8-pound tray, suggesting 200 pesos a day for 12.5 trays a day.

In addition to piece rate wages of 12 pesos a flat, growers pay 30-percent taxes on their workers' wages and, for migrants, they provide housing and sometimes food. There are also labor costs for checking and repacking, making total labor costs 20 to 30 pesos a flat or about $1.35. When raspberries are $15 a flat, growers may receive $8 to $9 after paying for plants and cooling and marketing costs, making harvest labor costs 16 percent of grower revenue.

Most hired workers on Jocotepec-area berry farms are local residents, but the availability of other jobs, including providing cooking and gardening services to the growing retirement community of Ajijic for 200 to 250 pesos a day, prompts growers to recruit often indigenous workers in poorer areas of Mexico to ensure they have enough workers. Recruiters visit poor areas with workers and, when they have a busload of recruits, request a grower-provided screener to select workers and a bus to transport the migrants to Jocotepec and their temporary housing. Migrants typically receive pay advances of 1,000 pesos ($53) so that their families have some money until they begin sending remittances.

The major issue for growers is the availability of labor for the continued expansion of the berry industry. There is pessimism about attracting more Jocotepec-area workers to fill seasonal jobs, and few near-term prospects for mechanical harvesting. There appear to be three major options to increase the labor supply. First would be hiring more local youth and women. Most export-oriented growers do not hire workers under age 18, even though the minimum school-leaving and working age in Mexico has been 15 since 2014, versus 16 in the US. Berry exporters do not hire Mexican youth aged 16 and 17 to avoid charges of using child labor. Women are attracted to the relatively high wages in export agriculture, but fear sexual harassment and complain of the lack of child care. Formal sector workers covered by IMSS should have access to low-cost and government-provided child care, but IMSS has few child-care facilities in areas with export-oriented agriculture, and the short opening hours of IMSS child-care centers are not conducive to farm work. Women farm workers often organize informal coops that involve one woman caring for children while the other women work (Escobar et al., 2019).

The second option is to recruit more internal migrants from poorer areas of Mexico, mostly in areas with subsistence farmers who speak indigenous languages and are willing to be seasonal farm workers away from home. One report suggested there were almost 26 million indigenous people in 2015, up from 16 million in 2010, with indigenous defined as speaking an indigenous language or self-identifying as indigenous, criteria that made two-thirds of the residents of Oaxaca and Yucatan indigenous. Berry growers are recruiting more indigenous workers to fill seasonal jobs, but there can be abuses during recruitment and while employed, primarily because of fees charged to workers, recruiters acting as supervisors and withholding wages, and workers provided with poor housing and inadequate food. Keeping the recruitment, employment, and housing of internal migrants "clean" is a challenge as the number of migrants increases.

The third option is more guest workers. Mexico allows farmers in Chiapas to employ Guatemalan guest workers, and a 2016 KNOMAD survey found that legal Guatemalan migrant workers had relatively low migration costs. The International Labour Organization (ILO) launched a project to promote the fair recruitment of Guatemalan guest workers in 2015 that aimed to expand knowledge, strengthen institutional capacities to improve recruitment and register private recruiters, and disseminate information on proper recruitment and registered recruiters.[22]

Guatemalan guest workers may spread to other areas of Mexico. Associations of growers that export commodities are exploring using the Guatemala–Chiapas program to bring Guatemalan guest workers into northern Mexico, and some of the Central Americans who sought asylum in the US in 2019, were rebuffed, and applied in Mexico may become seasonal farm workers.

Berry and Vegetable Workers 2019

A spring 2019 survey of almost 3,000 farm workers found that export-oriented Mexican berry and vegetable farms create good jobs for workers with little education, which reduces rural poverty and unauthorized Mexico–US migration. The farm workers were an average of 32 years old, had 7.2 years of schooling, and earned 200–300 pesos ($10–15) a day plus in-kind benefits, significantly higher than Mexico's minimum wage of 103 pesos a day. Harvest workers who are paid piece wages earn more, up to 500 pesos a day. Most workers are local residents, but a rising share are migrants from poorer mountainous regions of the Mexican states with export farms and southern Mexican states.

Second, more than 90 percent of the workers interviewed on export-oriented farms reported that their employers paid taxes to the comprehensive social-security system IMSS, compared with 48 percent of all Mexican workers who are covered by IMSS. However, IMSS often fails to deliver services to farm workers, especially child care and health care.[23] If IMSS provided more comprehensive child-care services, more local women could work on farms, reducing the need for internal migration.

Third, the expansion of export agriculture in Mexico creates jobs that reduce unauthorized Mexico–US migration but increase migration within Mexico. Migration to western and northern Mexico to fill farm jobs offers opportunities

---

[22] See   http://www.ilo.org/global/topics/labour-migration/projects/WCMS_355061/lang-en/index.htm.

[23] The Ministry for Social Development and the Ministry of Agriculture provided some housing, health care, child care, and other services to farm workers, but these programs are being reduced or eliminated under the AMLO (Andrés Manuel López Obrador) government elected in 2018.

for people in poorer areas to earn higher wages within Mexico and to send remittances to poorer areas, improving housing and increasing investment in their children's education and health care. Longer seasons are encouraging some migrants to settle near their export-oriented workplaces, which moves workers and their families from poorer to richer areas of Mexico that offer more opportunity.

Workers were interviewed between January and April 2019 in six states to collect data on (1) the characteristics of workers and their families; (2) the way in which workers were recruited and any worker-paid costs to get their jobs; (3) employment patterns and earnings, work-related benefits, and working conditions; (4) for migrants, housing, food, and living issues while employed away from home; and (5) plans for next season. Most of the workers were employed on large farms that belong to associations and account for most of Mexico's fruit and vegetable exports. The growers who were interviewed employed 97,000 workers; almost 3 percent of their were interviewed in spring 2019.

Table 4.5 shows that half of the workers interviewed were employed in berries, the commodity with the highest monthly wages; most of the berry interviews were in Jalisco and Michoacán. Vegetable workers who earned lower monthly wages were employed primarily in Sinaloa. Workers were 54-percent male and 46-percent female, and 56 percent were born in the state where they were working. There were two other groups of workers: settled or permanent migrants who were born outside the state in which they are working (14 percent) and temporary migrant workers whose usual home was in another state (30 percent).

Most workers had little schooling, including 10 percent of all workers and 18 percent of the indigenous workers who did not attend any school. Average years of schooling were 7.2, with berry and tomato workers having slightly more years of schooling than bell pepper and cucumber workers. Peak season harvesting wages can be 9,000 pesos ($473) a month, which attracts some university students to pick berries.

Mexico has a complex and comprehensive social-insurance system that requires formal-sector employers to provide their workers with contracts, pay taxes on behalf of their employees to IMSS and Infonavit, and provide employees with year-end bonuses and profit-sharing payments. IMSS benefits include health- and child-care services; paid sick leave and three months' paid maternity leave; and retirement, permanent disability, and widow(er) pensions. Workers accumulate benefits over time; employers and employees who contribute twenty-five years receive maximum benefits.

Since formal jobs in agriculture are a relatively recent development, most farm workers do not qualify for retirement pensions or housing mortgages. Instead, many workers try to maximize their earnings, changing employers frequently and thus reducing the chances that they will qualify for IMSS or Infonavit benefits.

Table 4.5 Workers employed on Mexican export farms, spring 2019

Commodity	Workers	Monthly wage (pesos)	Monthly wage ($)
Berries	1,426	7,234	379
Tomatoes	364	6,490	340
Bell peppers	495	6,366	334
Cucumbers	392	6,369	334
Total	2,677		

Demographics	Workers Interviewed	Share	Age	Men percent	Education years
Baja California	196	7%	30	72%	7.5
Colima	38	1%	35	42%	8.8
Guanajuato	316	11%	29	56%	8.8
Jalisco	678	24%	32	69%	8.2
Michoacán	654	24%	35	50%	7
Sinaloa	897	32%	33	46%	6.3
Total	2,779	100%			

Wages	Monthly wage (pesos)	Monthly male wage (pesos)	Monthly female wage (pesos)	Male premium
Baja California	10,120	10,220	9,856	4%
Colima	6,047	6,805	5,496	19%
Guanajuato	6,419	6,227	6,661	−7%
Jalisco	7,261	7,330	7,108	3%
Michoacán	6,159	6,529	5,799	11%
Sinaloa	6,406	7,267	5,677	22%

Benefits	IMSS	Infonavit	IMSS Day Care	Bonus	Vacation
Baja California	97%	25%	1%	72%	61%
Colima	100%	70%	21%	89%	86%
Guanajuato	99%	47%	9%	98%	96%
Jalisco	94%	46%	10%	85%	77%
Michoacán	91%	35%	5%	65%	46%
Sinaloa	92%	20%	14%	86%	36%

Access to Benefits	IMSS	Infonavit	IMSS Day Care	Bonus	Vacation
Baja California	89%	11%	1%	61%	46%
Colima	97%	55%	15%	82%	83%
Guanajuato	91%	11%	2%	92%	85%
Jalisco	79%	19%	4%	72%	58%
Michoacán	81%	15%	2%	58%	35%
Sinaloa	86%	10%	9%	80 %	30%

Source: Worker survey in spring 2019.

After the *Los Angeles Times* published a series of articles documenting poor working conditions in Mexican agriculture in December 2014, a combination of stepped-up enforcement of laws requiring growers to enroll their workers in IMSS and US buyer pressure on Mexican suppliers to comply with all labor laws increased the share of large Mexican farms that enrolled their workers in IMSS and Infonavit. There were several reasons to formalize jobs on large export farms, including the fact that they were visible targets for tax authorities, and US buyers pressured their Mexican suppliers to comply with Mexican labor laws. Over 90 percent of the workers interviewed in spring 2019 on large export farms reported that their employers enrolled them in IMSS and Infonavit.

However, enrollment in IMSS and Infonavit does not mean that workers have effective access to program services. Farm workers repeatedly said that they knew where IMSS health-care facilities were located, but they preferred to obtain health-care advice and drugs from pharmacies or private doctors rather than take time off from work and wait for hours for sometimes low-quality IMSS health-care services. IMSS was reserved for serious health issues and childbirth.

Very few workers had effective access to IMSS day care, in part because the hours of government-operated centers did not coincide with farm work hours. Many IMSS child-care centers close at 2 p.m., while most farm workers work until 4 or 5 p.m., encouraging informal child-care arrangements, as when five women worked and one watched their children.

There was even less access to other benefits supported by payroll taxes. Few seasonal workers qualify for IMSS pension benefits, which require twenty-five years of full-time work. Even fewer qualify for Infonavit housing subsidies. This means that after retirement, workers whose employers contributed 6.5 percent of wages for IMSS retirement benefits, and those whose employers contributed 5 percent of wages for Infonavit housing assistance, can receive a refund of 11.5 percent of their wages if they can navigate the IMSS and Infonavit bureaucracies.

Mexico's export-oriented agriculture is an economic success story, creating hundreds of thousands of jobs for local and migrant workers with little education in northern and central Mexico. A combination of media exposés, government audits, and US buyer pressure formalized the farm-labor market on large farms that export fruits and vegetables to the US after 2015, but this formalization is tenuous. Farmers were able to cover the increased cost of payroll taxes and rising minimum wages because of high prices due to expanding US demand for fresh produce. The success in formalizing jobs on export farms could reverse if a recession or trade dispute reduces US demand and grower prices, if government enforcement efforts and US buyer pressure ease, or if the supply of farm workers increases, as could happen if Central Americans who want to enter the US and apply for asylum remain in Mexico and seek farm jobs.

Most Mexican firms and jobs are informal: 90 percent of Mexican firms employ 55 percent of Mexican workers who are not registered with IMSS and Infonavit. Ex-IMSS Director Santiago Levy (2018) believes that Mexico's approach to protecting formal-sector workers is flawed because it raises costs for formal firms so high that most firms elect to remain informal. Since the productivity of workers in informal firms is half that of workers in formal firms, Mexico's payroll tax system allocates too much of Mexico's capital and labor to informal firms and requires formal firms to pay the most taxes.

Levy found that employers and workers value the health, pension, housing and other services that add 30 percent to wage costs at only two-thirds of their cost. Most workers will not qualify for pensions or health care in retirement because of frequent job changes and tough eligibility requirements (Levy, 2018, 37–8). Levy believes that, unless the payroll tax system and the incentives it creates are changed, there is little hope of raising productivity and wages for most Mexican workers.

Whither Mexican Farm Labor?

The 2019 worker surveys found that export agriculture creates good jobs for Mexicans with little education. However, there is a widespread and generally false belief that Americans who eat Mexican-grown avocados or tomatoes are eating fruits and vegetables picked by children and workers who are forced to work.

Media stories highlight poor conditions for Mexican farm workers. The *Los Angeles Times* published a four-part series December 7–14, 2014, that made four major charges (Marosi, 2014). First, the LAT argued that many migrant farm workers are effectively trapped in camps on or near the farms where they work. Some of the migrant camps offer very poor living conditions, including little furniture and inadequate sanitation.[24]

Second, migrant workers are often recruited and supervised by contractors from their area of origin who withhold workers' wages to discourage them from leaving for other employers who may offer higher wages. Some contractors retain workers' wages until the end of their three- to eight-month contracts, making the workers effectively indentured.

Third, some workers wind up in a form of debt peonage, owing money to in-camp stores for reasons that range from wages that are withheld until the end

---

[24] Some farmers told the reporters that camp residents did not want furniture, preferring to live as they did at home.

of contracts to buying supplemental food, alcohol, and other items at in-camp stores on credit; guards reportedly prevent residents from leaving the camp until camp-store debts are repaid.[25] Fourth, US buyers of Mexican produce have not enforced their social-responsibility guidelines that require Mexican farmers to pay their workers regularly and to provide migrants with decent food and housing.

The Los Angeles Times stories profiled mostly indigenous and sometimes non-Spanish-speaking workers recruited in poor areas of Mexico and employed on farms in northern and western Mexico that produce fresh fruits and vegetables for US consumers. The reporting emphasized that these internal migrant workers are expected to work six days a week for the equivalent of $8 to 12 a day, a wage that is low by US standards but well above Mexico's minimum wage.

The recruitment of migrant workers occurs in rural areas of extreme poverty. Contractors offer workers willing to migrate to Sinaloa daily wages of 100 pesos ($5.50 in June 2017) and housing and food where they work. The reporters encountered recruiters who were accused of trafficking or withholding wages; the contractors denied these charges. Recruitment is a bidding process, meaning that contractors offered the assembled workers in the Huasteca region spending money for the two-day bus trip from their homes to labor camps in Sinaloa. After forty workers boarded the bus for Sinaloa, they were read their three-month contracts, which included no wage payments until the end of the contract.

Withholding wages until the end of the contract can lead to conflict. The recruiter believes that pay at the end of three-month contracts ensures worker loyalty and ensures that workers return home with savings, and workers agree to end-of-contract pay at the place where they were recruited. However, Mexican law specifies that farm workers must be paid weekly, which makes end-of-contract pay agreements invalid.

Grower Agricola San Emilio provided the workers it housed with three meals a day, but some camp residents said this camp food was insufficient, explaining why they purchased supplemental food on credit from in-camp stores. Monopoly in-camp stores are a well-known problem, since company stores on haciendas sometimes kept peasants in perpetual debt in the nineteenth century. Some growers operate camps that sell items at cost, and the government has opened discount stores in some farm-labor camps, but the Los Angeles Times found many private stores with unmarked prices and expensive credit in farm-worker camps.

---

[25] Marosi (2014) reported that half of the thirty camps visited included workers who said at least some of their wages were withheld and required workers to repay debts incurred at in-camp stores before leaving, or both. There are reportedly 200 farm-labor camps in Mexico, including 150 in Sinaloa.

Several themes run through the *Los Angeles Times* series. First, the most exploited workers are indigenous workers recruited by indigenous contractors and bussed several days from their homes to labor camps on or near the farms where they work. Second, workers receive housing and food in the camps where they live while working, but the quality of these items varies, leading to examples of workers bathing in irrigation canals because showers do not function and workers purchasing supplemental food at high prices from in-camp stores. Third, a common worker complaint involved withheld wages, that is, not receiving wages until the end of their contracts. Contractors inform workers that they will not be paid for three months, and workers agree to these terms by getting on contractor buses, but such agreements violate labor laws that require regular payment of wages earned.

There were several reactions to the *Los Angeles Times* series. The Fresh Produce Association of the Americas (FPAA) , which represents Mexican exporters and US importers, called the stories one-sided. The FPAA stressed that its members have a "long and rich history of improving worker conditions…in Mexico" (FPAA, 2015–16, 2) and that the abuses detailed by the *Los Angeles Times* are the exception, not the rule. The FPAA asserted that increased regulatory vigilance, worker education, and peer pressure among employers have greatly reduced abuse of workers. Some suggested that third-party auditors who already visit farms to do food safety checks should also investigate labor conditions.

Worker advocates countered that farm-worker abuses on export-oriented produce farms are more systemic than occasional, and that top-down pressure from US produce buyers could effectuate lasting change. Some US buyers require Mexican producers to sign social-responsibility statements and undergo labor-standards audits, which often take the auditor a day and cost the grower $1,500. Critics allege that auditors can be misled by growers who take them to showcase labor camps and allow only preselected workers to be interviewed.

The International Fresh Produce Social Responsibility Alliance (AHIFORES), created by the Confederation of Agribusiness Associations in Sinaloa and the Fresh Produce Association of the Americas in December 2014, promised to ensure that Mexican labor laws are obeyed on its member farms that account for over 80 percent of Mexican produce-exports to the US. The alliance does not include US grocery chains, restaurants, or other food retailers, and its enforcement mechanisms are vague.

AHIFORES brings growers together with other stakeholders to discuss farm-labor conditions and ways to improve them each year. The second AHIFORES meeting in 2018 highlighted three themes. First, dependence on internal migrants is rising with increased Mexican production for export. Local workers who previously worked seasonally in agriculture have found nonfarm jobs, are staying in school, or are not available due to declining fertility and rural–urban migration. There is often a wide gulf between the indigenous migrants who do a rising share of work in export agriculture and the residents of local communities in the richer areas of Mexico where most export-oriented farms are located, which can lead to tensions as some indigenous workers settle. There were frequent references to farmers who offer housing to indigenous migrants having to teach them about toilets, appliances, and modern living.

Second, employers are frustrated with the work-related programs financed by their payroll taxes. Most harvest workers earn two or three times Mexico's minimum wage, but some growers do not enroll their workers in the IMSS and Infonavit systems as required.[26] There are two sides to the IMSS and Infonavit issue. On the one hand, Mexican law and US buyer social-responsibility guidelines require export farms to enroll their workers in IMSS and Infonavit and to pay taxes that add 30 percent to wages. On the other hand, most workers do not benefit from IMSS and Infonavit services, and some growers provide health-care, child-care, and other services that should be provided by government agencies. This makes the formalization of jobs in export agriculture since 2015 tenuous, since neither workers nor employers value the services that should be provided by government agencies financed by payroll taxes.

Third, many migrants are settling in areas where they do farm work, especially as periods of employment lengthen, which can increase tensions with local residents *and* local governments. Farmers who provided housing and food in on-farm camps typically do not provide services to employees who live in local communities. However, some local governments also fail to provide water and other services to current and ex-farm workers in the informal housing areas where some settle. The resulting frustration with growers *and* local governments can explode into protests, as in the San Quintín area of Baja California 200 miles south of San Diego in March 2015, where migrants who settled in local communities did not receive basic sanitation and water services from the local government. Government inspectors in March 2015 found some indigenous workers living under plastic tarps strung between trees.

On March 17, 2015, Baja berry workers went on strike, demanding an increase in wages. Strikers said that most of the area's 30,000 farm workers were earning 110 pesos ($8) a day picking strawberries at piece rates of 10 to 14 pesos a tray or box. The strikers, organized by the independent union Alianza de Organizaciones Nacional, Estatal y Municipal por la Justicia Social, demanded a minimum wage of 200 pesos ($13) a day from the area's twelve major farm employers, and shut down the Transpeninsular Highway in the area to prevent harvested berries from being shipped to the United States (Zlolniski, 2019).

Many of Baja's farm workers are Mixtec, Triqui, and Zapotec internal migrants from southern Mexican states. They were represented by unions affiliated with

---

[26] Some employers register their workers with IMSS, but at the minimum wage rather than the two or three times the minimum wage that workers actually earn.

the Confederation of Mexican Workers (CTM) and the Regional Confederation of Mexican Workers (CROM). The Alianza charged that these CTM and CROM unions signed collective-bargaining agreements with farm employers before any workers were hired, and did not inform the workers who were employed under these contracts that they had a union representative.[27] Leaders of CTM and CROM unions said they "worked with" growers to resolve worker complaints in order to preserve farm-worker jobs; some union leaders were paid by growers and grower associations (Zlolniski, 2019, ch. 5).

Some of the Alianza strike leaders gained experience mounting demonstrations while employed in the United States, and used this experience to organize protests in Baja. In June 2015, after twelve weeks of intermittent strikes and losses estimated at $80 million, Baja growers agreed to raise daily wages to at least 180 pesos ($11.50) a day on large farms and to 150 pesos ($9.50) a day on small farms.[28] The agreement also required farm employers to make IMSS contributions on behalf of workers and called on state and local governments to improve area schools, clinics, and other infrastructure for workers who had settled in towns and cities near the farms.[29]

Wages are higher in northern Mexican border regions to compensate for the higher cost of living near the US border. In the past, some migrants from southern Mexico continued to migrate northward into the United States after harvests ended in San Quintín Valley, but tougher US border controls reduced further migration and encouraged settlement in Baja farming areas.

BerryMex, which hires a peak 4,500 workers and markets berries through Driscoll's, is a wage and benefit leader in the San Quintín Valley. In March 2016, BerryMex was paying at least 226 pesos ($12) a day, with some workers earning $2 to $3 an hour under the piece-rate wage system (Marosi, 2016). Certified by Fair Trade USA in 2016 as having good conditions for its workers, BerryMex provided housing for 500 workers, and Costco and Whole Foods paid a 50-cent premium per tray for BerryMex berries to fund community projects. However, some workers complained that BerryMex required pickers to work seven days a week during peak harvests, and required workers who refuse seven-day work schedules to take unpaid days off.

The December 2014 *Los Angeles Times* series, the spring 2015 strikes in Baja, and concerns about wages and working conditions on both Mexican and US farms producing fruits and vegetables prompted the Produce Marketing

---

[27] Zlolniski (2019, ch. 5) reported that the wage system changed around 2000 from daily to piece-rate wages, with workers expected to work faster under piece rates.

[28] Some growers, including vegetable exporter Rancho Los Pinos, paid 150 pesos a day instead of the 180 pesos because they provided housing. Rancho Los Pinos provides its 1,200 workers with free housing, day care, and other benefits (Marosi, 2016).

[29] In November 2015, a new union, Sindicato Nacional Independiente de Jornaleros Agrícolas y Similares, was registered by the Mexican government to represent San Quintín-area farm workers. The Sindicato split from the Alianza, which it has disowned, exposing divisions among the protesters.

Association and the United Fresh Produce Association to release an ethical charter that calls on growers to abide by labor laws and to educate their employees about their rights and responsibilities. The UF-PMA Joint Committee consulted a wide range of stakeholders to "evaluate local, national and international standards, growers' best practices, and common customer expectations for labor practices to take advantage of the opportunity to harmonize this effort with other relevant frameworks. In doing so, industry members are coming together to identify, learn from, and leverage industry practice."

The UF-PMA ethical charter released in 2017 asserted that "responsible labor practices are the right thing to do and our success as an industry depends on it." The charter laid out goals for employers, including compliance with applicable wage, hour, and work-safety laws. It dealt with the management of workers, asserting that "direct communication between workers and management is the most effective way of resolving workplace issues and concerns." Ethical recruitment involves growers using only contractors who comply with labor laws and "seeks to mitigate the risks of forced labor, child labor and human trafficking in their [growers'] recruitment and employment practices." The charter also dealt with the fundamental rights of workers, including nonharassment and nondiscrimination, and called on growers to bar children below legal employment age (usually age 15 in Mexico) from working. The charter asserted that "All work must be conducted on a voluntary basis, and not under threat or menace of penalty." The charter called on growers to pledge to combat "forced labor, involuntary prison labor, bonded, debt bondage, indentured labor, or the trafficking of persons."

As stakeholders consider the future of export-oriented agriculture, it is important to remember that export agriculture creates jobs that pay more than minimum wages for Mexicans with little education and that almost all export growers enroll their employees in IMSS. An expanding export agriculture is drawing migrants from poorer areas to the richer areas that have export-oriented farms, which could help the migrants and their children to achieve upward mobility.

Growers and worker advocates agree that most growers enroll their employees in IMSS, but workers do not receive the services funded by grower contributions. This gap may set the stage for a grand bargain under which growers who provide the services receive credits against payroll taxes owed, IMSS provides missing services, or there is some combination of the credits and services.

No country has managed the recruitment of migrant farm workers well. Recruiting farm workers in Mexico is complicated by the fact that many of the migrants are minorities who may speak little Spanish, and most are moving far away from villages in mountainous areas within states that have export agriculture or from poorer Mexican states to richer states. Mexico has a wide range of protective labor laws, but they are not always enforced, especially if the contractor and the workers are indigenous. In most cases, indigenous contractors and crews move, work, and return without incident, but making growers jointly liable for labor-law violations by the contractors who bring workers to their farms would likely encourage the beneficiaries of the work to take greater interest in how workers are recruited, transported, housed, and supervised.

Mexico's export-oriented agriculture has a latecomer advantage. Many Mexican fruits and vegetables destined for export are produced under plastic-covered hoops, which increases yields, reduces pest pressures, and lengthens the season. Longer seasons in areas with more opportunities encourage migrants to settle near their jobs, where they expect government services and education. Some local governments are slow to recognize settled-out migrants as residents and provide them with services, a source of tensions. Local stakeholder forums would allow growers to cooperate with local governments to provide services to settled-out migrant workers, minimizing conflict and ensuring that children have access to education and health care.

Export-oriented agriculture may also strain local environments. Critics argue that planting the same crop year after year erodes soil fertility and allows disease and pest pressures to build, leading to the use of more chemicals that can taint water supplies and harm farm workers and local residents. Some producers of export crops lease virgin land for five to ten years that may have been pasture, promising to leave the irrigation wells and other improvements to the landowner. The result, according to critics, is Mexican and foreign producers using and abusing Mexico's scarce water and soil and leaving behind contaminated water and sick people (Gonzalez, 2019, 175).

Over 40 percent of Mexicans have below-poverty-level incomes, including 10 percent who live in extreme poverty. Poverty and extreme poverty have been declining, in part because of the growth of export-oriented agriculture. This suggests that the Mexican government should foster the continued expansion of export-oriented agriculture in ways that ensure workers are protected and benefit from a Mexican success story.

AMLO and the Future

Ex-Mexico City Mayor Andrés Manuel López Obrador (AMLO) was elected to a six-year term as president July 1, 2018. AMLO's Movement for National Regeneration or Morena party won 307 of 500 seats in the lower house and 68 of 128 seats in the senate, making AMLO the first president to have a congressional majority since 1997. AMLO is a symbolic politician with a genuine concern for the rural poor but without a clear strategy to help poor Mexicans who were left behind by economic growth.

AMLO promised a fourth transformation of Mexico, after the 1821 independence from Spain, liberal reforms in the mid-1860s, and the 1910 revolution.

He asserted that the "mafia of power" between politicians and business leaders keeps ordinary Mexicans poor. AMLO's specific proposals include a public-works program to employ 2.6 million young people at $160 a month, grants for 300,000 university students, and a doubling of pension payments. AMLO's New Deal is to be financed by saving $25 billion from reducing corruption and another $20 billion by cutting the salaries and benefits of high-government officials.

AMLO promised to make Mexico self-sufficient in corn,[30] wheat, rice, edible beans, and milk, and to encourage production of these commodities by small-scale farmers. In 1911, Emiliano Zapata's Plan de Ayala called for comprehensive land reform to benefit peasant farmers; during the 2018 campaign, AMLO endorsed a twenty-first-century Plan de Ayala developed by Mexican farmers' organizations that calls on government to favor small over large farmers.

AMLO's agricultural policy guarantees corn producers 5,610 pesos a ton or $7 a bushel for up to 20 tons of corn from farmers with up to 5 hectares of land for their spring/summer harvest, and 14,500 pesos a ton or $21 a bushel for up to 15 tons of edible beans produced by farmers with up to 5 hectares of land for the same harvest. There are also guaranteed prices for wheat, rice, and fresh milk, all providing above-market prices for the commodities produced by small farmers who sell their commodities to Seguridad Alimentaria Mexicana (SEGALMEX), which operates 34,000 community food-distribution centers across Mexico (Hansen-Kuhn, 2019).

Real average hourly wages in Mexico have been falling, and were an average $1.40 an hour in 2018. Mexico raised its minimum wage from 88 to 103 pesos a day ($5.10), or $0.64 an hour, on January 1, 2019, and doubled the minimum wage to 177 pesos ($8.80) in forty-three municipalities in the six northern states on the US border. Mexico's minimum wage rose again in January 1, 2020, to 123 pesos ($6.35), and to 186 pesos in the six border states. Most workers employed on the large farms that export produce to the US are paid more than minimum wages.

Higher minimum wages alone are unlikely to end poverty. Over 40 percent of Mexicans have incomes below the poverty line, and the share of persons in poverty has been relatively stable over the past decade. Poverty rates vary by state. In Chiapas, over 75 percent of residents are poor, while in Nuevo Leon the poverty rate is less than 15 percent. AMLO wants to reduce entrenched poverty in southern Mexico, but raising the minimum wage is unlikely to help, since most farm workers in southern Mexican states do not work in formal jobs covered by minimum-wage laws.

AMLO has focused attention on the southern Mexican states, which have mostly subsistence farms as well as some large farms that export coffee, bananas,

[30] Almost all corn exported by the US to Mexico is from genetically modified seeds. Mexico does not allow GM seed corn to be planted.

citrus, and other commodities. The expansion of export agriculture in southern Mexico could create good jobs for workers with low levels of education, reducing their need to migrate for opportunity. Past efforts to develop export-oriented agriculture in southern Mexico faltered, including the export coffee industry that evolved in the late nineteenth century in the coastal Soconusco area of Chiapas (Lurtz, 2019).

There are obstacles to expanding export agriculture in southern Mexico, beginning with a lack of irrigation facilities and transportation infrastructure. Building more infrastructure means overcoming distrust from past failures, as when over-filled dams led to downstream flooding, prompting protests from indigenous communities against outsiders. Instead of welcoming new projects that could create jobs, these communities often make demands on investors that can discourage investment. Section 22 of the Coordinadora Nacional de Trabajadores de la Educación (CNTE) often leads strikes and protests in Oaxaca, a state with below-average levels of education.[31]

There have been many analyses of the Mexican economic dilemma. Despite NAFTA and Mexico's location next to the world's largest market, the US, Mexico's economy expanded by only 1.2 percent a year in real per capita terms between 1996 and 2015, and labor productivity rose by only 0.5 percent a year. Without faster productivity growth, it will be hard to raise Mexican wages and incomes.

Economist Santiago Levy, the architect of Mexico's Progresa-Oportunidades-Prospera program that makes small payments to mothers who keep their children in school and ensure that they receive regular health checkups, believes that Mexico's slow growth is due to a persistent misallocation of resources that favors small and informal firms rather than large and formal firms (Levy, 2018). Small firms with less than 2 million pesos ($107,000) in annual revenue do not pay IMSS or Infonavit payroll taxes on the wages they pay their employees and cannot be sued for dismissing workers. Instead, such small firms pay a 2-percent tax on their revenues (up to $2,140), and their employees are entitled to free social services, which provides incentives for firms to remain small and to hire informal workers (Levy, 2018, 44).

Levy warns of the growing gaps between formal and informal firms, and between salaried and non-salaried workers, due to Mexico's social-insurance system, tax policies, and poor enforcement of contracts. Levy argues that larger formal firms with salaried workers subsidize informal firms with non-salaried workers, the wrong prescription to increase productivity and wages. Rising levels

---

[31] Some 15 percent of persons 15 and older in Oaxaca were illiterate in 2015, more than twice the Mexican average of 6 percent. http://www.milenio.com/opinion/varios-autores/corredor-fronterizo/la-cnte-y-la-reforma-educativa.

of education are "wasted" if the graduates who are are employed by small informal firms do not raise the productivity of their employees over time.[32]

Levy and the IMF (2018) recommend switching from payroll to general taxes to finance the social safety net. All workers, formal and informal, should be eligible for social benefits, severance pay for laid-off workers should be replaced with unemployment insurance, and all exemptions to the value-added taxes that are now paid mostly by formal firms should be eliminated. Making these changes would reduce the costs associated with informal firms becoming formal and could speed productivity and economic growth.

---

[32] Small firms with less than 2 million pesos ($107,000) in annual sales that hire non-salaried firms do not pay IMSS or Infonavit payroll taxes and cannot be sued for dismissing workers. They pay only a 2-percent tax on their revenues (up to $2,140), and their employees are entitled to free social services (Levy, 2018, 44).

5

Farm Labor in Other Countries

All countries with more than 50 percent of their workers employed in agriculture are poor, and all countries with fewer than 5 percent of workers employed in agriculture are rich. This chapter reviews the experiences of rich countries with less than 5 percent of their workers employed in agriculture, highlighting the vulnerability of the hired workers from poorer countries who do most of the work in labor-intensive crops on the farms of the richest OECD countries. The chapter contrasts the situation in non-US industrial countries with that in Brazil, the largest agricultural exporter among middle-income developing countries.

Shrinking farm workforces are associated with more vulnerable hired farm workers in both rich and poorer countries, largely due to rising shares of migrant, guest, and unauthorized workers. Farmers in both industrial and middle-income countries increasingly turn to unauthorized migrants or guest workers who are tied to them by contracts. Lack of local knowledge and fear of being fired and subject to deportation have led to abuse, as with Asians in British fisheries, Africans in Italian citrus, as well as Bangladeshis and Indonesians in Malaysian palm oil and Burmese in Thai agriculture and fisheries. Governments struggle to develop policies that allow farmers to fill vacant farm jobs and protect both local and foreign workers.

Canada

Canada is a net exporter of farm commodities and the world's leading exporter of canola and maple syrup. Canada exported farm commodities and food worth C$66 billion in 2018, dominated by grains and oil seeds. The most valuable farm exports were canola seeds, oil, and cake worth C$10 billion and spring and durum wheat worth C$5 billion. Canada's farm exports to the US were worth C$30 billion in 2017, followed by C$7 billion to China and C$4 billion to Japan. Canada also imports farm commodities and food worth about C$40 billion, with 60 percent coming from the US.

Primary agriculture, the production of food and fiber on farms, employed 275,300 people in 2014 to generate $56 billion in cash farm receipts (Canada Agriculture, 2016, 28 and 42). Farm operating expenses in 2014 were $50 billion, including $5 billion for cash wages and the value of farm-provided housing, about the same as expenditures on fertilizer and lime.

The Prosperity Paradox: Fewer and More Vulnerable Farm Workers. Philip Martin, Oxford University Press (2021).
© Philip Martin.
DOI: 10.1093/oso/9780198867845.001.0001

Canada had 193,000 farms in 2016, including 15,000 that had annual sales of C$1 million or more. Most farms produced wheat (52,000 farms), barley (25,000), and oat (24,000), but there were 3,200 farms with tree fruits, 9,300 with berries and grapes, and 10,000 with vegetables.[1] Canola was the largest acreage crop, 21 million acres, followed by 15 million acres of spring wheat and about 7 million acres each of barley, durum wheat, and soybeans.

Fruits and vegetables worth C$4.5 billion in 2014 employ most of Canada's farm workers, and their production is concentrated in three provinces. Ontario had horticultural sales of $878 million in 2015, led by greenhouse tomatoes; Quebec C$490 million led by field vegetables; and British Columbia $478 million led by fruits such as blueberries.

Over 75,000 farms reported cattle and calves; some also produce crops. Alberta dominates beef-cattle production, with cattle sales of C$7.4 billion in 2016, while Quebec and Ontario each had about C$2.5 billion in dairy and milk sales. Canada had about 15 million beef cows in 2016 and almost a million dairy cows.

Canada had 325,000 to 350,000 people employed in agriculture in 2008, including self-employed and hired workers (CAHRC, 2009). Livestock and poultry farms paid 42 percent of wages paid by Canadian farmers, greenhouses and nurseries paid 24 percent, and fruits and vegetables paid 16 percent; that is, fruits, greenhouses, and vegetables accounted for 40 percent of wages paid CAHRC (2009, 14). Ontario accounted for 35 percent of farm labor expenses, Quebec 19 percent, the prairie provinces 40 percent, and British Columbia 13 percent.

Labor law and hired-farm-worker data are province-specific. Ontario reported 12,300 farms that hired labor in 2016, and they reported hiring a total of 2.2 million weeks of hired labor in 2011, equivalent to 42,600 full-time equivalent workers. Two-thirds of these hired-worker weeks were worked by year-round workers.[2] Ontario's leading commodities by farm sales in 2016 were dairy products worth C$2 billion and vegetables and soybeans worth C$1.6 billion each.

Farm Labor and SAWP

Canada has a mostly Canadian-born farm workforce, but the share of farm work done by foreign guest workers is rising as farms get fewer and larger and the government makes guest workers available via more channels. The Seasonal Agricultural Workers Program (SAWP) has been admitting Caribbean workers since 1966 and Mexican workers since 1974 to fill farm jobs, and the SAWP is

---

[1] 2016 Census of Agriculture: http://www150.statcan.gc.ca/t1/tbl1/en/tv.action?pid=3210015401.
[2] See http://www.omafra.gov.on.ca/english/stats/agriculture_summary.htm#labour

often considered a model bilateral labor agreement.[3] Procedures to recruit workers and to protect them while they are employed abroad are spelled out in government-to-government Memoranda of Understanding (MOUs)[4] and employer–worker contracts.

The SAWP, according to the Canadian government, "matches workers from Mexico and the Caribbean countries with Canadian farmers who need temporary support during planting and harvesting seasons, when qualified Canadians or permanent residents are not available." There are about three Mexican workers admitted for each Jamaican, the second-largest sending country. Two-thirds of SAWP workers are in Ontario, almost 20 percent in British Columbia, and 10 percent in Quebec. Between 1974 and 2017, some 351,869 Mexican workers were employed in Canadian agriculture, including some who returned year after year.

The SAWP admissions process begins with Canadian farmers who try and fail to recruit Canadian workers by offering the higher of the minimum or prevailing wage.[5] Canadian minimum wages vary by province, and were C$14 in Ontario, C$13.85 in British Columbia, and C$12.50 in Quebec in 2019. If efforts to recruit Canadian workers fail, and the government determines that the presence of SAWP workers will not depress the wages of similar Canadian farm workers, farmers are certified by Service Canada to recruit SAWP workers by promising them at least 240 hours of farm work for at least 6 weeks in Canada.[6]

SAWP workers may stay in Canada up to 8 months between January 1 and December 15 each year, and they stay an average 22 weeks or 5.5 months, often working 60 to 70 hours a week. About 2,000 Canadian farms hire SAWP workers, including hydroponic or greenhouse farms that produce fresh tomatoes. Two-thirds of Canada's greenhouse tomatoes are in Ontario, where Leamington is the self-described tomato capital of the world. Tomato production peaks between April and November, when long hours of daylight contribute to average yields of over 500 metric tons per hectare.

Canadian farmers specify or "name" over three-fourths of the SAWP workers they want to hire, and rely on non-profit organizations created by farmers to transport SAWP workers to Canada: Foreign Agricultural Resource Management Service (FARMS) in Ontario and Fondation des Entreprises en Recrutement de Main-d'œuvre Agricole Étrangère (FERME) in Quebec. Mexico's Department of

---

[3] Some 264 Jamaican workers were admitted in 1966, and the Caribbean SAWP was extended to Barbados and Trinidad-Tobago in 1967, and expanded to other Caribbean islands in 1976.

[4] The MOUs between Canada and Mexico, Jamaica, and other Caribbean countries are intergovernmental administrative arrangements, not binding international treaties; http://www.canada.ca/en/employment-social-development/services/foreign-workers/agricultural/seasonal-agricultural.html.

[5] The prevailing wage can be that determined by Human Resources Development Canada (HRDC) for the work in question or the wage paid by the farmer to Canadian workers doing similar work.

[6] Farm employers receive a positive Labor Market Information Assessment that allows them to recruit foreign workers. Most discussions of available Canadian workers refer to insufficient "reliable" local workers, that is, there are unemployed Canadians, but they do not want to fill seasonal farm jobs.

Labor maintains a list of workers who would like to be selected to work in Canada, and employers can select from this list of prescreened workers if they do not have enough named workers. Many Canadian farmers ask current workers to refer friends and relatives if more workers are needed, so that networks of current workers are the primary means of recruiting additional workers.

Mexican workers are prohibited from paying recruitment fees to get jobs in Canada, but some do. On June 23, 2008, Canadian Border Services Agency (CBSA) inspectors asked eighty Mexicans arriving with SAWP permits whether they had paid recruitment fees in Mexico. When the workers responded yes, they were not admitted to British Columbia to work. CBSA says that workers who pay recruitment fees are denied entry into Canada because they may not leave at the end of their work contracts.[7]

Both employers and workers sign contracts that spell out wages, working conditions, and deductions. Most farmers advance the cost of airfare and visas, but deduct some travel and other costs from workers' wages.[8] Employers offer free housing to SAWP workers on their farms or in nearby commercial establishments that are inspected by Canadian authorities before workers arrive. Farmers must provide transportation between worker housing and workplaces at no charge.

Employers must enroll SAWP workers in provincial health-insurance programs, and SAWP workers and their employers pay premiums for the (un)employment insurance program, even though SAWP workers are generally not eligible for unemployment benefits because they cannot remain unemployed in Canada looking for jobs.

Farmers evaluate each SAWP worker at the end of the season. SAWP workers are required to present their employer's evaluation to a government agency at home to be selected for the next season. Farmers and farm organizations can "blacklist" particular workers and not hire them in the future, and government agencies in sending countries can blacklist particular Canadian famers and not approve sending workers to them. However, Canadian famers blacklisted by the Mexican government can turn to the Caribbean for workers, and vice versa.

FARMS, FERME, and other farmers' organizations that bring SAWP workers to Canada and deploy them to member farms are also involved in reviewing the operation of the SAWP program in periodic meetings with the Canadian, Mexican, and Caribbean governments. There is no formal role for workers' organizations in these review-of-SAWP-operations meetings, and sending country governments represent the interests of their workers.

[7] For details see http://migration.ucdavis.edu/rmn/more.php?id=1328.
[8] British Columbia does not allow farmers to recoup transportation costs from SAWP workers, but does allow farmers to deduct 6 percent of gross wages or a maximum C$450 to cover housing costs. The Mexican consulate in BC handles employer requests for SAWP workers and arranges for workers to travel to BC.

Caribbean government liaison officers interact with workers from their countries while they are in Canada,[9] and the Mexican government has consular officers who interact with Mexican SAWP workers. Some SAWP workers complain that their government's representatives are more interested in maximizing the number of Canadian jobs available than dealing with the grievances of particular workers.[10] If workers make complaints, labor attachés may discuss worker issues with employers, and the remedy may be returning the complaining worker to the country of origin.

Most Caribbean workers admitted under the SAWP are from Jamaica, which required SAWP workers to agree to have 25 percent of their Canadian wages deducted and sent to a liaison office in Canada, which kept 5 percent and forwarded 20 percent to the worker's account at home.[11] Some workers complain of delays in receiving these forced savings at home and of the low exchange rate used to convert Canadian dollars into Jamaican dollars. After January 1, 2016, the Jamaican government was allowed to deduct only C$5.45 a day from each worker's pay to cover its services, a policy shift that angered Jamaica.[12]

The Jamaican government's forced savings and deductions policy is an example of how some sending countries try to tax citizens selected to work abroad at higher wages, reasoning that the government should collect some of the guest worker's foreign earnings. The Jamaican example went further when it was revealed that members of Jamaica's parliament are allowed to nominate new workers to participate in SAWP, prompting complaints from Canadian farmers and a promise in 2004 to ensure that nominated workers have experience doing farm work.[13]

Agricultural Stream (NOC Low-Skill)

In addition to the SAWP, farmers can hire foreign workers under the agricultural stream,[14] which began as the Pilot Project for Occupations Requiring Lower

---

[9] The Jamaican Liaison Service is at http://jamliser.com/.

[10] Some workers and NGOs say that government liaison officers in Canada generally favor Canadian employers rather than their citizen workers because they value high-wage jobs and remittances more than worker complaints.

[11] The Jamaican government required Jamaican workers coming to the US with H-2A visas to agree to have 25 percent of their wages deducted, and promised to return 23 percent. The US ended this forced savings scheme before Canada (Mize, 2019, 137–8).

[12] The dispute over the Jamaican forced savings program is described at https://nationalpost.com/pmn/news-pmn/canada-news-pmn/minister-urged-to-press-jamaica-over-wage-deductions-of-migrant-workers-in-canada.

[13] Most Caribbean countries allow returning workers to bring $500 worth of electronics and other goods home duty-free at the end of their contracts; many pack these goods in barrels to send home. See http://migration.ucdavis.edu/rmn/more.php?id=824.

[14] http://www.canada.ca/en/employment-social-development/services/foreign-workers/agricultural/agricultural/requirements.html.

Levels of Formal Training (National Occupational Classification or NOC C&D Pilot), a unilateral program that offers fewer protections for guest workers. The NOC C&D Pilot began in 2002, and the number of migrants admitted more than doubled from 101,300 in 2002 to 251,200 in 2008. Most NOC C&D Pilot workers fill year-round nonfarm jobs.

The NOC C&D Pilot and later the agricultural stream of temporary foreign workers admitted 7,100 workers in 2013 (NOC 8431, 8432, 8611, 8251, 8252, 8254, 8256), mostly Guatemalans employed by Quebec farmers, compared with the SAWP's 27,600 admissions of mostly Mexican workers for Ontario farmers. Foreigners admitted under the SAWP can return to Canada indefinitely, while foreigners admitted under the NOC C&D Pilot can stay in Canada up to 24 months.[15]

The SAWP is governed by bilateral MOUs, and recruitment is overseen by a government agency in the sending country, while the agricultural stream is a unilateral program that allows Canadian employers to recruit guest workers anywhere. Agricultural stream employers must pay the workers round-trip transportation and not recoup transport costs in wage deductions, and must provide on-farm or off-farm housing for which up to $30 a week can be deducted from worker wages.

The Guatemala–Quebec program was developed with the help of the International Organization for Migration (IOM) to ensure clean recruitment, beginning with a pilot program in 2003. The program expanded, before ending in 2013 in the wake of charges that Guatemalans had to pay high fees to be selected and had to deposit $500 with IOM as a surety bond that they forfeit if they do not return to Guatemala (Gabriel and Macdonald, 2017, 1715). The Guatemalan government was supposed to take over the IOM-created clean recruitment system, but instead IOM quit acting as a labor recruiter and the ex-IOM director who developed the Guatemala–Canada program created a private labor recruiter, Amigo Laboral, which now sends most Guatemalan farm workers to Canada (Gabriel and Macdonald, 2017, 1717).

A proliferation of private recruitment agencies in Guatemala has led to widespread fraud as recruiters collect fees and deposits from rural Guatemalans for non-existent foreign jobs and disappeared. The Guatemala–Quebec program, begun with good intentions, appears to be an example of stimulating widespread interest in working in high-wage countries but leaving most rural Guatemalans with no way to access honest and legal channels to obtain work permits.[16]

---

[15] If they then leave Canada for at least four years, NOC guest workers can return for another four years.

[16] The Guatemalan government appears incapable of regulating recruitment. It announced that all private recruiters pay Q3,000 or C$500 to register, but did not establish a registry of recruiters, so many recruiters refused to pay and neither workers nor employers could check the list of registered recruiters (Gabriel and Macdonald, 2017, 1719).

In summer 2019, Guatemala signed a safe third country agreement with the US that requires Hondurans, Salvadorans, and other foreigners passing through the country to apply for asylum in Guatemala rather than continue to travel through Mexico to the US. As a "reward" for signing the safe third country agreement, a US official suggested that the number of H-2A visas issued to Guatemalans could triple from the 4,000 issued in FY18, reportedly spurring a new round of recruitment fraud.

Issues with the agricultural stream, such as temp agencies recruiting workers and moving them from one Canadian farm to another, prompted a federal review published in February 2018. Almost 500 stakeholders submitted comments. Farmers asked for fewer barriers between themselves and the guest workers they want to hire, while unions emphasized the potential for recruitment fraud abroad and exploitation in Canada.[17]

The SAWP and the agricultural stream of the NOC C&D Pilot are limited to fruits, vegetables, horticultural crops, tobacco, and sod, while the general NOC C&D is open to all farm employers, including livestock producers. SAWP allows farm employers who pay for worker transportation to Canada to deduct from worker wages half of the airfare to get to Canada and requires employers to offer housing to workers at no charge. The agricultural stream of the NOC C&D Pilot allows employers to require guest workers to cover their transport costs to Canada, and farm employers can charge guest workers up to C$30 a week for employer-provided housing, which can be off the farm.[18]

Data on SAWP and NOC primary agricultural admissions are scarce. Table 5.1 shows that NOC primary agriculture admissions rose faster than SAWP admissions between 2002 and 2013. Since then, admissions data for the SAWP and NOC agriculture are combined. However, the number of positive Labor Market Impact Assessments (LMIAs), the certification from Service Canada that is necessary to hire SAWP or NOC workers, has continued to increase, reaching almost 70,000 in 2017.

Unions and Development

Most farmers are satisfied with the SAWP, but the United Food and Commercial Workers (UFCW) union calls the SAWP "Canada's dirty little secret." The UFCW operates Agriculture Workers Alliance support centers for SAWP and other guest workers to inform them of their rights and to solicit their complaints.

---

[17] http://www.ohscanada.com/migrant-farm-worker-review-prompts-renewed-calls-reforms-protections/.

[18] SAWP housing must be on the farm where the migrant works.

Table 5.1   SAWP and NOC admissions and positive LMIAs for agriculture, 2002–17

	Admissions	Admissions	LMIAs
	SAWP*	NOC Primary Ag	Primary Ag
2002	18,622	123	
2003	18,698	341	
2004	19,049	430	
2005	20,282	877	
2006	21,253	2,231	
2007	22,571	3,170	
2008	24,188	4,513	
2009	23,386	4,844	
2010	23,933	5,161	
2011	24,693	6,209	37,945
2012	25,710	6,632	40,271
2013	27,566	7,099	45,361
2014	40,033		47,474
2015	43,394		53,298
2016	41,881		54,260
2017	47,166		60,578
2002–13	48%	5672%	69,775
2010–13	15%	38%	
2013–17	18%		28%

* 2014–17 data include SAWP and NOC primary ag admissions.

Source: https://www.canada.ca/en/employment-social-development/services/foreign-workers/reports/overhaul.html#h2.1-3.1.

The UFCW organized some SAWP workers. Mayfair Farms in Portage la Prairie, Manitoba, signed a three-year contract with UFCW local 832 in June 2008 that linked future wage increases to the provincial minimum wage and provided a C$1-an-hour overtime premium for work done after 70 hours a week. Mayfair's SAWP workers were dissatisfied, complaining that the UFCW negotiated a C$0.15 an hour raise on their behalf but charged them $4 a week in union dues. Some Mayfair workers wanted to work twelve to fourteen hour days and seven days a week, but Mayfair limited them to seventy hours a week to avoid the overtime pay required by the contract (Russo, 2018). Mayfair's SAWP workers voted 26–0 to decertify UFCW in August 2009, a vote that migrant advocates charged was influenced by the Mexican consul's warning to Mayfair's SAWP workers they could be blacklisted if they did not vote for decertification.[19]

The UFCW has also had mixed experiences in British Columbia, which has a provincial standard contract for SAWP workers. UFCW Local 1518 won the right to represent SAWP workers at Greenway Farms in Surrey and Floralia Plant Growers in 2008, and at Sidhu & Sons Nursery in 2010. The UFCW achieved

---

[19] For details on the Mayfair Farms case see http://migration.ucdavis.edu/rmn/more.php?id=1488.

collective bargaining agreements (CBAs) with Floralia and Sidhu by way of arbitration that included provisions specific to the SAWP workers, such as return trips if there was a death in the family and storage for work equipment while SAWP workers were at home (Vosko, 2018, 896–7).

The CBAs included seniority recall after completing the first season and provisions for speedy arbitration if a SAWP worker was fired, since losing a job in Canada normally requires a worker to return to her home country. Seniority recall may not be observed strictly because Canadians have priority to fill jobs, so some SAWP workers may not be recalled if the employer recruits more local workers, and the Mexican government can block the return of particular workers.

This is what happened in Sidhu, where the UFCW complained that the Mexican government in 2011 blocked the return of some pro-union SAWP workers. The UFCW filed charges against the Mexican government with the British Columbia Labor Board, which countered that it was a sovereign immune from labor suits and won (Vosko, 2018, 900–1; Vosko, 2016). Workers at Sidhu voted to decertify the UFCW in an election that some workers said was tainted by Mexican labor attachés warning workers to vote out the UFCW in order to keep their jobs, an example of the Mexican government acting on behalf of Canadian employers rather than Mexican SAWP workers.[20]

The North-South Institute supported several studies that evaluated the SAWP program's impacts on Canada and sending countries. The overall conclusion is that the SAWP helps Canadian farmers to recruit and employ reliable low-skilled workers, but cannot avoid depressing Canadian wages and working conditions because SAWP migrants are vulnerable and can lose their jobs and the right to be in Canada if they complain (Verma, 2002). Worker vulnerability is highlighted by Vosko et al., (2019), who used the Ontario Ministry of Labor's Employment Standards Information System to determine that labor law enforcement depends on complaints, and SAWP workers rarely complain.

The Institute for Research on Public Policy (IRPP) interviewed 600 Mexican and Jamaican farm workers in 2012 and found that most had returned to Canada for an average of eight seasons. Many SAWP workers noted their isolation on the farms where they worked, but two-thirds said they would like to return next season and eventually to become Canadian immigrants (Hennebry, 2012).

The SAWP is an example of a circular migration program that fills seasonal jobs with workers from lower-wage countries, most of whom return year after year. The Mexican government in a 2015 press release called the SAWP "a model of bilateral cooperation between the two countries, guaranteeing employment to farm workers and making it possible to maintain a temporary migration flow that

---

[20] https://migration.ucdavis.edu/rmn/more.php?id=1893.

is orderly, circular and secure, and above all, one that fully respects the workers' labor, social and human rights."[21]

Researchers often point out gaps between migration policy goals and outcomes. Some call SAWP workers "unfree" because they are dependent on Canadian employers to remain in Canada and to be recalled for next season (Choudry and Smith, 2016).

Farmers benefit from the fact that over 85 percent of SAWP workers have been employed in Canada previously, reducing training costs and ensuring high worker productivity that may not result in higher wages for experienced workers. Hennebry and Preibisch (2012) praise the cooperation between governments to regulate recruitment and employment, transparent processes used to select workers, and the availability of health insurance for SAWP workers while they are in Canada. However, they note that there is no formal program to recognize worker qualifications in Canada, or after they return to Mexico, and no path for SAWP workers to become Canadian immigrants. If the alternative to SAWP is illegal migration and contractors assembling crews of workers to fill seasonal farm jobs, as in California and other areas of the US, the SAWP can be considered a "model despite flaws" (Basok, 2007).

There is less evidence that the SAWP has promoted stay-at-home development in worker areas of origin, as may occur if returned workers invest their remittances to expand small farms and start small businesses. Most returned SAWP workers improved their housing and spent more on their children's health and education than similar families that did not receive remittances, but many household heads continue to migrate year after year to Canada. Upward mobility may be intergenerational, as the children of SAWP workers who obtained more health care and education due to their parents' remittances get the education and skills and find good jobs in Mexico.

European Union

The European Union (EU) had farm sales of €365 billion in 2018, including €205 billion from crops and €160 billion from animals.[22] France led EU member states in farm sales, accounting for almost 18 percent of the EU total, followed by Italy and Spain with over 12 percent each and Germany with over 11 percent. The EU is the world's leading importer of farm commodities, and is also an important exporter, especially of wine and beer and processed food.

---

[21] http://embamex.sre.gob.mx/canada_eng/index.php/press-releases/573-jan2015/5453-ptat15begins.
[22] https://ec.europa.eu/info/sites/info/files/food-farming-fisheries/farming/documents/agri-statistical-factsheet-eu_en.pdf.

The EU had 10.5 million farms in 2016, down from 13.8 million in 2007. Romania had the most farms, 3.4 million, followed by 1.4 million in Poland, 1.1 million in Italy, and 950,000 in Spain. The decrease in the number of farms over the past decade was largest in countries such as Bulgaria and Slovakia, and smallest in Ireland and Portugal. In many of the ex-communist countries, 90 percent or more of farms have less than 5 hectares, compared with a quarter of French farms and less than 10 percent of German farms.

Most EU farms are hobby, retirement, or part-time operations. Table 5.2 shows that full-time equivalent employment or annual work units (AWUs) on farms in the EU-28 countries fell from 10.3 million to 9.1 million between 2010 and 2019. These AWUs included 2.4 million that were filled by hired or salaried workers. The share of hired or salaried workers among the AWUs in EU-28 agriculture rose slightly, from 23 to 27 percent, as the number of farmers and family members declined.

The share of hired workers among AWUs in agriculture was highest for some Eastern European countries such as the Czech Republic and Estonia, where two-thirds of AWUs were hired. By contrast, less than 10 percent of AWUs were hired in Ireland, Malta, and Slovenia, and only 10 percent were hired in Poland and Romania, the two countries with a third of EU AWUs or full-time farm jobs.

The EU's Farm Structure Survey (FSS), conducted every decade, has more detailed country data. Romania had the most people employed in agriculture, 7.2 million or almost 30 percent of the total 25 million employed in EU agriculture in 2010, followed by 3.8 million workers in Poland and 3.4 million in Italy (these numbers include part-time workers). The highest share of non-family regular hired workers was in the Czech Republic, 68 percent of 133,000, followed by Slovakia, 49 percent of 91,000, and France, 44 percent of a million. When standardized to 9.8 million AWUs or year-round jobs, Poland, with 1.9 million year-round equivalent hired workers, and Romania, with 1.6 million, accounted for 36 percent of full-time equivalent (FTE) jobs in EU agriculture.

The Farm Structure Survey distinguishes between non-family regular workers with contracts and non-family and non-regular workers. The highest share of non-family and non-regular workers, often immigrants, was in Spain, where they were 19 percent of all AWUs or year-round jobs in agriculture, followed by Greece and Italy.

Another survey, the Economic Accounts for Agriculture (EAA), reported 10.1 million AWUs in the EU-27 in 2012, including 2.1 million in Poland, 1.6 million in Romania, and 1.2 million in Italy. The EAA finds the highest shares of salaried or hired workers in the Czech Republic and Slovakia, over 70 percent, and the lowest shares in Ireland and Poland, less than 10 percent.

A third source of farm labor data is from the Labor Force Surveys conducted by EU member states that involve interviews with 1.5 million people each quarter. Labor Force Surveys found an average 9.9 million workers employed in agriculture in 2012, including the self-employed.

Table 5.2 Employment in EU agriculture, 2010 and 2019

	Total Annual Work Units		Family or non-salaried (000's)		Hired or salaried		Hired share	
	2010	2019	2010	2019	2010	2019	2010	2019
Belgium	62	56	47	43	10	12	16%	22%
Bulgaria	407	190	303	124	70	66	17%	35%
Czech Republic	109	104	26	30	83	74	76%	71%
Denmark	54	54	28	24	25	30	46%	56%
Germany	522	473	303	263	214	210	41%	44%
Estonia	25	20	13	6	12	13	47%	68%
Ireland	166	161	153	148	13	13	8%	8%
Greece	441	417	377	348	76	69	17%	17%
Spain	964	862	511	450	401	412	42%	48%
France	809	741	529	452	268	289	33%	39%
Croatia	202	175	188	160	12	15	6%	9%
Italy	1,164	1,126	786	750	336	375	29%	33%
Cyprus	25	22	18	15	7	6	29%	29%
Latvia	86	69	71	52	16	17	19%	25%
Lithuania	143	138	104	98	39	40	27%	29%
Luxembourg	4	3	3	2	1	1	21%	32%
Hungary	444	384	329	261	109	123	25%	32%
Malta	5	5	4	5	0	0	9%	9%
Netherlands	153	158	85	83	68	74	44%	47%
Austria	128	115	111	95	15	20	12%	17%
Poland	1,915	1,676	1,804	1,504	111	172	6%	10%
Portugal	310	234	231	151	72	83	23%	36%
Romania	1,639	1,400	1,326	1,245	210	155	13%	11%
Slovenia	77	78	71	71	8	6	11%	8%
Slovakia	56	44	16	16	40	28	72%	64%
Finland	82	59	65	47	16	12	19%	21%
Sweden	65	55	42	33	22	22	33%	40%
United Kingdom	291	296	194	197	99	99	34%	33%
EU-28	10,348	9,113	7,736	6,674	2,352	2,440	23%	27%

Source: Eurostat; https://appsso.eurostat.ec.europa.eu/nui/setupDownloads.do.

The fewer and larger farms that produce most of the EU's agricultural output rely mostly on hired workers, many of whom are immigrants. Nori (2017, 3) reports that at least a third of hired farm workers in southern European countries are immigrants, including over half in Greece, a third in Italy, and a quarter in Spain. Foreigners move to agricultural areas in EU countries for many reasons, including easier access to jobs if they are unauthorized and lower living costs in agricultural areas, but they can face exploitation and abuse, especially at the hands of the contractors who often assemble work crews (Nori, 2017).

All reports agree that dependence on migrants from outside the country is highest in Greece, Italy, and Spain, but Rye and Scott (2018) emphasize that there are also many non-nationals employed in the agricultural sectors of northern European countries, from Britain and Scandinavia to Poland. Migrant farm workers in northern European countries are more likely to be intra-EU migrants who may legally switch from one farm employer to another or accept nonfarm jobs. Legal non-EU migrants, on the other hand, are obliged to remain with one employer.

The EU's Common Agricultural Policy (CAP), begun in 1962, absorbs 40 percent of the EU's total budget, which was €134 billion for payments in 2017 and €158 billion for commitments.[23] CAP spending totaled €58.5 billion in 2018, including €41 billion for direct payments to farmers and €14 billion to support rural development. Direct payments to farmers are based on the size of farms and the extent of sustainable farming practices, and provide an additional payment for young farmers.

Direct payments to 7 million EU farmers are most important, absorbing about three-fourths of CAP spending. Four countries received half of CAP monies in 2018: France €9.5 billion, Spain €6.8 billion, Germany €6.4 billion, and Italy €5.8 billion. Some EU member states offer additional support to particular types of farms and farmers (EU, 2017).

Britain

The UK's 185,000 farms sold commodities worth €28 billion in 2018, including 37 percent from crops and 58 percent from animal products.[24] Milk accounted for 18 percent of farm sales, followed by 15 percent for cattle, 13 percent for grain, 11 percent for vegetables, and 10 percent for poultry.

The UK is a net importer of all types of food, but a net exporter of beverages, primarily because of the high value of Scotch whisky exports. For example, the UK exported fruits and vegetables worth $1 billion in 2017, and imported fruits and vegetables worth $11 billion.[25] Overall farm exports, including processed

---

[23] https://ec.europa.eu/info/food-farming-fisheries/key-policies/common-agricultural-policy/cap-glance_en.

[24] https://ec.europa.eu/info/sites/info/files/food-farming-fisheries/farming/documents/agri-statistical-factsheet-uk_en.pdf.

[25] http://www.gov.uk/government/publications/food-statistics-pocketbook-2017/food-statistics-in-your-pocket-2017-global-and-uk-supply.

Table 5.3 Employment in UK and English agriculture, 2016

	UK	England
Number of workers in agriculture	######	301,500
Number of farmers and unpaid family	######	173,100
...of which, full-time	######	88,800
...of which, part-time	######	84,300
Regular and casual employees	######	128,400
Regular, full-time workers	71,400	54,900
Regular, part-time workers	40,900	29,600
Seasonal/casual/gang workers	64,200	43,900

Source: http://www.ons.gov.uk/peoplepopulationandcommunity/populationandmigration/
internationalmigration/articles/labourintheagricultureindustry/2018-02-06.

food and beverages, were €26 billion in 2018, when imports were over twice as much, €55 billion.[26]

Table 5.3 shows that 466,000 people were employed in British agriculture in 2016, including two-thirds in England. Farmers and unpaid family members were over 60 percent of agricultural employment. There were 176,000 hired workers, including 40 percent who were regular full-time workers, a quarter who were regular part-time workers, and 35 percent who were casual or gang workers, that is, brought to farms by labor contractors or gangmasters.[27] Crop production is concentrated in East Anglia (Norfolk, Suffolk, and Cambridgeshire), and livestock production is concentrated in the southwest (Bristol, Cornwall, Devon, Dorset, Gloucestershire, Somerset, and Wiltshire).

SAWS

After World War II, the British government launched a Seasonal Agricultural Workers Scheme (SAWS) to allowed farmers to recruit foreign workers to fill seasonal jobs for up to six months. Farmers had to provide housing to SAWS workers and pay them at least the minimum wage, established in an agricultural wages order.[28] The SAWS quota peaked at 25,000 in 2004, and then was gradually reduced after May 1, 2004, when Eastern Europeans could work in the UK without visas before ending in 2013 in anticipation of Bulgarians and Romanians gaining free access to EU labor markets (Consterdine and Samuk, 2015).

---

[26] https://ec.europa.eu/info/sites/info/files/food-farming-fisheries/farming/documents/agri-statistical-factsheet-uk_en.pdf.

[27] http://www.ons.gov.uk/peoplepopulationandcommunity/populationandmigration/internationalmigration/articles/labourintheagricultureindustry/2018-02-06.

[28] http://www.daera-ni.gov.uk/topics/countryside-management-and-managing-your-business/managing-your-business/employing-people.

In 2016, British farms employed 27,000 non-British EU workers year-round and another 75,000 seasonally. Voter approval of Brexit in June 2016 prompted farmers to warn of farm labor shortages. The government responded by allowing up to 2,500 non-EU workers to work on British farms for up to six months in 2019 and 2020, and may consider a new NAWS.[29]

During Covid-19 lockdowns in spring 2020, agriculture was considered an essential industry, and farmers and farm workers were expected to continue to work. Leaders including Prince Charles urged jobless Britains to "Pick for Britain" in 2020 by applying for jobs that pay about $125 a day, and added that the UK needed "pickers who are stickers." Many jobless British residents applied for farm jobs, leading to predictions that a third of seasonal jobs in 2020 could be filled by Britons. However, British labor recruiter Concordia said that only 10 percent of the 1,000 British workers who responded to the "Pick for Britain" campaign in April 2020 went to work on farms; the others cited the short duration of the job, difficulties getting from their homes to farms with jobs, and the need to care for children. Many British farmers said they preferred experienced Romanians to first-time British farm workers.

Gangmasters

The UK has struggled to regulate labor providers or gangmasters, who provided at least 30,000 workers to the British horticulture industry in 2017, including two-thirds from Romania and Bulgaria and one third from the EU-8 countries, such as Poland, that joined the EU in 2004.[30] The British Growers Association estimated that there were 75,000 non-British citizens employed seasonally in British horticulture in 2016, suggesting that most foreign workers are hired directly rather than via contractors.

The drowning of twenty-three illegal Chinese migrants picking cockles, a seafood delicacy similar to clams, in Morecambe Bay in February 2004 led to the Gangmasters (Licensing) Act that required gangmasters to obtain licenses from a new Gangmasters and Labour Abuse Authority (http://www.gla.gov.uk). The Ethical Trading Initiative—a group of buyers, NGOs, and unions—developed an industry-based code of good practice for labor providers that supply temporary labor to growers or packers (http://www.ethicaltrade.org).

When the Gangmasters Act was enacted, there were an estimated 10,000 gangmasters in the UK, including 3,000 active in agriculture. Their crews, which

---

[29] http://www.gov.uk/government/news/new-pilot-scheme-to-bring-2500-seasonal-workers-to-uk-farms.
[30] http://www.ons.gov.uk/peoplepopulationandcommunity/populationandmigration/internationalmigration/articles/labourintheagricultureindustry/2018-02-06.

include foreigners and some British citizens who may be working for cash while drawing benefits, often start in the Cornish flower sector before moving on to other labor-intensive jobs in Devon harvesting crops like cabbages, lettuces, spring onions, and strawberries. East Anglia's vast flatlands are ideal for growing vegetables and flowers, explaining why Spalding, in Lincolnshire, has many packinghouses.

Investigations of gangmasters reveal problems. For example, gangmaster Victor Solomka, who arrived in the UK from Ukraine in 2000 and was granted refugee status, was convicted in February 2005 of sending 700 Eastern European migrants to fish-processing plants at below-standard wages and pocketing the difference. In some cases, Solomka received £6 per hour for workers, paid them £4 an hour, and recouped some of their reduced wages in fees for room and board.[31] Other enforcement actions highlighted the mix of legal and unauthorized workers among those provided by gangmasters.[32]

Staffmasters Ltd, an agency supplying legal South African workers to Empire World Trade, a produce packer, charged each migrant £1,500 for visas and travel to the UK, so that migrants arrived in debt for their two-year work assignments and repaid loans at high interest rates while having 25 percent of their £200-a-week earnings deducted for room and board. Migrants were told that they could not leave Staffmasters for other UK jobs until they repaid their loans, which anti-slavery groups said made them bonded labor in the UK. Staffmasters had pledged to adhere to good practices as a member of the 350-member Association of Labour Providers (ALP), which says its members provide 70 percent of the temporary workers to the UK's food-growing and food-processing sector.[33]

Farmers and food processors say that they need more foreign workers to continue to produce food in the UK. Mark Boleat, chairman of the Association of Labour Providers, said migrant labor is "fundamental to the running of our agricultural economy." Competition between gangmasters keeps commissions low, which encourages "cheating," such as hiring British workers who are also collecting welfare or unemployment benefits and paying them less than the minimum wage in cash. Many gangmasters charge foreign workers for jobs or other services. The ALP website touts its links to NGOs that aim to extirpate labor trafficking through initiatives such as Stronger Together.[34]

---

[31] See https://migration.ucdavis.edu/rmn/more.php?id=987.
[32] For example, Monarch Catering Agency, a Portuguese-owned labor provider based in London, sent Brazilians to work at Nature's Way with Portuguese documents. MCA has a series of affiliates, some of which did not pay all of the taxes that they owe: https://migration.ucdavis.edu/rmn/more.php?id=987.
[33] https://migration.ucdavis.edu/mn/more.php?id=3002.
[34] https://labourproviders.org.uk/resources/?_sft_sub-category=agricultural-wages.

Italy

Italy's 1.1 million farms had sales of €52 billion in 2018, including 60 percent from the sale of crops and 30 percent from the sale of animal products. Wine was the most valuable crop, accounting for 18 percent of farm sales, followed by vegetables and horticultural specialties, also 18 percent, and fruits and olive oil, 13 percent. Most farms are small, 60 percent had less than 5 hectares, and over 40 percent of farmers were 64 and older.[35] The EU provided €5.8 billion in Common Agricultural Policy support to Italian agriculture in 2018, including €3.6 billion in direct payments and €1.5 billon to promote rural development.

Italian agriculture employs about 4 percent of Italian workers and generates 2 percent of Italian GDP, suggesting downward pressure on farm wages and incomes for the 1.2 million people employed in the sector, including 900,000 annual work units or full-time equivalent workers in 2018.

Italy is a net food importer, exporting almost €3 billion worth of farm commodities in 2018 and importing farm commodities worth €10 billion; it has a trade surplus in processed-food products. Italy is the second-largest exporter of olive oil, supplying a quarter of the world's olive-oil exports; Spain which provides half of olive-oil exports. However, Italy gets twice as much per liter for its olive oil as Spain. The farm price of olive oil is €5 per kilo in Italy, €2.50 in Greece, and €2.20 in Spain, prompting protests in Andalusia, which produced 80 percent of Spain's 1.8 million tons of olive oil in 2019. Spain exports three-fourths of its olive oil, and has almost a million tons in storage. Italy is the leading importer of Spanish olive oil, and some is reportedly blended with Italian olive oil and sold for higher-than-Spanish prices.[36]

As in many other sectors of the Italian economy, there is a difference between agriculture in northern Italy, where grains and livestock commodities predominate, and southern Italy, which specializes in fruits, vegetables, olive oil, wine, and durum wheat.

Italy has a Mediterranean climate that allows the production of fresh fruits and vegetables that are shipped elsewhere, similar to California agriculture. A major difference is that most Italian farms are smaller than the factories in the fields of California, and the coops to which most Italian farmers belong cannot guarantee a steady supply of high-quality produce to major buyers, which limits their bargaining power.

---

[35] https://ec.europa.eu/info/sites/info/files/food-farming-fisheries/farming/documents/agri-statistical-factsheet-it_en.pdf.

[36] See https://migration.ucdavis.edu/rmn/more.php?id=2355. Olive-oil labeling can be confusing. Extra virgin is oil from the very first pressing of the olives, but this is often meaningless because most olive oil is from centrifuges that produce cleaner and purer oils than presses. Most olive oil has a best-by date on the label that is usually two years from when it was bottled. Residents of Greece, Italy, and Spain consume an average 20 liters of olive oil per person per year, compared with 1 liter per person in the US.

The weak bargaining power of farmers and their coops leads to low farm prices that put downward pressure on wages, which can be further lowered by the widespread use of labor intermediaries. Most farm-labor reformers favor a campaign against supermarkets to persuade them to raise the prices they pay to farmers rather than encouraging the consolidation of farms into fewer and larger units to achieve economies of scale and lower production costs. Fewer and larger farms may have more bargaining power with buyers.

Labor and Foreign Workers

Almost 8.3 million workers were employed in Italy's agriculture in 1950, 42 percent of the Italian labor force. Agricultural employment fell sharply over the next four decades, to 3.2 million or 17 percent of the labor force in 1971, and to 1.6 million or 8 percent of the labor force in 1991. By 2011, there were about 1.3 million people employed in Italian agriculture, 4.3 percent of the Italian workforce (Corrado et al., 2018, 5).

There are several estimates of hired workers in Italian agriculture. The Italian agricultural economics association INEA in 2008 estimated there were 895,000 seasonal farm workers, including 720,000 Italians, 116,000 non-EU foreigners, and 58,000 workers from Eastern European EU-member states such as Romania.[37] A more recent estimate was 843,000 hired farm workers in 2015, including 405,000 or almost half who were foreigners (Corrado et al., 2018, 3). Some 430,000 hired farm workers, or over half, who did not have official contracts, which means that payroll taxes were not paid on their wages and the workers were not entitled to social-security and other work-related benefits. By one estimate, 80 percent of Italian farm workers without contracts are foreigners (Corrado et al., 2018).

National Institute of Social Security (INPS) data suggest that foreigners were almost 30 percent of the 1 million agricultural workers in 2016, up from less than 20 percent in 2006. Corrado et al. (2018, tables 2 and 4) report that these foreign farm workers included over 150,000 intra-EU migrants from Eastern European countries such as Romania (112,000), and 135,000 non-EU foreigners, including 27,000 from India, 25,000 from Albania, and 24,000 from Morocco. The migrant share of farm workers is higher in northern Italy, largely because there are more Italians employed in southern Italian agriculture.

Researchers warn that government data on hired farm labor may be misleading for several reasons, including Italians who want credit at the INPS for farm work in order to receive social-security benefits (Corrado et al., 2018). The INPS allows employers to report days worked well after the work occurred, which can

---

[37] https://migration.ucdavis.edu/rmn/more.php?id=1552.

lead to farmers overreporting days worked by Italians and underreporting days worked by foreigners.

Italy sets an annual quota of non-EU foreigners to fill seasonal jobs that last up to nine months. The quota was 80,000 in 2009, including 70,000 for agriculture and 10,000 for tourism. The quota is supposed to be set by November 30 for the following year, but is often set only in the spring of the year to which it applies.

Legal non-EU seasonal farm workers are from many countries, including nearby Albania and Tunisia and South Asian countries such as Bangladesh and Sri Lanka. The best estimates are that over 40 percent of seasonal guest workers are employed in fruits and 30 percent in vegetables (Corrado et al., 2018). Non-EU seasonal farm workers can also be in Italy as students or asylum seekers, and such workers are half of foreign farm workers in Apulia, Sicily, and Calabria.

The normal farm workday is 6.5 hours a day or 39 hours a week; overtime wages of 1.5 times the usual wage are paid for hours in excess of 39 a week. Employers are supposed to pay taxes of 35.3 percent of farm-worker wages for workers' compensation, social security, and unemployment benefits, and workers contribute 8.8 percent of their wages for these work-related social-insurance programs. Beginning in 2008, farms with annual sales of less than €7,000 were able to hire workers and pay them with vouchers bought at the post office for €10 each. Workers receive the vouchers as their pay, and obtain €7.50 for each one, with the remaining €2.50 used for social-security taxes and workers' compensation insurance payments. Italian farm employers must provide housing to non-EU seasonal foreign workers.

Southern Italy

Many of the most vulnerable foreign workers are in southern Italian regions including Apulia, Calabria, Campania, Basilicata, and Sicily, where small to medium-sized growers produce fruits and vegetables for Italians and northern Europeans (Corrado et al., 2016). Unauthorized farm workers who were able to legalize their status during regularizations in 1990, 1995, 1998, and 2009 often left southern Italy for nonfarm jobs in northern Italy. However, the 2008–9 recession led to layoffs in northern Italy, encouraging some regularized foreigners to return to southern Italian agriculture (Corrado et al., 2018, 3), where they competed with unauthorized foreigners and Italians for jobs.

Cavanna (2020) argues that unauthorized migrants are vulnerable because labor exploiters know that most migrants will not complain to avoid coming to the attention of immigration-enforcement authorities. Labor courts are not required to report the status of workers who file charges to immigration authorities, but most unauthorized migrants do not understand distinctions between government agencies and avoid all of them.

Workers are matched with seasonal jobs in southern Italian agriculture via a variety of intermediaries that range from labor contractors to temp agencies to employer coops to *caporalati* or criminal gangmasters. *Caporalati* have a long history in southern Italy, but they became more important as the seasonal workforce became more diverse, with some contractors using Romanians to supervise Romanian workers and Albanians to supervise Albanian workers. *Caporalati* match most seasonal workers with jobs in some commodities, including tomatoes, oranges, and strawberries.

A third of the workers employed in the greenhouses around Acate on the southeastern coast of Sicily are migrants, including Romanians who replaced the Tunisians who had previously been employed in these greenhouses.[38] Wages are €15 to €25 for 10- to 12-hour days, well below minimum wage levels (Corrado et al., 2018, 9). Workers are often housed on or near the farm where they work, making them especially dependent on their employers.

In January 2010, there were protests in the 16,000-resident municipality of Rosarno, part of the city of Reggio Calabria in Calabria, by some of the 900 African migrants who picked oranges to be processed into juice; the protests were mounted by colleagues of an African migrant who was attacked by a local resident. The migrants earned wages of €20 to €30 a day, less a deduction of up to 25 percent of earnings that was taken by the contractors who hired them. Subsequent analysis attributed the violence to the falling profitability of orange-growing at a time when more local workers competed for orange-picking jobs.[39]

Orange prices fell in 2009–10, reducing the profitability of the 32,000 hectares of oranges amidst rising Brazilian orange-juice imports. The local Mafia, the 'Ndrangheta, controls the transport and processing of oranges into juice and taxes labor contractors. The EU in 2009 switched its orange subsidy from yield, or a payment of €10 per 100 kilograms of oranges, to easier-to-count trees, which reduced the EU subsidy to Italian orange farmers by half.

Calabria, the region in which Rosarno is located, has a high unemployment rate. There are 135,000 farm workers registered with the INPS, and 75 percent were unemployed before the INPS in 2008 began to eliminate from its rolls workers who did not do sufficient farm work to qualify for benefits. The mix of legal and unauthorized African migrants competing with Italians for orange-picking jobs helped to set the stage for conflict in Rosarno.

Produce buyers for supermarkets are the key actors in the Italian food system, and they have more bargaining power than farmers because food retailing is far more concentrated than food production. Most Italian farmers belong to coops, such as Conrad and Coop, that deal with produce buyers on their behalf, but the

---

[38] The Tunisians who were employed around Acate were reportedly more skilled and well organized, demanding higher wages and better working conditions than the Romanians, who consider working in Italy a short-term seasonal job.

[39] Christophe Ventura, "Italy's Blood Oranges," *Counterpunch*, January 4, 2011; http://www.counterpunch.org/2011/01/04/italy-s-blood-oranges/.

dominance of a handful of supermarket chains has reduced the farmer's share of the average retail price of commodities. Farm coops and other sellers use Dutch-style reverse auctions to sell produce, beginning with a high price and tempting buyers to purchase as the price falls.

The southern Italian farms that produce many of the fruits and vegetables that are exported to northern Europe are too small and lack effective cooperatives to persuade supermarket buyers to raise the prices they pay for commodities. Many of those who want to reduce the exploitation of vulnerable farm workers blame the power of supermarket buyers and the lack of cooperation among producers for low farm prices (Corrado et al., 2018, 11).

The so-called agro-Mafia compounds problems for farm workers. One study examined southern Italian vineyards and found that more migrants are associated with more uncompensated work hours in agriculture (Seifert and Valente, 2018). The agro-Mafia may also put downward pressure on wages indirectly, as when some of the proceeds of drug trafficking and other illegal activities are invested in agriculture to produce counterfeit versions of Protected Designation of Origin (DOP) cheeses and olive oil, increasing the supply and putting downward pressure on prices for farmers who sell genuine commodities.

Some economists believe that Italy's dualistic economy and labor market make the country ill-suited to integrate low-skilled migrants (Bonatti, 2019). Less than 50 percent of Italians aged 15 to 39 were employed in 2017, meaning there were 23 million workers employed in a country of 60 million instead of the 26 million that would be employed if Italy had the average employment rate in the EU. Per capita GDP in southern Italy was only 55 percent of the Italian average in 2017, about the same ratio as in the early 1970s, reflecting both low productivity and low labor-force participation, especially of women in southern Italy.

Half of the 5 million foreigners in Italy work, including 500,000 irregular for-eigners, mostly in low-skilled jobs that pay less than €800 a month. Low earnings, high remittances, and employment in the informal economy mean that adding immigrants may not help Italian public finances because neither the migrants nor their employers pay taxes. Bonatti (2019) believes that adding more low-skilled migrants would perpetuate Italy's dualistic economy, bolstering the low-skilled and small-firm segment of the economy that prefers informal labor markets.

Spain

Spain had farm sales of €51 billion in 2018, including 62 percent from crops and 36 percent from animals. The most valuable crops were fruits worth 20 percent of farm sales, vegetables worth 19 percent, and pork worth 14 percent.[40] Like Italy,

---

[40] https://ec.europa.eu/info/sites/info/files/food-farming-fisheries/farming/documents/agri-statistical-factsheet-es_en.pdf.

Spain has a trade deficit in farm commodities, with exports worth €3.3 billion and imports worth €10 billion, but has a trade surplus in processed food products, exporting €11 billion in 2018 and importing €4 billion.

Spain's 945,000 farms have 12.5 million hectares of arable land, including 4.7 million hectares planted in trees and vineyards; 80 percent of the orchards and vineyards are irrigated.[41] The 30 percent of Spanish farm land that is irrigated accounts for over half of the value of Spanish crops and most of the country's farm exports. Much of Spain's central plateau is semiarid, and some crop land is fallowed each year for lack of water. Animals are concentrated in northern green Spanish regions including Galicia, Asturias, and Santander, while vegetables grow under a "sea of plastic" in southern Spain.

Farm Labor

The agricultural labor force in Spain was 890,000 in 2013, when the total labor force was 23 million, making the farm work force less than 4 percent of the Spanish labor force.[42] By 2018, there were an estimated 812,000 people employed in agriculture, including three-fourths men and two-thirds hired workers. Spain's total labor force in 2018 was 19.3 million.[43]

The number of farmers and family members fell from 666,000 in 2001 to 440,000 in 2018, while the number of hired farm workers was relatively stable, falling from 432,000 to 421,000 over the same period.[44] Some 9,500 foreigners received work permits for employment in agriculture in 2018, including almost 90 percent men. Work permits issued to foreigners to work in agriculture peaked at 113,000 in 2008, and fell by more than 90 percent over the past decade.[45]

There were 100,000 internal migrant farm workers in 2000; many moved with the harvest from southern coastal areas producing fruits and vegetables to the orange groves of Valencia and then to the vineyards of Rioja. Seasonal farm earnings were supplemented by unemployment benefits that allowed farm workers in poorer regions of Andalusia and Extremadura to collect up to 75 percent of the

[41] These data are from FAO: http://faostat.fao.org/CountryProfiles/Country_Profile/Direct. aspx?lang=en&area=203.
[42] FAO data: http://faostat.fao.org/CountryProfiles/Country_Profile/Direct.aspx?lang=en&area=203). Another source reports 1.1 million full-time equivalent employment in Spanish agriculture in 2004 and 2.3 million farm workers, a 2 to 1 ratio of workers to jobs. Almost 70 percent of agricultural workers were men: http://www.eurofound.europa.eu/observatories/eurwork/comparative-information/national-contributions/spain/representativeness-of-the-social-partners-agricultural-sector-spain).
[43] http://www.mapa.gob.es/estadistica/pags/anuario/2018/CAPITULOSPDF/CAPITULO05/pdfc05_7.pdf.
[44] http://www.mapa.gob.es/estadistica/pags/anuario/2018/CAPITULOSPDF/CAPITULO05/pdfc05_12.pdf.
[45] http://www.mapa.gob.es/estadistica/pags/anuario/2018/CAPITULOSPDF/CAPITULO05/pdfc05_30.pdf.

minimum wage in benefits for six months after thirty-five to sixty days of farm work (Mendoza, n.d.).

After this benefits system was made less generous and more jobs were created closer to home, foreign-born workers came to dominate Spain's seasonal work force. Internal Spanish migrants, farmers complained, would work only long enough to qualify for unemployment benefits, making foreigners who were eager to maximize their earnings preferred workers.

Labor-intensive agriculture in southern Spain has expanded to provide fruits and vegetables for northern Europe. Almeria has hundreds of greenhouses, often described as a sea of plastic, that produce vegetables for domestic consumers and for northern Europeans. Spanish strawberries are concentrated in the southwestern province of Huelva, with most harvested between April and June. Most of the farms producing labor-intensive commodities rely on a mix of legal and unauthorized migrants to perform labor-intensive tasks.

Spain has one of the most diverse migrant farm workforces among industrial countries. Most legal foreign farm workers are Eastern Europeans, followed by Africans (mostly Moroccans), and Latin Americans, especially Ecuadorians. The Latin Americans have the advantage of knowing Spanish, but their higher transport costs, partially paid by employers, mean that most are employed in commodities with longer seasons, such as greenhouse vegetables. Many of the Eastern Europeans and Moroccans are women who are employed during the shorter strawberry harvest.

Interviews with almost 200 legal migrant farm workers in 2014 included workers from Bulgaria, Ecuador, Morocco, Poland, and Romania who generally had low migration costs to get to Spain.[46] The EU nationals who dominate the migrant farm workforce had zero costs for items that are common in other migration corridors, from visas to medical exams. All of the workers interviewed had previous Spanish work experience, which also lowers migration costs. Most reported that regulations requiring employers to pay at least half of worker transportation costs were enforced. Worker-paid migration costs were generally less than half of a migrant's monthly earnings of $1,000 a month for full-time work.[47]

Since the migrant farm workers who were interviewed had worked in Spain previously, and intra-EU migrants do not require visas or medical checks to seek jobs in Spain, fewer than half of the migrants reported any costs for passports and even fewer reported costs for visas and medical checks. Travel costs were also low, an average of less than $30 for internal travel costs in the home country and $300 for international travel costs. There were marked differences: Moroccans had

---

[46] These interviews were conducted by Piotr Plewa in 2014 for the Global Knowledge Partnership on Migration and Development (KNOMAD) and summarized in Martin (2017a).

[47] Earnings data were not collected. If workers earned the minimum wage of €39.5 or $54 for a 6.5-hour day, they earn $270 for a 5-day week or $324 for a 6-day week, and $1,080–1,300 a month.

$100 in average travel costs, East Europeans $350, and Ecuadorians, who can stay nine months in Spain, $1,100.[48]

Focusing on worker-paid costs incurred by at least forty migrants finds that transportation costs were two-thirds of average total costs of $530, with a wide variance reflecting the cost of getting to Spain. Employer organizations often arranged transportation on chartered buses to lower transport costs, although some experienced Eastern European migrants elected to fly to save time, even though their travel costs were higher. Three-fourths of the migrants interviewed in Spain did not take out loans to cover migration costs. The quarter that took out loans reported relatively small loans averaging $350 but debts of over $500, suggesting high interest rates.

Most of the migrants were from rural areas in Morocco and Latin America; the Eastern Europeans had agricultural backgrounds but included some workers who had been laid off from state-owned factories. Migrating to Spain to do farm work is, for some, an alternative to rural–urban migration within their countries of origin. Most of the guest workers in Spain had less than secondary-school education.[49] For example, the Moroccan women often had less than nine years' schooling, suggesting that migrating to Spain to do farm work was one way to remain within agriculture while working in a higher-wage country. Many of the Moroccans wanted to settle in Spain, while most of the Eastern Europeans wanted to return to their countries of origin.

Migrants harvesting fruits and vegetables in Spain were mostly unemployed or self-employed in agriculture at home, making it hard to calculate the average wage gap between Spain and migrant countries of origin. Less than a seventh of the migrants interviewed in Spain had wage-paying jobs before migrating to Spain (Martin, 2017a). Of the 40 percent who reported *any* income before migrating to Spain from wage work or self-employment, mean and mode monthly earnings at home were $160 a month, suggesting that work in Spain increased earnings by an average six times.

Strawberries and Workers

In Huelva, there are over 6,000 hectares of strawberries producing about 300,000 tons a year. Most berry growers belong to cooperatives such as Freshuelva, which

---

[48] Spanish employers must pay half of the transportation costs of the inbound workers they recruit. Most advance the entire cost of inbound transportation and then deduct the worker's share from earnings over the duration of their contract, typically at the rate of €90 a month. With employers advancing transportation costs, there is less need for workers to borrow money to travel to Spain.

[49] The Eastern Europeans were best educated, but most did not complete secondary school. Many of the Moroccans had less than five years' schooling, and the Ecuadorians averaged less than seven years' schooling.

estimates Huelva strawberry revenues at €250 million a year.[50] Strawberries, called "red gold" in southwestern Spain, are often picked by women. A 2001 bilateral Morocco–Spain agreement facilitates the migration of Moroccan mothers with children to pick strawberries in Spain. The children remain in Morocco, encouraging mothers to return at the end of the season.

Moroccan women who pick strawberries in Spain must be paid €34–37 a day for 6.5 hours, receive employer-provided housing,[51] and have employer-provided medical insurance while in Spain for three to six months.[52] Moroccan workers must be provided with at least eighteen days of work a month, employers must pay required social security taxes and ensure that workers retain their passports, and employers must pay the return travel costs of workers who are terminated in their first two weeks in Spain. Perhaps because of these requirements, most strawberry pickers are from Eastern Europe; Moroccans are less than 20 percent of the harvesting labor force.[53]

The main complaint of Moroccan guest workers in Spain is too little work. Employers recruit too many workers, so that many are employed only the minimum 18 days a month rather than the 25 or more days they want to work; some workers reported working less than 6.5 hours a day and earning less than the €38 daily wage of 2011. With workers scrambling for more work, unpaid days off are a frequent disciplinary tool, especially because employers set productivity standards in spite of contracts that stipulate a per-day wage rather than a piece rate. Workers pick berries into eight-box trays.

Some of the Moroccan women complain of sexual harassment by managers on Spanish farms, but fear being fired and returned to Morocco if they file formal complaints. After 100 Moroccan women were fired and returned in May 2018, nine found advocates to help them file formal complaints. They remained in Spain to testify against the managers who they allege harassed them.

There have been several experiments that involved recruiting workers in particular countries in exchange for that country accepting the return of unauthorized citizens from Spain. A Spain–Senegal agreement anticipated the admission of 4,000 Senegalese guest workers, including 700 for Huelva strawberries, with Senegalese unions involved in the selection of guest workers. Farmers seeking guest workers make their requests to provincial labor authorities that send farmer requests to immigration authorities in Madrid, which announces the *contingente*, or quota, by December for the following year. Agricultural guest workers receive

---

[50] Spain's strawberry revenues were reportedly $650 million in 2018: https://www.nytimes.com/2019/07/20/world/europe/spain-strawberry-fields-abuse.html. Some Huelva growers are producing in Morocco, where daily wages of €5 a day are an eighth of the €40-a-day wage in Spain.

[51] Representatives of the Spanish unions CCOO and UGT can inspect grower-provided housing to ensure that it has hot and cold water, electricity, and toilets.

[52] Spouses and children of workers with contracts in Spain are eligible for health-care services in Morocco, although many of those eligible report difficulties obtaining benefits.

[53] See http://migration.ucdavis.edu/rmn/more.php?id=1305.

seasonal (*de temporada*) permits for three to nine months that must be renewed outside Spain. Most recruitment of strawberry workers is done by the four employer organizations, Freshuelva, ASAJA, COAG, and UPA-CORA.

Guest workers arrive without their families and must stay with the employer who recruited them. After completing three seasonal work contracts, they can apply for a twelve-month temporary (*estable*) permit, and after another twelve months can have their families join them in Spain. Employers can request workers by name, and most do. There is a fifteen-day probationary period, during which workers can be terminated and sent home.

Legal workers are to be employed at least 18 days a month, and the work week is six 6.5 hour days, with a 30-minute lunch break and rest periods, for 39 hours a week. Workers pick berries into 8-box trays (each box is 2.5 kilograms), and most harvest 10 trays in a 6.5 hour day. Harvesters in 2007 were paid €5.42 ($8) an hour, €35 a day and €211 a week. There are relatively few illegal workers, in part because employer organizations can obtain sufficient guest workers and because sanctions range from €6,000 to €60,000 for each illegal hire. In most cases, supervisors (team masters) are of the same nationality as the pickers they supervise, and they allegedly take the employer's side in any disputes to avoid being forced to return to picking.

Spain has an export-oriented agriculture that is increasingly dependent on migrant workers. Internal migrants have been replaced by vulnerable foreign citizens in Spanish agriculture.

Australia

Australia has a Seasonal Worker Program (SWP) that allows workers from eleven Pacific Island Countries (PICs) to fill seasonal farm jobs, and New Zealand has a similar Recognized Seasonal Employers (RSE) scheme. Both of these guest-worker programs have similar objectives, viz., to fill jobs in destination countries, to enable PIC guest workers to earn higher wages and send home remittances, and to promote development on Pacific Islands that often offer few opportunities for low-skilled workers to increase their earnings.

Australia's hired horticultural workforce includes mostly legal temporary and unauthorized foreign workers. However, fewer than 10 percent of Australia's horticultural workers are guest workers admitted after employers test the labor market for local workers. This makes Australia different from Canada, New Zealand, and the US, where most temporary foreign workers are admitted only after farm employers try but fail to recruit local workers under government supervision.

Estimates of the peak number of hired horticultural workers center on 75,000, including 40,000 Working Holiday Makers (WHMs) or backpackers who are able to stay in Australia a second year if they worked at least three months in fruit-and-vegetable agriculture during their first year of work-and-vacation in

Australia; 15,000 foreign students who may work 40 hours a fortnight while studying and full time during study breaks; and perhaps 10,000 unauthorized workers. Over 12,000 PIC guest workers were admitted under the Seasonal Worker Program in 2018–19.

Australians used to migrate seasonally from north to south to pick fruit crops, including Queensland cane cutters who migrated south to join local workers who were unable to obtain full-time nonfarm jobs. There are also legal Asians and Pacific Islanders such as Samoans who became citizens of New Zealand and thus could move to Australia under the two countries' freedom of movement regime. Farm employers say they must rely on foreign-born workers because native-born "Ozzies" have lost their work ethic and desire to be seasonal farm workers.

Some believe that the number of unauthorized and quasi-authorized workers could be reduced with aggressive enforcement of labor and immigration laws, which would force employers to choose between backpackers and SWP guest workers. In 2005, Australia allowed backpackers who did at least three months of work in regional or agricultural Australia to remain a second year as an alternative to a guest worker program. This policy encouraged foreign youths aged 18 to 30 to perform three months of farm work in order to stay in Australia a second year and work in nonfarm jobs.

In 2017–18, some 36,000 backpackers obtained a second-year visa, almost always by working in agriculture during their first year in Australia. New Zealand also allows backpackers to extend their stay if they work in agriculture during their first year in the country, but only for three months, and in New Zealand backpackers must continue to work in agriculture during their second year. There were 4,100 second-year backpackers in New Zealand in 2016–17.

Many backpackers in Australia want to obtain skilled worker (482) visas that allow them to remain longer in nonfarm jobs and eventually to become immigrants; a seventh of backpackers have been able to become Australian immigrants. Backpackers seeking extended stays are attractive to employers because they pay their own way to Australia and are often housed in hostels, paying for their accommodations and paying hostels to transport them to the fields. In this way, hostels often act as contractors or gatekeepers to seasonal farm work.

Studies and surveys find that backpackers are often paid less than Australia's minimum wage or the typically higher award wage for a particular commodity and sector. However, few backpackers complain because of the complexity of the complaint process to the Fair Work Ombudsman and a sense that their employer or contractor will not provide back pay even if ordered to do so. Backpackers willing to move on rather than complain of labor-law violations make WHMs an attractive workforce to employers, albeit not totally "reliable" in the sense that backpackers may change employers.

The Australian government approved a pilot program in 2008 that offered 2,500 visas to Pacific Islanders to do farm work in Australia. Farm employers sought fewer than 100 Pacific Island guest workers in each of 2008–9 and 2009–10, less than 450 in 2010–11, and about 1,100 in 2011–12. The cap was raised to 3,250 in 2014–15, when 3,200 guest workers were admitted, and lifted entirely after 2015–16. About 8,500 SWP guest workers were admitted in 2017–18. The largest source countries are Vanuatu and Tonga. Half of guest workers from these countries reported that they would rest at home before returning to Australia to work again.

Farmers complained in July 2018 that they faced a shortage of 100,000 workers for the 2018–19 crop year. There is little evidence of wage spikes to suggest labor shortages, but the government responded by allowing backpackers to stay in Australia a third year after January 1, 2020, if they do at least six months of farm work during their first two years in Australia. In addition, more backpackers from Southeast Asian countries will be admitted, and the eligible age range was extended from 18 to 30 to 18 to 35. Backpackers are permitted to work for the same employer for up to twelve months during the three years they are in Australia, up from the previous maximum six months, and some do not have to pay taxes on their Australian earnings.[54] Farmers who believe there are not enough legal workers to harvest crops persuaded the Liberal-National government to provide labor-supply insurance in the form of making farm work ever more attractive to backpackers.

A 2019 report from the Australian Bureau of Agricultural and Resource Economics and Sciences (ABARES) surveyed 2,500 farms, and found that 18 percent of vegetable farms and 14 percent of fruit and nut farms had difficulty filling vacant jobs. Farmers reported that they recruited to fill 20,000 jobs, and filled 19,300 of them.

Why does Australia admit half as many Pacific Island guest workers as NZ? Curtain et al. point to three factors. First, the two countries horticultural sectors differ. Australia produces fruits and vegetables primarily for the domestic market, and the country's two dominant supermarket chains, Coles and Woolworths, account for three-fourths of sales and can exert downward pressure on producer prices, which encourages growers to cut costs. Neither buyer requirements for producers to abide by all laws, nor labor law enforcement, appear sufficient to ensure that all Australian growers pay the A$18.93 minimum wage in 2018 and abide by other labor laws.

Second, backpackers are cheaper and readily available in Australia. Backpackers pay their own transportation to Australia, often arrange their own housing, and are generally quick to learn the work. On the other hand, backpackers may be less

---

[54] Australians are not taxed on earnings up to A$18,200, but WHMs were until a 2019 decision of a federal court declared that taxing WHMs was unlawful if Australia had double-taxation treaties with the WHM's country of citizenship. Australia has such tax treaties with Chile, Finland, Germany, Japan, Norway, Turkey, the UK, and the US; http://www.abc.net.au/news/rural/2019-10-30/federal-court-rules-backpacker-tax-invalid/11653928.

"reliable" or "loyal," since they are not required to remain with one farm employer, and backpackers may be less willing than guest workers to work extra hours. Studies suggest that, after two or three years' experience, guest workers are more productive than backpackers.

Third, a range of other factors encourages more backpackers in Australia. Australia is more attractive to backpackers because it has a larger economy and allows nonfarm work during years two and three in the country. Most of New Zealand's fruit is exported, encouraging growers to ensure that they are in compliance with food-safety and labor laws to attract and retain buyers. Australian horticulture may be more fragmented, with less grower input into the development of the SWP program than New Zealand growers have in the RSE. Finally, Australian growers may face less pressure from their associations to abide by labor-law norms that New Zealand exporters believe help them to sell abroad.

Recent declines in the number of backpackers in Australia may expand the number of SWP guest workers. If the number of guest workers grows, what will be the effects on Pacific Islands, which offer few jobs? Vanuatu has found that growers prefer to rehire experienced workers, limiting the number of residents able to earn A$10,000 ($7,200) by working seasonally in Australia. The Vanuatu government has discussed limiting how many times the same worker may depart. There are also concerns that the already limited agricultural output on the islands may fall as workers depart, prompting proposals to require departing migrants to do a certain amount of farm work at home.

New Zealand

The New Zealand Recognized Seasonal Employer program began April 30, 2007, after farmers complained of too few workers to harvest wine grapes, kiwifruit, and apples. New Zealand exports half of the commodities produced on its 5,500 commercial horticultural farms with the help of a peak 60,000 seasonal workers in March–April, including 60 percent who are hired in the Hawke's Bay and Bay of Plenty regions.

With too few unemployed and underemployed New Zealand workers, and not enough Working Holiday Makers available to harvest their crops, gangmasters or contractors filled the gap with crews of foreign students and other migrants, some of whom were not authorized to work. Reports of unauthorized farm workers and contractors taking advantage of them prompted the government to launch the RSE as a way to fill farm jobs and promote development on the Pacific Island Countries that are home to guest workers.

The World Bank was a catalyst in prompting the New Zealand government to launch the RSE. Half of the populations of the PICs are under 24, and that 60 percent of youth are NEETs, that is, not in education, employment, or training.

The World Bank believed that wage work in richer Australia and New Zealand would generate win-win-win outcomes, for workers, farmers, and both sending and receiving countries (Luthria, 2008; Haque and Packard, 2014). The New Zealand government was also motivated to act by the UN's High-Level Dialogue on migration and development, which urged governments in fall 2006 to open more channels for migrants from lower-wage countries to increase remittances and speed development in migrant-sending countries.[55]

As with other seasonal farm labor programs, the New Zealand RSE gives priority to local workers to fill farm jobs. This means that farmers must try and fail to recruit local workers by offering at least the minimum wage or the prevailing wage for the work to be done. There have been few complaints of New Zealand farmers refusing to hire available local workers, and the government has reduced the use of labor contractors who in the past provided unauthorized farm workers.

Once certified to employ Pacific Island Countries' workers, New Zealand farm employers must offer contracts that guarantee guest workers at least 240 hours and 30 hours a week of work at the minimum wage. Farm employers must provide guest workers with housing, health insurance, and pastoral care, such as transportation for banking and religious services. Employers may charge guest workers for housing and health insurance. Farmers must also pay half of the cost of a return ticket for PIC migrants, and must post bonds of NZ$3,000 ($2,000) for each worker that can be used by the government to return fired workers to their countries or origin or detect and remove runaways.

New Zealand employers can recruit Pacific Island workers directly, usually with the help of recruitment agents, or select workers from lists prepared by local governments. For example, the Tongan government used village committees to rank the "work-ready" men and women who wanted to work in New Zealand by criteria such as honesty, being a hard worker, and knowing some English. About 5,000 of Tonga's 67,000 working-age adults registered to work in New Zealand in 2008, representing 20 percent of Tongan men between 20 and 60.

Before departing for New Zealand, migrant workers must obtain passports and undergo health checks and police clearances, as well as complete a pre-departure orientation. PIC migrants may remain in New Zealand for up to seven months, but migrants from Kiribati and Tuvalu can stay in New Zealand up to nine months because of their higher travel costs.

The number of RSE migrants was capped at 4,500 in 2007–8, but has since been raised, and was 12,850 for 2018–19.[56] Pacific Island countries' workers earned an average NZ$2,400 ($2,000) a month during their five months in New

---

[55] This development benefit was highlighted in a New Zealand government submission to an Australian parliamentary inquiry in 2015, which highlighted the triple wins from the RSE: filling vacant jobs in New Zealand, generating more jobs for New Zealand workers, and promoting development in the Pacific Islands (New Zealand Government Submission, 2015).

[56] See https://migration.ucdavis.edu/rmn/blog/post/?id=2232.

Zealand and remit half of what they earn to their families. The major skills acquired by migrants in New Zealand include better English, improved abilities to manage time and money, and perhaps an improved work ethic. However, the fruit and wine grapes produced in New Zealand are not produced in the Pacific Islands, making experience with these crops of limited use at home.

Employers say that, because most RSE migrants do not have experience picking fruit, newly arrived workers require training to become proficient workers. However, since most RSE migrants return year after year, employers recoup their training expenses via the higher productivity of returning workers. The workers have few complaints, although some note that they incur living costs when there is no work and that some employers set piece-rate wages so low that workers earn only the minimum wage. Piece-rate workers normally earn more than the minimum wage, giving them an incentive to work fast without close supervision.[57]

Evaluations suggest the RSE has been successful in filling jobs with rural and less educated Pacific Islanders who earn more in New Zealand than they would earn at home. The third win is faster development. If migration speeds development, its effects should be visible in migrant-sending villages. Gibson, McKenzie, and Rohorua (2008) found that RSE migrants averaged seventeen weeks of work in New Zealand and had average net earnings of NZ$5,700 ($3,400) after paying for half of their airfare and their living expenses in New Zealand.

A December 2010 evaluation concluded that per capita incomes in Pacific Island households with at least one member in the RSE were 40-percent higher than incomes similar households without migrants, suggesting that migration to New Zealand raised incomes far more than microfinance and conditional cash transfers in other developing countries. Households with participants in the RSE were also more likely to improve their homes, buy durable goods, and keep 15 to 18-year-old children in secondary school.

Vanuatu provided over a third of RSE migrants in recent years, followed by 20 percent from Tonga, 15 percent from Samoa, and almost 10 percent from Thailand; over 80 percent of RSE migrants are from seven Pacific Island countries. Most are men: 85 percent of those admitted from Vanuatu under the RSE were men in 2012–13, as were 88 percent of those from Tonga admitted to Australia under the SWP (ILO, 2015).

There are several challenges. First, farm employers prefer experienced workers to benefit from their higher productivity. However, rehiring experienced workers can mean fewer opportunities for new Pacific Islands workers to participate, which may slow the development impacts of working abroad.

Second, more workers want to be employed in New Zealand than there are jobs. If the pool of workers from which New Zealand employers can select

---

[57] Some New Zealand employers had to raise piece rates so that RSE workers earned at least the minimum wage at the rate at which they were able to work.

increases faster than New Zealand job opportunities, the result may be slower development if workers who anticipate being selected shun local opportunities in anticipation of going to New Zealand. Pacific Island countries may compete with each other to send workers to New Zealand, which could erode labor standards and worker protections over time.

The third issue is the future of the RSE. If New Zealand fruit and wine exporters can achieve some kind of a fair trade certification for commodities produced with the help of Pacific Island countries' workers, they may continue to hire them in order to receive premium prices. GLOBALG.A.P., a European organization that certifies compliance with Good Agricultural Practice (GAP) in food safety, sustainable production methods, worker and animal welfare, responsible use of water, and compound feed and plant propagation materials, has accredited ten times more farms in New Zealand than in Australia.

The Horticulture and Viticulture Seasonal Working Group, which includes representatives of government, employers, and unions, is charged with developing medium- and long-term strategies for the New Zealand horticultural industry. New Zealand industry groups say that the availability of reliable guest workers encouraged farmers to expand production and exports of horticultural commodities.

Brazil

Brazil is an agricultural superpower that produced food for 210 million Brazilians and exported food worth $102 billion in 2018. Brazil accounted for almost 80 percent of global orange-juice exports in 2016–17, 45 percent of sugar and soybean exports, 35 percent of poultry exports, and a quarter of global coffee exports. China is the major destination for Brazil's farm exports.

Brazilian agricultural output and exports rose with higher productivity and because more land was brought into production; farm output quadrupled between 1975 and 2016 (Daglia Calil, 2019). More farmers began to use modern seeds and more fertilizers and there was much more mechanization, especially in the new farmlands of the cerrado region of the center-west or midwest Brazil, where many farmers harvest two crops a year.

Environmental laws aim to stop deforestation in the Amazon and to keep much of the cerrado in native vegetation. However, the Ministry of Agriculture (MAPA) expects new land to be brought into crop production in the midwest and the area to its north known as MATOPIBA. Some farmers plant soybeans, followed by corn and grass. Farmers harvest the corn and allow cattle to graze on the grass before replanting with soybeans and beginning the soybean and corn and grass cycle again.

Brazil was in the news in 2019 due to fires in the Amazon rainforest, which contains over half of the world's rainforest in 2.1 million square miles. About 60 percent of the Amazon rainforest is in Brazil, where cattle ranchers and farmers sometimes burn the rainforest during the drier June through September period to clear land for ranching and soybeans. Deforestation prompted the major buyers of cattle and soy to pledge not to purchase from farmers who recently cleared rainforest, slowing deforestation for a time.

Amazon deforestation peaked at 11,200 square miles in 1995, fell due to buyer pressure and government monitoring, and rose to 11,000 square miles again in 2004 in response to increased beef and soy prices. There was fewer than 2,000 square miles of deforestation in 2012 in the aftermath of the 2008–9 recession, but deforestation doubled to 4,000 square miles in 2019 as President Jair Bolsonaro seemed to encourage agricultural expansion.

Brazil has 5 million farms, but the largest 10 percent account for 90 percent of the value of the farm commodities produced. Some 51,000 farms had more than 1,000 hectares in 2017, and they had almost half of the country's farm land. Large acreage and modern farms are prominent in the southeast, south, and center-midwest of the country.

Brazil is an unequal society, with a richer south and southeast and a poorer north and northeast. About 10 percent of Brazilians live in the largest metro area of São Paulo and 5 percent are in metro Rio de Janeiro. Many poor residents of Brazil's northern and northeastern states move to metro São Paulo in the southeast. Other cities attract rural–urban migrants as well, including Goiana, a midwest city of 2.5 million in Goiás state whose farms specialize in cattle, soybeans, and sugar.

Farm Workers and Slavery

Some 15 million people were employed in Brazilian agriculture in 2017, down from a peak 23 million in 1985. Many are subsistence farmers in the poorer north and northeast, some of whom migrate seasonally to the south and southeast as hired workers. A quarter of persons employed in agriculture are wage workers, and 1.4 million of the almost 4 million wage workers were in the formal sector and thus entitled to at least the minimum wage of 998 reais ($258) a month (Garcia and Maia, 2019).

Brazil's constitution of 1988 extended labor-law protections to all workers in all sectors, which raised farm-labor costs and encouraged labor-saving mechanization over the past three decades (Garcia and Maia, 2019). Coops help workers to deal with farmers, as with coop crews that harvest oranges, but some coops are fraudulent and cheat workers (Catholic Relief Services, 2016). Brazil's orange industry is dominated by a few large processors that export frozen concentrated orange juice, which encourages them to demand compliance with labor laws on farms that produce oranges. Declining orange-juice consumption and citrus-tree diseases have reduced the acreage of oranges, but rising yields have kept orange production stable at 450 million 40.8-kilogram boxes per year.

About 40 percent of the 11 million African slaves brought to the Americas went to Brazil, which was the last New World country to abolish slavery with the so-called Golden Law of May 13, 1888. Freed slaves with no education were concentrated in the north and northeast, where their descendants still live. Some become victims of what is often called modern slavery, which Article 149 of Brazil's penal code defines as holding "someone in a condition analogous to that of a slave." Slavery includes forced labor, enduring very hard working conditions or poor housing, and employing workers who are in debt bondage to employers.

The Ministry of Labor and Employment (MTE) has had a Special Mobile Inspection Group since 1995 to detect Article 149 slavery, and identified over 53,000 workers who satisfied one of the four definitions of modern slavery, viz., forced labor, very hard working conditions, poor housing, or debt bondage.[58] Most victims were found in metro São Paulo in factories and construction, and some were migrants from Bolivia and other countries. However, agriculture is often associated with modern slavery in Brazil, especially when workers are prevented from leaving remote cattle or crop farms by armed guards. The number of victims had been declining, but rose to 1,700 in 2017, perhaps as a result of Brazil's 2016–18 recession.

The MTE has 3,000 labor inspectors to find forced labor and other poor working conditions; MTE agents who find slavery require employers to pay workers any back wages owed and to offer victims assistance to return to their homes.[59] However, only prosecutors can bring charges against employers believed by MTE agents to have enslaved workers, and only a third of MTE investigator charges of slavery result in court prosecutions. Since 2004, MTE's Division of Inspection for the Eradication of Slave Labor (DETRAE) has had a "dirty list" of employers found by investigators to have violated Article 149, a list that included 186 employers in mid-2019.[60]

Brazil's definition of slavery is broader than that of the ILO and the labor laws of most countries. For example, hard working conditions and poor housing may be violations of labor laws, but few countries consider them indicators of slavery. Similarly, wage advances are common for migrant workers, and employers may take steps to avoid having workers leave until they recoup such advances, but it is not clear whether wage advances are debt bondage that prevents workers from ever paying off their debts.

---

[58] http://www.reuters.com/article/us-brazil-trafficking-dirtylist/brazil-to-issue-dirty-list-of-employers-using-slave-labor-based-on-court-findings-idUSKCN1TX30L.
[59] http://www.ilo.org/labadmin/info/WCMS_114935/lang--en/index.htm.
[60] http://www.reuters.com/article/us-brazil-trafficking-dirtylist/brazil-to-issue-dirty-list-of-employers-using-slave-labor-based-on-court-findings-idUSKCN1TX30L. Another list of employers convicted by courts was announced in 2019.

The line between exploitative working conditions and slavery is often grey, which is one reason why firms in Brazil have resisted being placed on the dirty list and losing access to credit and customers. A second list, an employer monitoring or observation list, was created in 2016 for employers who were found to be in violation of Article 149 but are taking steps to remedy deficiencies. Employers on the monitoring list do not face the same sanctions as those on the dirty list.[61]

Most victims identified by labor inspectors are poor Afro-Brazilian men with little education who migrate away from their homes to clear land for cattle and crops and to harvest sugar cane. NGOs estimate that up to 150,000 farm workers were in some form of slavery in Brazil in the 1990s, with up to a third freed after MTE and other investigations over the past two decades.

Most forced labor victims were recruited by contractors (*gatos*) who make promises to workers about wages, housing, and food that are often not fulfilled. One *gato* told Catholic Relief Services (CRS) that he earns 6 percent of what "his workers" are paid. Problems regulating labor contractors are not new, nor are they confined to Brazil.[62] The 2019 US Department of State Trafficking in Persons report (p. 109) highlighted the role of *gatos* who used various forms of debt peonage to maintain crews for harvesting sugar and coffee.

Coffee

There were 15 coffee farms on the MTE dirty list in 2013, which prompted Catholic Relief Services (2016) to investigate the working and living conditions of the 400 workers that MTE agents freed from forced labor, very hard working conditions, poor housing, and debt bondage. CRS reported that mid-sized coffee farms in mountainous areas were most likely to have abused and exploited workers. Small coffee farms rely on family labor, while large farms mechanize many farm tasks and often seek certification of their compliance with labor and other laws in order to export their coffee.

Coffee mechanization is most advanced in the Triângulo Mineiro region of Minas Gerais, where the land is flat and a coffee harvester can harvest a hectare of coffee in four hours, much faster than a crew of thirty workers who take a day to harvest a hectare of coffee. Cooperative Cooxupé estimated the cost of machine harvesting at 25 reais a 60-kilogram bag, a fourth of the 100 reais a bag for hand harvesting. Machines have shortened the area's coffee harvest from four to two months (Catholic Relief Services, 2016).

Many coffee farms no longer provide housing to migrant farm workers, with mixed results. On the one hand, workers are less likely to be under the thumb of

[61] http://news.trust.org/item/20190617004224-nkhob.
[62] https://migration.ucdavis.edu/rmn/more.php?id=104.

the farm employer, but they must now find their own housing and rides to work, which adds to their living expenses. In the Triângulo Mineiro area, only 20 percent of farm workers are housed where they work, while 80 percent of the so-called *boias-frias*, or cold-lunch workers, rent housing in nearby communities.

Brazil had 287,000 coffee farms, with 2.3 million hectares of arabica (70 percent of farms) and robusta coffee trees, in 2006. Half of coffee production is in Minas Gerais, where the coffee capital of Patrocínio is located, and a quarter of coffee production is in Espírito Santo, which has many robusta farms. Almost 90 percent of arabica growers, and 85 percent of robusta growers, have fewer than 20 hectares, and these small growers produce about 45 percent of the arabica coffee and two-thirds of the robusta. However, the largest 20 percent of coffee farms. account for three-fourths of Brazil's coffee production.

Brazil is one of the few countries with an expanding agricultural sector, bringing new land into production in sparsely populated areas. One side effect of agricultural expansion is more farm-worker migration, mostly from the poorer north and northeast to the south, southeast, and midwest (Garcia and Maia, 2019). The Brazilian government has struggled to regulate the contractors who move farm workers from their homes to farm jobs.

The Brazilian experience with farm labor mirrors that of other countries, viz., as the share of workers employed in agriculture declines, the importance of hired workers to the large and modern farms that account for most farm production increases. Hired workers are diverse, but they include many low-skilled and vulnerable workers unable to find nonfarm jobs. Brazil's prosperity paradox is complicated by illegal deforestation that moves very poor Brazilians into remote areas where the government has little presence, making it difficult to protect vulnerable farm workers.

Lessons

Industrial and middle-income developing countries have rising shares of hired farm workers who do most of their farm work. Many of these hired workers are more vulnerable to exploitation than previous generations of farm workers because they include domestic workers who are unable to find better nonfarm jobs and a mix of legal, quasi-authorized, and unauthorized foreigners. Governments use a variety of strategies to protect farm workers, but often seem to be in a losing battle as vulnerability rises faster than new laws and their implementation can keep up with farm-labor markets that are dominated by intermediaries such as labor contractors.

The most protected farm workers are in countries with few unauthorized workers, strong labor laws, and unions and NGOs committed to protecting hired farm workers, as in Britain and Canada. Countries such as Spain are further away from the protection end of the spectrum, with mostly legal internal or intra-EU migrant workers and a relatively robust system of protections for workers. Countries with higher shares of unauthorized workers and labor contractors linked to crime, such as Italy, find it hardest to protect farm workers. Scale also makes a difference. Italy and Spain have more small farms that hire workers compared to Britain and Canada.[63]

Agriculture and farm workers are often found in the poorer areas of rich countries, such as in southern Spain and Italy. But some labor-intensive agriculture is found in richer areas of rich countries, as in Salinas south of Silicon Valley in California and in southern Ontario.

---

[63] Eurostat reports that 40 percent or more of all workers in Italy and Spain are employed in workplaces with fewer than ten employees, compared with 10 percent of US workers.

PART III
MOVING FORWARD

The two chapters in Part III focus on how to protect the vulnerable hired workers employed in modern agriculture. International-development organizations such as the World Bank emphasize that economic growth enables fewer and more productive farmers and workers to produce ever more food and fiber to feed growing populations at home and abroad. Agricultural development means that farmers plant improved seeds, use fertilizers and irrigation, and have access to modern transportation and storage infrastructure so that harvested crops reach consumers with minimal losses.

United Nations agencies such as the International Labour Organization aim to protect all workers, including farm workers, and regularly decry the child and forced labor found in some agricultural systems. The ILO encourages governments to adopt top-down economic policies that create decent jobs for all workers and to enact and enforce labor laws in bottom-up fashion to protect workers. Unions organize farm workers and bargain on their behalf, collecting dues from the workers they represent to negotiate contracts that raise wages and protect workers. NGOs can also advocate on behalf of farm workers in a bottom-up fashion, as when legal-aid groups help farm workers to make complaints, or act in a top-down manner, as when they advocate for tougher labor laws and more enforcement.

Buyers of farm commodities have enormous influence over conditions on farms because they can refuse to purchase commodities from farmers who do not abide by food safety protocols and labor laws. Buyers sometimes insist that farmers adhere to labor standards that protect small farmers and farm workers, as exemplified by fair-trade labels for coffee, cocoa, and other commodities, including fruits and vegetables. Fair-trade labels have so far been a niche rather than a mainstream phenomenon, but mainstream buyers could wind up as the champions of farm workers by buying only from compliant employers.

6
Protecting Farm Workers

The UN system, most governments, and many unions and NGOs aim to ensure that the human rights of all residents are protected and that all residents benefit from economic development. The development policies advocated by the World Bank and UN agencies have changed over time, from encouraging governments to neglect agriculture in favor of industry during the 1950s to the Washington consensus since the 1990s that urges governments to allow private markets to allocate limited resources, to foster free trade, and to encourage foreign investment and new technologies.

The market-led development strategy of the past three decades has accelerated the expansion of export-oriented agriculture in many developing countries. Colombia, Ecuador, Kenya, and Ethiopia are leading flower exporters; India, Ecuador, Vietnam, Indonesia, and Thailand are leading shrimp exporters; and Mexico is the leading exporter of avocados and fresh tomatoes. Most farms in developing countries that export commodities are larger than average farms in the country and rely on hired workers. The ILO and other UN agencies assist governments in developing countries to protect the workers employed to produce high-value commodities for consumers in richer countries. Fair-trade NGOs aim to ensure that farmers and workers employed in export agriculture benefit from their work.

Export-oriented farm employers are generally more powerful than the workers they employ. When governments face a choice between supporting farm exporters or farm workers, they often favor exporters because of the jobs that exporters provide to local residents and the foreign currency they earn. Many governments downplay or ignore reports of gaps between labor-protection laws and realities on export-oriented farms, treating any problems that are uncovered as exceptions rather than systemic. Governments are moved to action when refusals to buy their exports because of poor labor practices threaten the loss of jobs.

Unions bargain on behalf of the workers they represent, negotiating contracts that establish wages and working conditions and grievance systems that allow workers to complain or file grievances when the contract is not being obeyed. NGOs can play roles similar to unions when they act in bottom-up fashion to solicit worker complaints, or by pressuring employers and buyers in a top-down manner to improve conditions for farm workers by insisting on wage premiums or particular benefits.

The Prosperity Paradox: Fewer and More Vulnerable Farm Workers. Philip Martin, Oxford University Press (2021).
© Philip Martin.
DOI: 10.1093/oso/9780198867845.001.0001

ILO Labor Standards

The International Labor Organization is a specialized agency of the United Nations created in 1919 to improve labor conditions and living standards throughout the world. The ILO became the UN's first affiliated specialized agency in 1946, and was awarded the Nobel Peace Prize in 1969 for its efforts to promote decent work and social justice. The ILO is unique among intergovernmental organizations because its 187 member states are represented by government, employer, and worker-union delegates at the annual International Labor Conference, which elects a 56-member Governing Body.

This tripartite governance structure makes the ILO different from other UN agencies, where government representatives set policies. Governments provide most of the ILO's funding, but employer and union representatives have equal voices in determining ILO policies and priorities.

The ILO develops and promotes international labor standards in the form of Conventions and Recommendations that establish basic labor rights, including freedom of association and the right to organize and bargain collectively with employers, no forced or child labor, and equality of opportunity and treatment in the labor market. To promote these standards, the ILO provides technical assistance to governments to develop laws and programs that protect workers, to combat child labor and human trafficking, and to create more and better jobs for all workers, with special attention to women and minorities. The ILO works with associations of employers to improve safety at work, and works with governments to expand the coverage and benefits under social security and to adopt economic policies that increase the number of decent jobs.[1]

The International Labour Office, which is the secretariat to the ILO, has several major divisions, including Labour Standards, Employment Policy, and Social Protection. The ILO adopted 189 Labour Conventions by 2020, international treaties that are expected to be ratified and implemented by the member States, and 205 Labour Recommendations, which are nonbinding instruments that often deal with the same subjects as a convention and establish guidelines for national policy.[2] Eight of the ILO Conventions are considered "fundamental" to the rights of human beings at work, including those that guarantee freedom of association (nos. 87 and 98), the abolition of forced labor (29 and 105), equality in the workplace (100 and 111), and the elimination of child labor (138 and 182).

---

[1] The ILO has a decent work agenda that aims to create opportunities for work that is productive and delivers a fair income, offers security in the workplace and social protection for families, leads to personal development and social integration and freedom for people to express their concerns, organize and participate in the decisions that affect their lives. http://www.ilo.org/global/topics/decent-work/lang—en/index.htm.

[2] http://www.ilo.org/dyn/normlex/en/f?p=NORMLEXPUB:12010:0::NO:::.

Migrant Conventions

The ILO has two major conventions and two major recommendations on migrant workers, that is, workers who are employed outside their country of citizenship. When these were adopted, the drafters of the migrant conventions asserted that their purpose was to regulate labor migration and to protect migrant workers by having governments organize international labor migration to meet the needs of countries of employment, provide information to migrants so they can make informed decisions about whether to migrate for employment, and to ensure equality of treatment in destination countries so that both migrant and local workers were protected.

The ILO's Migration for Employment Convention of 1949 (no. 97) outlines minimum standards for recruiting, transporting, and employing migrant workers. Convention 97, enacted as people were being reshuffled across European borders in the aftermath of World War II, stressed the need to treat migrant workers the same as local workers to avoid a race to the bottom, as might occur if migrant workers received lower wages and fewer benefits than native workers. Convention 97 is supplemented by Recommendation 86, which emphasizes the need for governments to operate no-fee employment exchanges where workers can seek jobs and employers can seek workers at home and abroad. Recommendation 86 contains a model bilateral labor agreement to guide governments that send and receive migrant workers.

The Migrant Workers Convention of 1975 (no. 143) outlines steps governments can take to protect the basic human rights of migrants and to guarantee equality for migrants in social-security systems. Convention 143 also urges governments to implement policies to prevent illegal migration and employment by sanctioning employers who hire irregular workers. Recommendation 151 urges governments to help settled migrants to integrate into their host societies.

Fewer than a quarter of ILO member states have ratified Conventions 97 and 143, and most of these ratifications are from labor-sending rather than labor-receiving countries (Ruhs, 2017). Once ILO conventions are ratified, countries report periodically on what they have done to implement them.

The ILO has an office dedicated to improving conditions for hired workers in agriculture.[3] There are two agriculture-specific conventions, Convention 129 (1969) on Labour Inspection and Convention 184 (2001) on Safety and Health in Agriculture. Convention 129 calls on governments to cover workers employed on farms under protective labor laws that establish minimum wages, regulate child labor, and promote health and safety at work. Convention 129 calls on governments to hire inspectors on the basis of merit to enforce labor laws and to publish

---

[3] http://www.ilo.org/global/industries-and-sectors/agriculture-plantations-other-rural-sectors/lang—en/index.htm.

annual reports on the results of enforcement inspections. Convention 184 similarly calls on governments to enact safety and health laws that protect workers employed in agriculture, to hire labor-law inspectors, and to report the results of their inspections.

The ILO provides assistance to governments to detect and prevent discrimination against migrants, conducts studies of legal and irregular migration for employment in particular countries, examines emigration pressures in sending countries, and issues manuals that provide guidance to governments in middle-income developing countries that are new to the employment of migrants. For example, the ILO's 1996 manual for labor-receiving countries recommends that the Labor Ministry determine whether and how many migrant workers are needed and ensure that employers abide by the terms of migrant workers' contracts. The manual recommends that migrant labor policies be flexible, since they must "balance nationals' legitimate expectation of some preferential treatment against [the] human, economic and social rights that foreigners can justifiably claim to be theirs" (Böhning, 1996, 87).

Countries that send migrant workers abroad have policies that range from laissez-faire (the US and UK) to a state agency that checks migrant worker contracts to ensure that citizens going abroad will not be exploited (Philippines). Most labor-sending governments have policies between these extremes, regulating the recruitment of workers for jobs abroad but not checking individual worker contracts. Since there are often more workers who want to go abroad than there are jobs, it is hard for governments to regulate the maximum fees that recruiters can charge migrants because many workers believe that, by paying more to recruiters, they will get preference to depart for a high-wage job abroad.

Regulatory agencies must weigh trade-offs between competing goods in migrant-sending countries such as the Philippines. Should governments try to protect women who want to go abroad from abuse by requiring them to be at least 25 and to receive training on how to do household work to minimize their vulnerability, even if some women who want to go abroad are prevented from departing? Abella (1999) warned policymakers to be careful about such protective policies, since "too much" protection may have the unintended consequence of pushing migrants into unofficial channels where they have few or no protections.

The ILO is active in middle-income developing countries that attract migrant workers from neighboring countries, including Thailand and Malaysia, Poland and Hungary, Ivory Coast and South Africa, and Argentina and Costa Rica. Policies toward migrant workers in these countries are often ad hoc, zigzagging between generosity to register irregular workers and enforcement policies that aim to remove unauthorized workers from the country.

Some countries send workers abroad to higher-wage countries, such as Thais who migrate to Israel to do farm work, while simultaneously employing migrants from poorer neighbors to work in the same jobs that their citizens perform abroad, as with Burmese who work in Thai agriculture. The Thai government struggles to protect its workers abroad and migrants from other countries employed in Thailand.

The UN's International Migrants Day is December 18, the date in 1990 that the UN General Assembly approved a Migrant Workers Convention that went beyond ILO Conventions by calling on governments to extend rights to unauthorized workers and their families. On December 18, 2001, the ILO Director General declared that "Migrant workers are an asset to every country where they bring their labor...[but] the fate of these immigrants runs contrary to the ILO goal of promoting decent work for all." The Director General asked governments to give migrants "the dignity they deserve as human beings and the respect they deserve as workers."

ILO conventions are often aspirational, laying out ideals that governments should strive to achieve rather than urging incremental improvements in the labor markets of member countries. The conventions are most relevant in middle-income developing countries that recognize they have incomplete protections for workers employed in agriculture, and where governments are torn between the need to create jobs and the desire to protect workers. In such circumstances, governments may enact laws that are close to ILO recommendations but not enforce them aggressively, setting the stage for reports of worker abuse and exploitation.

Helfer (2019) reviewed a century of ILO accomplishments and noted the mismatch between the ILO's "lofty aspirations and practical achievements," a criticism of the ILO's tendency to focus on creating more protections for workers rather than persuading governments to implement protections already included in conventions and recommendations. Helfer noted that unions have become weaker in most countries, and are usually stronger in the public rather than in the private sector, making them less representative of all of the country's workers. Many efforts to improve worker protections are mounted by NGOs that are not represented officially in the ILO alongside governments, employers, and unions.

The world of work is changing rapidly, as artificial intelligence,[4] autonomous systems, and robotics eliminate jobs in a wide range of industries and occupations. Labor-market dynamics are speeding up as robots and algorithms replace human workers, especially to perform repetitive tasks.[5] The traditional employer–employee relationship is being eroded by new forms of work, including self-employment in the gig economy and more workers with short-term and part-time contracts that sometimes require employees to be "on call" to their employers. Gig-based workers

---

[4] Artificial or machine intelligence means the ability to mimic human minds to learn and solve problems. AI includes teaching machines a variety of skills including reasoning, knowledge representation, planning, learning, natural language processing, perception, and the ability to move and manipulate objects.

[5] The word robot was coined by Czech writer Karel Capek in 1920 to describe machines that replace human labor; robot is the Slavic word for work.

may not meet one another, making collective action difficult, and must usually save from their earnings for social and pension benefits instead of relying on employers to pay taxes or make contributions to fund social safety net programs.[6]

The postwar social contract is also changing due to rising inequality and more workers who do not benefit from economic growth. Economic inequality is rising for many reasons, including technology and market factors that concentrate revenue and profits among a relative handful of firms and entrepreneurs. First-mover advantages, market-leader dominance, and other factors may be increasing monopoly power in output markets and monopsony power in labor markets,[7] widening economic gaps between workers and owners.

An ILO Commission in 2019 (ILO, 2019b) examined the future of work and urged governments to invest more to help workers adapt to ever-faster labor-market changes by promoting lifelong learning that keeps worker skills fresh and relevant to new jobs, to develop mechanisms to ease transitions from school to work and between jobs, to promote gender equality, and to create universal safety-net protections for workers who are unable to find jobs and those who are injured or disabled. The ILO Commission's recommendations are aspirational. Many ILO member states do not provide unemployment insurance or other assistance to jobless workers, so the call to provide all workers (including migrant workers) with unemployment insurance and opportunities for lifelong learning in order to ease transitions between jobs and occupations is an ideal likely to be achieved only over time.

Garments and Seafood

The ILO often engages in very practical actions that help workers, especially after particular incidents of worker exploitation. The ILO's activities in the Bangladeshi garment and Thai seafood industries are examples of how the ILO can improve worker protection while preserving jobs in an important export industry.

On April 24, 2013, the eight-story Rana Plaza building in Savar that housed five sewing factories collapsed, killing a third of the 3,000 workers who made clothes for export. The Bangladeshi government responded to the deadliest

---

[6] About 10 percent of the 20 million workers in California are independent contractors responsible for their own safety net. Most are not app-based workers—fewer than 1 percent of the state's workers report that they are employed full-time using apps to find work. Instead, most independent contractors are owner-operator truck drivers, insurance agents and translators, and hairdressers and barbers. Developing policies that distinguish between employees and independent contractors is proving very contentious.

[7] Monopoly is one seller in an output market that can charge a higher-than-competitive price, and monopsony is one buyer or employer in an input market whose hiring decisions affect wages paid. Monopsony employers typically hire fewer workers and pay lower wages than competitive employers.

accident in its garment industry by stepping up inspections of buildings that housed sewing factories and promising to better enforce its labor laws.

Garments were 80 percent of Bangladeshi manufacturing exports in 2012, when $18 billion worth of clothing from 5,000 factories that employed 4 million workers was exported.[8] After the Rana Plaza collapse, the Walt Disney Company stopped having licensed clothing made in Bangladesh, prompting a discussion of whether sewing jobs that offered the Bangladeshi minimum wage of 3,000 taka ($38) a month reduced poverty or added to the misery and danger of poor workers.[9] Sewing jobs provide a first rung up the job ladder for many rural women who move to cities, and low wages are one reason many fashion labels and stores buy clothing from Bangladesh.

The ILO played a major role in persuading most clothing brands to continue to buy from Bangladeshi sewing factories by coordinating efforts to ensure that factories were made safer. However, ensuring that factories are safe sometimes requires fixes to larger issues. For example, one reason that the Rana Plaza building collapsed was because some sewing factories place heavy generators on the top floors of the factory to provide electricity during regular brownouts, reflecting a failure of the government power company to ensure a regular supply of electricity. The ILO cannot ensure the regular provision of electricity, but it can insist that factories place generators on the ground floor and that buildings are inspected regularly to ensure they are safe for workers.

The ILO played a similar improve-rather-than-boycott role to improve conditions for the mostly migrant workers employed in Thailand's shrimp and seafood export sectors. Many seafood sector workers are migrants from neighboring Myanmar (Burma), and they find jobs in Thailand with the help of brokers. These brokers may offer Burmese workers jobs that pay $750 to $1,000 a month in Thai manufacturing, construction, or services, but transfer workers to Thai brokers who instead place them on Thai fishing boats, where pay is sporadic and discipline can be harsh. Workers on fishing boats may be in debt peonage, unable to leave the boat until they pay off recruitment fees.[10]

Thailand is a leading shrimp and seafood exporter, and migrant Burmese dominate the fishing-sector labor force. NGOs such as the Issara Institute (2017) paint a grim picture of life for migrant Burmese workers employed on Thai fishing boats. One Issara survey found that 38 percent of the migrant workers had

---

[8] China, the world's leading clothing exporter, shipped clothing worth $154 billion in 2012. See https://migration.ucdavis.edu/mn/more.php?id=3851.
[9] Bangladesh raised its minimum wage to 5,300 taka in 2018 and to 8,000 taka ($95) in 2019.
[10] *The Guardian* in June 2014 described Burmese migrants who were sold to fishing-boat captains who fished for low-value fish that was ground into fish meal to sell to shrimp farms, including those owned by Charoen Pokphand (CP) Foods, which calls itself "the kitchen of the world." http://www.theguardian.com/global-development/2014/jun/10/supermarket-prawns-thailand-produced-slave-labour.

been trafficked, a seventh were physically abused by their employers, and three-fourths were in debt before they began to work in Thailand.

Given such a stark picture of labor exploitation, what is the optimal response? Should NGOs organize a boycott of Thai seafood exports to decrease demand and thus reduce the number of jobs in which Burmese migrants can be exploited, or is the better strategy to support the Thai fishing industry and government to improve wages and working conditions for migrant workers?

The response in Thailand was combined government and industry pressure to improve wages and working conditions. The first step was to survey more workers to determine if conditions were as bad as portrayed by the NGOs. These surveys found widespread compliance with Thai labor laws. For example, a 2013 survey of 527 migrant workers employed in 13 Thai tuna-processing factories found few violations of Thai labor laws. Some of the migrants interviewed were underage, but the passports they presented when they were hired showed them to be at least 18. Similarly, some migrants paid recruiting fees of 12,000 to 20,000 baht, double or triple the normal charge of 6,000 baht, but the overall finding was that migrants felt they were treated fairly.

Some NGOs challenged the results of the 2013 survey, pointing out that the workers were interviewed at work with the permission of the employers who paid for the survey.[11] However, the dueling NGO and employer-approved surveys highlight a fundamental problem, viz., which worker surveys should be considered representative of workers in a sector? Many NGOs solicit worker complaints and interview workers who complain, which is analogous to trying to determine the health of a population by visiting hospital emergency rooms. On the other hand, employers who want to protect export markets may tell workers what to say to interviewers.

The ILO took a middle ground, acknowledging problems but aiming to preserve jobs and export markets. A 2018 report based on a survey of 434 workers in 11 Thai provinces found only 1 percent of workers under age 18 and heard few reports of physical violence against workers (ILO, 2018a). Conditions need more improvement. The ILO reported that a third of fishery workers received less than the Thai minimum wage, over half of the women reported being paid less than men, and a quarter of workers reported that their pay was withheld by vessel owners, sometimes for months.

The ILO's efforts in Bangladesh and Thailand highlight the dilemma of how to respond to poor wages and working conditions. In both cases, the ILO's role was to preserve export markets and jobs while working with employers and governments to improve wages and working conditions. This middle way may be the most realistic option for an organization dedicated to protecting workers but also seeking to maximize the number of decent jobs.

---

[11] https://migration.ucdavis.edu/mn/comments.php?id=3906_0_3_0.

Decent Work

The ILO took a mend-rather-than-end approach to substandard jobs in the Bangladeshi garment and Thai seafood sectors, endorsing a policy of giving employers second chances to improve wages and working conditions for workers rather than embracing boycotts that could lead to layoffs. The ILO as an organization has been committed to decent work since 2000, arguing that both better-paid jobs and worker rights are desirable and necessary to foster development. However, Nattrass and Seekings (2019) argue that the ILO's decent work agenda can slow economic growth and preserve high unemployment, especially in countries with strong unions and robust labor-law enforcement such as South Africa.

South Africa has 57 million people in a country the size of California and Texas combined. Farming provides 10 percent of South Africa's formal-sector jobs, and the country produces commodities that range from fruit to wine. Whites own three-fourths of South Africa's farm land, prompting the governing African National Congress (ANC) party in 2018 to call for amendments to Article 25 of the constitution to allow the government to expropriate privately owned farm land without compensation, ending the current "willing buyer, willing seller" policy that has not distributed much farm land from whites to blacks.

South Africa has a very unequal economy. The poorest residents get most of their income from an extensive welfare system that, combined with a national minimum wage of R20 ($1.40) an hour or R3,500 ($240) a month in 2019, helps to explain the 27-percent unemployment rate. Wages are much higher for more skilled workers, $6 an hour for high-school graduates and over $12 an hour for college graduates. Employers complain of too few skilled workers, and the government encourages them to train unemployed blacks rather than recruit foreign workers. However, there are millions of migrants from other African countries in South Africa, and they are sometimes attacked by local residents who resent their success in small business.

The first ANC government elected in 1994 promised to create widespread prosperity via Black Economic Empowerment (BEE) policies that required most businesses to have black partners in order to obtain government contracts and mining licenses. BEE enriched a few well-connected blacks, including President Cyril Ramaphosa (since 2018). However, in most cases BEE resulted in token blacks being paid to serve on corporate boards without taking any active role in management, fueling corruption, especially under President Jacob Zuma (2009–18), who helped the Indian Gupta brothers to obtain government contracts in exchange for $4 billion in bribes and favors to friends and relatives.

State-owned companies, from South African Airways to power utility Eskom to the South African Post Office, incurred huge debts under contracts made with favored firms while failing to invest in the capacity to deliver basic services. Eskom, which generates 95 percent of South Africa's electricity, uses rolling blackouts to compensate for the failure to invest in power generation, including the failure of Gupta-linked firms to supply coal to power plants. Government efforts to restructure debt-ridden state-owned firms are opposed by unions that fear the loss of good jobs.

Nattrass and Seekings (2019) criticize the ILO's decent work agenda for allowing ANC-led governments and unions representing entrenched workers in the large-firm garment industry to destroy smaller and less productive clothing factories that often provided the only wage jobs available to women in poorer rural areas. The garment sector employed 10 percent of South Africa's manufacturing workers in 1994, but lost three-fourths of these jobs as minimum wages were raised and all garment firms had to pay union-negotiated wages.

Nattrass and Seekings (2019) argue that the South African government should have fostered and promoted the small-scale labor-intensive garment industry to preserve and create jobs, even if the jobs in small garment factories did not offer all of the features of decent work. They argue that labor-intensive development is needed to absorb workers in developing countries with high unemployment. Nattrass and Seekings say that "better work," such as safety and health at work, creates more jobs than "decent work" that demands ever rising wages as the number of jobs shrinks (2019, 8).

The result of what Nattrass and Seekings call decent work fundamentalism in South Africa are islands of high wages and high productivity in large and unionized garment factories and hundreds of abandoned sewing factories in poor areas; less productive sewing factories closed when the wages negotiated by the most productive firms were extended to all firms, raising wages for workers who kept their jobs but leading to widespread layoffs. Some unemployed garment workers have formed cooperatives that sew garments, since cooperatives are not subject to negotiated wages.

Forced Labor and Trafficking

Smuggling people over borders and forcing them to work or engage in sex are actions that the UN system and most governments aim to minimize with the 3-P strategies, viz., prevention, prosecution of violators, and protection of victims. Developing an effective 3-P framework to prevent trafficking, to prosecute traffickers, and to protect victims has proven to be difficult, especially in middle-income developing countries such as Malaysia and Mexico.

Smugglers generally move willing participants over borders, while traffickers may move migrants who want to travel but are enslaved or exploited in the destination. One distinction holds that smuggling is a crime against the state, with the smuggler as well as the person being smuggled subject to prosecution, while trafficking is a crime against people because of the force, fraud, or coercion used by the trafficker against the victim, who may be eligible for government assistance and protection.

The UN approved three Palermo protocols in 2000 to deal with smuggling, trafficking, and firearms, and made the UN Office on Drugs and Crime[12] responsible for monitoring the implementation of the protocols. The Protocol against the Smuggling of Migrants by Land, Sea and Air defines smuggling as "the procurement, in order to obtain directly or indirectly, a financial or other material benefit, of the illegal entry of a person into a State Party of which the person is not a national or a permanent resident."

The Protocol to Prevent, Suppress and Punish Trafficking in Persons defines trafficking as "The recruitment, transportation, transfer, harboring or receipt of persons, by means of the threat or use of force or other forms of coercion, of abduction, or fraud, of deception, of the abuse of power or of a position of vulnerability or the giving or receiving of payments or benefits to achieve the consent of a person having control over another person, for the purpose of exploitation. Exploitation shall include, at a minimum, the exploitation or the prostitution of others or other forms of sexual exploitation, forced labor or services, slavery or practices similar to slavery, servitude or the removal of organs."[13]

These UN protocols are widely credited with making governments aware of trafficking and enacting laws to detect and prosecute traffickers and to protect their victims. The US went further in 2000 with the Victims of Trafficking and Violence Protection Act (TVPA) which, inter alia, requires the US Department of State to issue an annual Trafficking in Persons (TIP) report that rates each country's efforts to prevent trafficking, prosecute traffickers, and protect victims.[14] The TIP report classifies countries in Tier 1 if their governments have implemented and enforce the 3-P framework of prevention, prosecution, and protection. Tier 2 governments are not in full compliance but making "significant efforts" to achieve implement and enforce the 3-Ps, and Tier 3 countries are not in compliance and not making significant efforts to implement and enforce the 3-Ps.

The Tier 2 "watch list" of countries gets attention because it includes countries that have a significant or an increasing number of trafficking victims, few government efforts to combat trafficking, and weak commitments to implement and enforce the 3-Ps. Countries that are on the Tier 2 watch list for two years, and would be designated to be on the Tier 2 watch list for a third consecutive year, are automatically designated Tier 3, which can lead to reductions in US aid and US efforts to deny World Bank and IMF assistance to the country. This means that the governments of Tier 2-watch countries often take steps against trafficking to avoid a Tier 3 listing.

---

[12] See http://www.unodc.org.

[13] See http://www.unodc.org/unodc/en/human-trafficking/index.html?ref=menuside.

[14] The report, normally released in June, is available at http://www.state.gov/trafficking-in-persons-report/.

The thirty-nine Tier 1 countries in 2018 included the richer industrial countries of Western Europe and Asia, while the eighty-plus Tier 2 countries include Mexico, which has been a Tier 2 country over the past five years (US Department of State, 2019). The TIP report noted that the Mexican government identified and supported trafficking victims and convicted several traffickers, but did not deal effectively with complicity by local officials in trafficking and had an inadequate number of shelters for victims. It recommended that the Mexican government increase efforts to detect and assist victims of trafficking and strengthen efforts to prosecute traffickers, improve anti-trafficking laws, increase cooperation between enforcement agencies, improve the training of police and prosecutors, and collect and publish more data on forced labor and trafficking. The TIP report noted the wide gap between NGO estimates of the number of forced laborers in Mexico (375,000) and the 1,500 victims identified between 2013 and 2017.

Categorizing countries by tier is hard, reflecting the debate over what to measure. Most funding for anti-trafficking activities goes to NGOs that train police and other front-line personnel to improve their abilities to detect trafficking victims. NGOs also operate hotlines for victims to report suspected trafficking and offer legal aid and other services to trafficking victims. Many NGOs measure progress by the number of police trained and calls to hotlines. The US Department of State, on the other hand, prefers evidence of government enforcement, such as how many traffickers were prosecuted and convicted, how many victims were assisted, and how many anti-trafficking laws were enacted or amended.

The debate between those who favor general education and training to prevent and detect trafficking versus specific anti-trafficking actions plays out in many areas that foreign aid seeks to influence. For example, should foreign aid aimed at coping with climate change be dedicated solely to projects that help countries to cope with the effects of rising temperatures, such as building seawalls to protect low-lying cities, or should climate-change aid be used to promote development generally under the theory that better educated and higher income residents will be better able to cope with climate change? Similarly, what is the optimal balance between focusing limited resources on anti-trafficking campaigns versus helping to improve wages and working conditions in migrant areas of origin so that residents have options and are less likely to be tempted by traffickers?

The ILO estimates the extent of forced labor, modern slavery, and human trafficking, reporting 25 million workers in forced labor in 2016, including 16 million in private-sector workplaces, almost 5 million in forced sexual exploitation, and 4 million in forced labor imposed by governments, as with prison labor.[15] The ILO estimated that 21 million people worldwide were in some form of forced labor during the period 2002–11, including 14.2 million who were "victims of forced

---

[15] http://www.ilo.org/global/topics/forced-labour/lang--en/index.htm

labor exploitation" in the private sector, generally for six months or less (ILO, 2012, 13). The private-sector victims were 60 percent men and 73 percent adults. Some 18 percent were international migrants, while 15 percent were internal migrants, meaning that most trafficking victims were local residents who did not cross international or internal borders.

ILO estimates are based on "reported cases" of forced labor that include the event, number of victims, place, and time. The methodology is capture–recapture, which means comparing the number of cases of forced labor in two samples and determining how many cases are in both. Capture–recapture requires four critical assumptions: (1) there was no change in the universe over the period studied, (2) victims were identified correctly, (3) the probability of case selection was equal in the two samples, and (4) the samples were drawn independently (ILO, 2012, 22). The total number of cases is estimated to be the number in sample 1 times the number in sample 2 divided by n, the number of cases reported in both samples. For example, if sample 1 had 50 cases and sample 2 had 30, and 10 cases appeared in both samples, the total number of cases would be 150 (50 × 30 = 1,500/10). If the average case had 10 victims, then the total number of victims would be 1,500.

The ILO sampled by geographic region, and used both recorded incidents of forced labor and data extracted from media reports, NGOs, police and court reports, and union and other reports. The result was seventy-two variables in each case, including twenty-eight variables that dealt with forced labor as signi- fied by people working against their will and facing penalties for nonperform- ance. The ILO assumed that data from government sources, international organizations, and international NGOs were valid. Two independent teams then validated 7,500 cases of forced labor between 2002 and 2011. The critical assump- tion is that each reported case represents twenty-seven unreported cases, so that the ILO analysis assumed it identified 3.6 percent of the total number of cases of forced labor, and multiplied its findings by twenty-seven to get an estimated total number of trafficking victims.

The ILO estimates leave the impression that sex and labor trafficking are wide- spread, and that more trafficking would be detected and victims rescued if there were more enforcement. Critics counter that the number of victims identified is far smaller than the ILO estimates, which are based on a range of assumptions that may be questioned. For example, one motivation for the US TVPA was a CIA estimate derived from foreign media accounts that 50,000 victims of trafficking arrived in the US each year (Markon, 2007). The TVPA provided funds to the Department of Health and Human Services to distribute to groups fighting traf- ficking, and these groups used HHS funds mostly to operate hot lines and educate law enforcement and others about how to recognize victims rather than finding and helping victims.

There are many critics of the TVPA and the role played by the TIP report. Feingold (2010, 47) concluded that estimates of trafficking victims are marked by "numerical certainty and statistical doubt," meaning that victim estimates are not based on reliable data. Feingold noted that anti-trafficking advocates attacked Simon Baker's study of socioeconomic changes in northern Thailand that led to more girls than boys going to secondary school, so that fewer girls were available to be enticed into the sex industry. Advocates feared that Baker's optimistic conclusion of fewer potential trafficking victims could reduce the funds available to them for anti-trafficking campaigns (Feingold, 2010, 51–2).

Mahdavi (2018) reinforced skepticism about the US role in preventing trafficking via the TIP Tier 2 watch list. Governments in the United Arab Emirates and Japan took steps to avoid being placed on the TIP Tier 2 watch list that increased the vulnerability of some migrants. For example, additional police targeted sex workers in both countries, some of whom voluntarily worked in the sex industry, which took police resources away from monitoring labor exploitation. Mahdavi concluded that government efforts to deter trafficking in the UAE and Japan to avoid the Tier 2 watch list made some migrants worse off, especially the irregular foreigners who were detected and removed by the UAE and Japanese governments during anti-trafficking campaigns.

Many NGOs exaggerate the number of trafficking victims they identify or assist. For example, the Coalition of Immokalee Workers reported helping 400 workers escape from labor contractors Miguel Flores and Sebastian Gomez in 1997, while the decision in US vs. Flores reported 25 victims.[16] The CIW claims credit for helping to expose Global Horizons, a Beverly Hills-based labor contractor that charged Thai workers high fees for H-2A visas to fill seasonal farm jobs in the US. The Thai workers were told in Thailand that they would earn at least $2,500 a month picking apples in Washington. Instead, they worked only a few months, and earned far less.

In September 2010, Global Horizon's president, Mordechai Orian, was charged with human trafficking for bringing 400 Thai farm workers to Washington and Hawaii under the H-2A program and forcing them to repay their recruitment debts from their earnings. Five Thais based in Los Angeles and Thailand were charged in what US authorities called the largest-ever case of human trafficking. However, the human-trafficking charges in Hawaii were dismissed when the government conceded that it could not prove its case.[17]

MacDonald et al. (2018, 87) reviewed US and UN efforts to reduce human trafficking since 1990 and concluded that "the impact has been minimal at best." Comparing global efforts to end slavery, piracy, counterfeiting currencies, and the hijacking of aircraft, MacDonald predicted that ending trafficking "will never

[16] http://www.unodc.org/cld/case-law-doc/traffickingpersonscrimetype/usa/1998/united_states_v._flores.html.
[17] AP, July 21, 2012: "Human Trafficking Case Against Executives Is Dismissed." http://www.nytimes.com/2012/07/22/us/human-trafficking-case-dismissed-against-global-horizons-officials.html.

succeed to the extent that other global prohibition regimes have done" (MacDonald et al., 2018, 89).

One trafficked worker is one too many, but estimates of trafficking are based on weak statistical foundations. Groups seeking funds to reduce trafficking have incentives to exaggerate the number of victims. Even more difficult is drawing the line between labor exploitation and trafficking in industries such as agriculture, where some regular features of the workplace can be considered indicators of trafficking, such as housing in employer-owned camps that workers can leave only with employer-provided transportation.

Misunderstanding agriculture hampered the Urban Institute's analysis of 122 trafficking cases, including 19 percent or 23 cases in agriculture (2014). Of the 169 suspected perpetrators of trafficking identified, two-thirds were farm-labor supervisors. The Urban Institute acknowledged the difficulty of separating labor exploitation, defined as not paying minimum wages or adhering to labor standards, from labor trafficking, which involves force, fraud, or coercion. The Urban Institute study (2014, 77) noted that "many victimization experiences appeared to be only exploitative labor situations" rather than trafficking. One table (2014, 80) notes that the most common exploitation involved paying less than promised wages or making unlawful deductions, whereas labor trafficking included threats to use violence or to report unauthorized workers to authorities.

Indicators of trafficking highlighted by the Urban Institute included workers living in isolated camps with only the employer providing transportation away from the camp, as well as employers calling workers derogatory names or providing them with poor housing. Many of the victims did not know they were trafficked until NGO service providers informed them of their rights.

The Urban Institute recommended changes to US guest-worker programs, so that workers are not tied to one employer; greater enforcement of labor laws; and the expansion of state laws, such as California's Transparency in Supply Chains Act that hold buyers at the top of supply chains liable for forced labor among suppliers in the chain. The study also recommended more training for those who could identify victims of trafficking, the creation of a Department of Homeland Security agency that focuses on anti-trafficking activities, and improved services for trafficking victims, including housing and vocational training.

Governments

The major asset of most of the world's workers is their own time. Converting personal time into wages via the labor market is the central economic activity of most workers, which is why almost all governments regulate the labor markets where effort is exchanged for reward. Governments seek to ensure that employers offer safe jobs that pay at least the minimum wage and provide work-related benefits to workers who earned them. Labor-law agencies investigate complaints filed by workers and others and conduct targeted enforcement operations in sectors and areas where labor-law violations are most common.

Governments have the responsibility to protect their citizens and workers. Labor-law enforcement is needed most when workers are in a weak bargaining position, as when unemployment is high or workers are vulnerable due to their lack of legal status and knowledge of their rights and responsibilities. Many hired farm workers are internal or international migrants who do not know their rights and may fear that complaints lead to layoffs and removal from higher-wage areas.

Agriculture is the largest sector of employment in poorer countries with incomplete labor-law protection and welfare systems. As economies develop, most governments implement protective labor laws and social-security systems for workers employed in the modern urban sector, but these laws may exempt most or all workers in agriculture.

Protecting workers employed in agriculture requires two steps. First, exemptions in labor laws for agriculture need to be reviewed and reduced so that farm workers become eligible for work-related benefits on the same basis as other workers. Second, labor laws must be enforced, which requires strategies in addition to relying on worker complaints because vulnerable workers rarely complain of labor-law violations.

The process of eliminating exemptions from labor laws for farm workers is often slow. As the number of farms declines, policymakers are sensitive to complaints that raising labor costs will accelerate the demise of small farms, making them reluctant to aggressively raise minimum wages or to require family farms to pay the taxes to provide social security and other benefits for hired workers. However, in an agriculture with small, medium-sized, and large farms, trying to slow the demise of small- and medium-sized farms by keeping farm-worker wages and payroll taxes low often fails, as other factors accelerate the consolidation of farm production on fewer and larger farms that benefit from economies of scale. Small farms often continue as hobby or retirement operations.

Most labor-law agencies say they lack staff to fully investigate complaints, giving them few resources to conduct targeted enforcement. Detecting and remedying violations of labor laws in low-wage sectors is often difficult, as records may be incomplete, workers may not speak the same language as enforcement staff, and employers often contest penalties. Enforcement incentives may also be perverse. Labor-law agencies that announce how much in back wages they recovered for workers during the past year are more "successful" in a higher-wage sector such as construction rather than a low-wage sector such as agriculture.

Many hired farm workers are international migrants. There is widespread agreement that the best way to protect native workers from "unfair" migrant-worker competition is to protect migrant workers, so that employers do not prefer migrant to native workers because they are easier to underpay or cheaper because employers do not have to pay taxes on migrant wages for work-related benefits. However, there is less agreement about whether the *number* of international migrants should be restricted in order to protect migrant and native workers, especially if many of the international migrants are unauthorized.

In the US, a quarter of all foreign-born workers, and over half of the foreign-born farm workers, are unauthorized. Labor law covers unauthorized workers and requires employers to pay them minimum wages and payroll taxes for work-related benefit programs, even if unauthorized workers are not eligible for benefits from these programs because of their status. Similarly, unauthorized workers may not be eligible for all remedies when employers violate their labor rights, as when employers cannot be forced to rehire unauthorized workers who are wrongly fired for union activities. The US Supreme Court in the 2002 Hoffman Plastic Compounds case compared the wrong of an unauthorized worker using false documents to get hired with that of the employer unlawfully firing the worker for union activities, and concluded that the immigration violation was worse. In this case, the fired worker did not receive back wages despite being fired unlawfully.[18]

Fresh produce is perishable, and one authority given to US labor-law enforcers is to declare farm commodities to be "hot goods" that cannot be shipped over state lines. This is a seemingly powerful enforcement tool, since 60 percent of fresh produce is from the western states and is destined for the 60 percent of Americans in the eastern states. However, when DOL invokes its hot goods authority, growers may prevail.

DOL in 2012 charged that blueberry growers Pan-American Berry Growers and B&G Ditchen Farms paid workers less than the minimum wage, and threatened to put a hot-goods hold on their blueberries so that they could not be shipped across state lines unless the farms agreed to settle the charges by paying $200,000 in back wages to 1,100 workers and penalties of $30,000.[19] The Fair Labor Standards Act allows DOL to seek a court order to prevent the interstate shipment of goods that were produced in violation of the statute's minimum-wage, overtime, or child-labor provisions.

Pan-American said it had 280 pickers for 165 acres of blueberries, and B&G had 310 workers for 150 acres, an average of almost 2 workers per acre. FLCs

---

[18] Chief Justice William H. Rehnquist, in a 5–4 decision, wrote that the unauthorized worker who was unlawfully fired was not entitled to back pay because "awarding back pay to illegal aliens runs counter to policies underlying" immigration law. It would encourage the successful evasion of apprehension by immigration authorities, condone prior violations of the immigration laws, and encourage future violations. He rejected the NLRB's plea for authority "to award back pay to an illegal alien for years of work not performed, for wages that could not lawfully have been earned and for a job obtained in the first instance by a criminal fraud." See https://migration.ucdavis.edu/rmn/more.php?id=575

[19] For more details: https://migration.ucdavis.edu/rmn/comments.php?id=1872_0_3_0.

supplied workers to both farms, and the workers were paid piece-rate wages. The farms protested that DOL assumed that workers could pick only 50 to 68 pounds of blueberries an hour, so that DOL believed that workers for whom farmers reported picking at a higher rate likely involved several workers employed under one Social Security number. DOL used worker productivity data to assert that the farms had hundreds of "ghost workers" who worked but were not on payroll lists.

Oregon's Cooperative Extension estimated hand-harvesting costs to be $0.55 a pound for yields of 16,000 pounds of blueberries an acre. If growers received $1.35 a pound for their blueberries, labor costs are 40 percent of grower revenue (hours per acre were not provided). California Cooperative Extension in 2009 estimated that 1,000 hours per acre were required to harvest blueberries that yielded 10,000 pounds per acre worth $3 a pound to growers, making harvesting costs a third of grower revenue.[20]

The Oregon blueberry growers wanted to place DOL back wages and penalties in an escrow fund and contest the DOL charges. DOL refused, so the growers paid and then sued DOL in August 2013, arguing that they were forced to settle in order to sell their berries. In January 2014, a federal magistrate agreed with the berry growers that DOL "unfairly stacked the deck" against them by invoking the hot-goods threat that their berries could not be shipped unless they signed the consent decree. A federal district judge agreed in April 2014 and invalidated the grower–DOL settlements, returning the monies to the growers.

Between FY09 and FY13, DOL conducted 7,500 investigations on US farms and collected over $20 million in back wages for 40,000 workers. DOL said that the number of times that farm producers voluntarily withheld their goods from interstate commerce after an investigation, plus the number when DOL obtained court orders limiting shipments, was two in FY13; three in FY12; two in FY11; and three in FY10—that is, hot-goods holds on perishable commodities are rare.

One debate is whether labor laws can be enforced effectively without enforcing immigration laws; that is, are employers tempted to violate labor laws in a labor market with unauthorized workers? Most economists believe that the supply of labor influences labor-law compliance, since employers who do not pay minimum wages or offer safe working conditions have difficulty recruiting and retaining workers. Some labor lawyers believe that, with sympathetic labor-law agencies and cooperation between labor-law enforcement and community groups, there can be effective labor-law enforcement even in labor markets with many unauthorized workers (Fine and Lyon, 2017).

---

[20] See: https://migration.ucdavis.edu/rmn/more.php?id=1837.

Unions

Many observers hope that unions can push up farm wages and improve protections for farm workers. The purpose of unions is to negotiate wage and benefit improvements for the workers they represent, with workers paying for their union's activities via dues that are usually 2–3 percent of gross wages. Farm-worker unions have generally failed to effectuate lasting wage and benefit improvements in agriculture for several reasons, including worker characteristics, union leadership, legal obstacles, and structural issues.

The most fundamental problem for farm-worker unions is that agriculture is an exit industry, meaning that dissatisfied workers tend to move on to nonfarm jobs rather than remain in agriculture and fight for better conditions. Indeed, the workers who would be most effective in fighting for change in agriculture are usually the first to exit, leaving unions to represent workers who have few opportunities for jobs outside of agriculture.

The characteristics of farm workers affect union leadership. Organizing workers scattered across diverse farms is difficult, so many union leaders are missionary-type figures who toil against long odds to inspire workers and overcome employer reluctance to sign contracts that raise wages and improve conditions. Cesar Chavez of California's United Farm Workers struggled against long odds to win contracts in the 1970s. However, when some of the best-paid UFW members challenged Chavez, he eliminated union locals in order to avoid having local union leaders challenge his authority. Chavez argued in court that only he could appoint union staff and won; the UFW remains one of the few US unions without locals to train future leaders.

Pawel (2009, 2014) emphasizes Chavez's austerity and authoritarianism, noting that he escaped from low-wage farm work by becoming an organizer for the Community Service Organization, a California Latino civil-rights organization, but quit the CSO when he realized that most poor people wanted to become middle-class rather than continue to struggle for broader social change.[21] Chavez moved the UFW's headquarters away from most farm workers, but retained authority to approve all contracts that were negotiated by UFW staff with input from workers on the farm. The UFW does not allow workers to vote on the contracts under which they work (Pawel, 2009, 2014).

There is similar distance between union leaders and the farm workers they represent in other countries. Mexico's 11,000 unions that are associated the dominant CTM federation often sign agreements with factories and farms before they

---

[21] Pawel suggests that Chavez wanted to lead a poor people's movement rather than a union. Chavez worried that resolving labor disputes through legal procedures would diminish the participation of people in the movement, preferring demonstrations, fasts, and boycotts to bargaining and legal procedures.

begin operations. These "protection agreements" require all newly hired workers to join the union and work under contracts that the workers may not be aware exist. When workers learn about the contract, they sometimes strike to protest what they see as unfair terms that they had no hand in negotiating or approving. CTM-affiliated unions have been associated with the dominant ruling political party, the PRI, and they generally joined with governments and employers that wanted to restrain wage growth to attract foreign investment to Mexico.

The US–Mexico–Canada (USMCA) trade agreement negotiated in 2018 to replace NAFTA requires Mexico to change its labor laws in ways that may result in faster wage growth. A labor law reform bill signed May 1, 2019, gives Mexican workers the right to vote by secret ballot on whether they want to be represented by a union and to elect their union's leaders. The Mexican government has promised to create an agency to enforce worker rights to unionize. There is hope on both sides of the border that the new Mexican law will lead to unions that negotiate higher wages and more effectively protect the workers they represent.

Lessons

The ILO establishes labor standards and encourages member states to implement them. The ILO envisions governments cooperating with employer and union stakeholders to determine appropriate labor laws and enforcement mechanisms. ILO conventions and recommendations are often aspirational, urging governments to promote decent work, defined as jobs that are safe and fulfilling and provide a decent life, but rarely lay out the policy trade-offs that may be needed to achieve such aspirational goals.

Labor-law enforcement is necessary but not sufficient to protect farm workers, especially when many farm workers are immigrants. Vulnerable immigrant farm workers tend not to complain, and there are unlikely to be enough enforcement agents to ensure compliance when employers believe that their violations are unlikely to be detected. Legal guest workers rarely complain about violations because they want to be invited to return next season, and making complaints could get them placed on a blacklist and not recruited in the future.

Unions are an alternative or supplement to labor-law enforcement. Union collective bargaining agreements set wages and working conditions for covered workers, and unions can file grievances to resolve disputes privately or complain to labor-law agencies if employers violate worker rights. However, unions in agriculture tend to be weak, and they have rarely represented or protected farm workers effectively.

The worst violations of worker rights involve trafficking. There are many NGOs, often funded by governments and international organizations, that educate police and other front-line agencies on how to detect trafficking victims and operate hotlines for victims to seek help. There is a wide gulf between estimates of trafficking victims made by NGOs and others seeking to extirpate forced labor and debt peonage and the number of victims detected and assisted, making it hard to assess progress in eliminating the worse labor abuses. Many of those believed to be trafficked are employed in agriculture.

7
Buyers, Consumers, and Farm Workers

Most of the fruits and vegetables handled by hired farm workers pass through intermediaries en route from farmers to consumers. Over the past half-century, the number of layers between farmers and consumers has shrunk as fewer and larger supermarkets have come to dominate grocery retailing. Supermarket buyers prefer to deal with a relative handful of large farm suppliers who can provide them with commodities year-round, an example of how concentration in grocery retailing encourages concentration in farm production.

Some consumers buy directly from farmers via farmers' markets, participate in community agriculture programs that deliver boxes of produce weekly, or connect directly with farmers in other ways. But direct farmer–consumer transactions are a very small share of the $700 billion a year in retail US food sales. Walmart is the largest US retailer of food, followed by supermarket chains Kroger, Albertsons, Ahold Delhaize, and Publix; general merchandisers that also sell food include Amazon, Costco, and Target.[1] The twenty largest food retailers account for 80 percent of US grocery store sales, including 45 percent from the largest four retailers.[2]

Food buyers can influence how farmers and other suppliers treat workers who produce farm commodities. For example, consumers want fresh produce to be safe, especially if it is not cooked before being eaten. Farmers also want fresh produce to be safe because of externalities: if one farmer's contaminated spinach makes consumers sick, many others will avoid spinach, reducing demand and the farm price of spinach and leading to losses for all spinach farmers.

The best way to ensure that food is safe is to develop good agricultural practices that are followed by all farmers and workers all of the time. One method to ensure compliance with food-safety protocols is to require farms to develop food-safety programs that monitor water and temperatures and rely on third-party auditors to ensure that the farm has proper systems in place and is accurately recording data. By buying only from farms in compliance with food safety standards, buyer behavior encourages farmers to have food-safety plans and to comply with them.

---

[1] Progressive Grocer's list of the top fifty food sellers in 2019 is at https://progressivegrocer.com/top-50-grocers-amazon-falls-below-aldi-while-independent-grocers-show-strength.
[2] http://www.ers.usda.gov/topics/food-markets-prices/retailing-wholesaling/retail-trends/.

The Prosperity Paradox: Fewer and More Vulnerable Farm Workers. Philip Martin, Oxford University Press (2021).
© Philip Martin.
DOI: 10.1093/oso/9780198867845.001.0001

Buying only from farms whose food-safety practices are audited and certified does not guarantee safe food. The Centers for Disease Control and Prevention defines a food-borne disease outbreak as occurring when two or more people get the same illness from the same food or drink, and counted ten to twenty outbreaks a year linked to leafy greens such as lettuce and spinach between 1998 and 2016 (CRS, 2019). The Food Safety Modernization Act of 2010, which makes adhering to food-safety practices mandatory for most fresh produce growers, is making food safety a top priority of farmers and food buyers, but has not eliminated food-borne disease outbreaks.

Could produce buyers and consumers effectuate a revolution in labor compliance similar to that underway in food-safety compliance? There were food-safety protocols before spinach's 9/14/06 moment when spinach contaminated with Escherichia coli O157:H7 (E. coli) sickened 205 people and killed 3, but these protocols needed to be strengthened and made a central focus of farm management in order to restore public trust in the safety of fresh fruits and vegetables. Similarly, there are labor laws in place even as labor-law inspectors and media reports expose low wages and child labor. Could a buyer-imposed labor protocol on farmer suppliers increase labor-law compliance?

There are other options to improve labor protections, but they affect only a small share of fresh produce. The Coalition of Immokalee Workers in Florida mounted boycotts of fast-food chains and retailers until they agreed to require their tomato producers to abide by the labor protocols that were developed and enforced by the CIW. There are several fair-trade-certifying organizations that charge growers fees to audit and certify their compliance with the organization's labor protocols. Finally, buyers and consumers can influence farm-labor practices with their purchasing decisions.

The Food-Safety Model

Government and voluntary efforts to assure a safe food supply have a long history, but they have not eliminated food-related illnesses. The Centers for Disease Control and Prevention estimates that tainted food sickens 48 million Americans a year, sends 128,000 people to the hospital, and kills 3,000.[3] The number of multistate food-borne illnesses has been increasing, reflecting centralized food processing facilities (GAO, 2017). Salmonella is the number-one food-borne killer, and fresh produce accounts for half of food-borne illnesses.

The federal government has periodically intervened in the farming and food industries to protect Americans from unsafe food. The Pure Food and Drug Act of

[3] See http://www.cdc.gov/foodsafety/cdc-and-food-safety.html.

1906 was inspired by descriptions of unsanitary meat processing plants in Upton Sinclair's 1906 novel *The Jungle*. In 1938, the US Food and Drug Administration (FDA) was given enhanced enforcement powers after some food companies were found to have doctored rancid meat and vegetables to make them more palatable.

Food-safety compliance systems in fresh fruits and vegetables were defensive reactions to food-borne illnesses that sickened consumers and reduced the demand for and prices of affected commodities (Cook, 2011). Consumers do not want to get sick from the food they eat, retailers do not want to be sued for selling bad produce, and farmers want their competitors to be in compliance with food-safety protocols so that one producer's unsafe food does not adversely affect all producers by reducing demand for the product.

Food safety became a major issue in 1993 when 623 people, mostly young children, were sickened by Escherichia coli (E. coli) O157:H7 bacteria in undercooked beef patties at 73 Jack in the Box restaurants in western states (Andrews 2013). Four children died and almost 200 were left with permanent injuries. The subsequent litigation resulted in individual and class-action settlements totaling over $50 million, the largest payments made until that date as a result of food-borne illnesses. Jack in the Box began having the meat it bought tested every fifteen minutes and stopped buying from meat suppliers with systemic E. coli contamination problems.

After the Jack in the Box incident, USDA made the presence of E. coli in ground beef an illegal adulterant and the FDA raised the minimum recommended temperature for cooking hamburger from 140°F to 155°F. Most meat producers introduced Hazard Analysis and Critical Control Point (HACCP) systems to ensure that their food was safe at each point in the production process. The beef industry invested $30 million in HACCP systems in the two decades after 1993, almost all to prevent E. coli contamination (Andrews, 2013). A steam pasteurization process that killed E. coli was approved by USDA in 1995, and was soon adopted by most major meat processors.

Bill Marler, who represented some of the Jack in the Box victims, said that E. coli-related illnesses linked to ground beef accounted for 90 percent of his firm's food-borne illness revenue between 1993 and 2005 and then practically disappeared as the beef industry reduced contamination (Andrews 2013).

Fresh produce has replaced beef as a frequent source of food-borne illness. The number of produce-linked illnesses doubled between 1980–7 and 1987–95, prompting government and industry efforts to adopt an approach similar to the HACCP with Good Agricultural Practices (GAPs) to reduce the chances of fresh produce causing illnesses. The "Guide to Minimize Microbial Food Safety Hazards for Fresh Fruits and Vegetables," issued in October 1998 by the US Food and Drug Administration's Center for Food Safety and Applied Nutrition (FDA CFSAN), established guidelines for monitoring water, manure, worker hygiene, and the traceability of commodities sold by each farmer.

Many buyers of fresh produce required their growers to implement a version of these GAP guidelines and to undergo third-party audits to ensure that their farms were in compliance with food-safety protocols as these guidelines were established (Minor et al., 2019). This changed the culture of many produce firms, encouraging them to treat food safety as an ongoing challenge and to develop risk-reduction programs. However, there was a proliferation of guidelines, certifying organizations, and buyer requirements that led to grower complaints, since a farm selling to six buyers might be required to adhere to six different food-safety protocols and undergo six grower-paid audits. The Food Marketing Institute in 2003 tried to standardize food-safety guidelines by developing a benchmark Safe Quality Food certification program.

This benchmark was not completed when bagged spinach contaminated with E. coli killed 3 people and hospitalized over 100 on September 14, 2006. The contaminated spinach was less than 1,000 pounds of the 680 million pounds of spinach consumed by Americans each year, but led to the recall of all bagged spinach, a sharp drop in demand, and a slow recovery in fresh spinach sales and prices. The contaminated spinach was eventually traced to a 51-acre field in California that had been leased by a spinach grower from a cattle rancher. E. coli found in nearby cattle and wild pig feces and river water was likely absorbed by the spinach plants. The fact that the contaminated spinach was mixed with spinach grown on farms where there was no contamination meant that, instead of the contaminated spinach sickening a few people, thousands became ill (Calvin, 2007).

Spinach's so-called "9/14 moment" convinced industry leaders that fresh produce needed better food-safety standards to restore consumer confidence. The seventy-one handlers who supplied 99 percent of leafy greens such as lettuce and spinach in California agreed to deal only with growers who were in compliance with the protocols developed by the California Leafy Green Products Handler Marketing Agreement (LGMA) of 2007. LGMA protocols sought to ensure that produce was safe by requiring growers to test irrigation water regularly, to ensure that workers followed sanitation guidelines, and to establish trace-back systems so that any commodity that caused a food-borne illness could be traced back to the field where it was grown and the crew that handled it. Audits were conducted to ensure compliance with the LGMA protocols.

The Food Safety Modernization Act of 2010 (FSMA, PL 111-353) translated many of the best practices developed by the LGMA into law. The FSMA, which governs how US fruits and vegetables are grown, harvested, cooled, and transported, includes standards for worker training and health and hygiene and establishes guidelines to monitor irrigation water, fertilizer usage, animal manure near fruit and vegetable fields, and equipment sanitation (Collart, 2016). The FSMA gave the FDA new powers to require food producers to take steps to prevent contamination by monitoring the water used to irrigate and wash produce and by ensuring that workers do not contaminate produce. Farmers need to document their on-farm food-safety efforts.

Calvin et al. (2017) examined the costs of seven fresh produce firms that implemented the LGMA and found that labor costs, including the cost of food safety staff and field supervisor time to monitor safety protocols, accounted for two-thirds of these firms' compliance costs.[4] The cost of food safety audits was one-sixth of the produce firms' safety-related costs, and lost product due to safety concerns was another 10 percent. In other words, most of the cost of compliance with the LGMA were labor costs to implement and monitor safety protocols, not the cost of being unable to sell suspect produce.

Bovay et al., (2018) estimated the costs of implementing the FSMA, and found that costs of compliance are lower for larger farms that can spread costs over more production. Farms with annual produce sales of $3.4 million accounted for almost 60 percent of total fresh fruit and vegetable sales, and their cost of complying with the FMSA was estimated to be less than 0.5 percent of sales. Farms that sold less than $500,000 worth of produce a year, on the other hand, had FMSA compliance costs that were 6 percent or more of their sales.

The importance of large farms in particular commodities explains why FMSA compliance costs are lower for lettuce than for snap beans, since most lettuce is from very large farms, and lower for honeydew melons than for pears (Bovay et al., 2018, iv). Complying with FMSA is yet another reason why fewer and larger farms produce most fresh fruits and vegetables.

The evolution of food-safety standards suggests three lessons for labor compliance systems. First, food-safety protocols have both bottom-up and top-down qualities. Good Agricultural Practices were a bottom-up response by industry leaders to food-safety issues on individual farms, and were quickly mandated by produce buyers and adopted by the relative handful of large farms that account for most fresh produce. When these private GAPs proved to be effective mechanisms to minimize food contamination, a top-down law, the FSMA, made them minimum standards for all producers.

Similarly, labor-compliance systems can be the result of top-down pressure, as when the threat of federal and state penalties for violations or the inability to sell produce to preferred buyers induce growers to comply with labor laws. Labor compliance can also be bottom-up, as when a union organizes the workers employed by a grower who pays low wages and negotiates higher wages, or the grower cannot recruit or retain workers until he or she raises wages and improves conditions.

[4] The average salary of the harvest foremen who monitor their workers, toilets, and hand-washing facilities, and ensure that harvest knives are sanitized several times a day, was reported to be $47,000 a year (Calvin et al., 2017). Foremen also look for animal intrusions that could contaminate the vegetables.

Second, whether inspected by governments or third parties, audits are snap-shots of food safety and workplace practices at a point in time. More important is motion-picture compliance, the systems and cultures that ensure food-safety protocols and labor laws are obeyed consistently. The problem with snapshot audits is that a farm can be certified as compliant one day, but have food-safety and farm-labor violations the next day. Collecting data and recording and responding to problems and complaints create the motion-picture record of com-pliance with food-safety and farm-labor protocols (Mortimore et al., 2019).

Management responses to problems and complaints influence day-to-day farming operations. If managers ignore or minimize food-safety warnings or worker complaints, they send a signal that production is more important than compliance, which may erode respect for food-safety and labor protocols over time. If managers take steps that reduce production in order to ensure compli-ance, they send a signal that compliance is a top priority.

Third, food-safety audits and certifications were developed primarily as a defen-sive reaction to illnesses that imposed negative externalities on all producers. Some of the first food-safety certification systems offered access to particular buyers and sometimes price premiums to compliant growers, but these premiums disappeared after "everyone complied." Buyers and consumers expect food to be safe, making it hard to sustain premium prices for compliant farms (Crespi and Marette, 2001).

Farm-labor compliance systems today are in the premium-price, good seal-of-approval phase, meaning that the relatively few growers who participate often receive preferred access to particular buyers and sometimes premium prices. However, if all farmers comply with labor requirements, these benefits are likely to disappear. In other words, it is only the early adopters of food-safety and labor-compliance systems that typically receive special benefits.

Labor-Certification Systems

If governments cannot effectively enforce labor laws that protect farm workers, and unions are unable to organize workers and negotiate collective bargaining agreements that protect farm workers on most farms, can private organizations develop and enforce labor-protection systems with the support of produce buy-ers? Private labor-certification systems believe that the answer is yes; several models are assessed below.

Coalition of Immokalee Workers

Perhaps the best-known and longest-running private labor-certification system is operated by the Coalition of Immokalee Workers in southwestern Florida.

The CIW began in the 1990s as a bottom-up effort to win a wage increase from major Florida tomato growers. It sought to double the piece-rate wage from $0.35 for picking a 32-pound bucket of mature green tomatoes to $0.70 a bucket with its penny-a-pound campaign.[5] CIW supporters engaged in hunger strikes and enlisted the help of ex-President Carter, who promised to mediate direct talks between workers and tomato growers for higher piece-rate wages in 1998.[6]

The CIW's bottom-up approach failed to convince tomato growers to raise wages, so the CIW switched to a top-down strategy, organizing boycotts of Taco Bell outlets on college campuses because Taco Bell bought tomatoes from Florida farms that refused to meet with the CIW and discuss wage increases. Taco Bell owner Yum! Brands in 2005 became the first major tomato buyer to require the Florida growers from whom it bought tomatoes to comply with the CIW-developed Fair Food Program (FFP).

Taco Bell also agreed to pay tomato growers an extra 1.5 cents a pound for the Florida tomatoes it bought to cover the higher piece-rate wages required by the FFP.[7] The FFP prohibits growers from requiring workers to cup or overfill their buckets, which the CIW estimates adds 5–10 percent to worker earnings because workers can fill more buckets that are level-full rather than overfull.

The Fair Food Program includes a code of conduct that requires participating growers to comply with all applicable labor laws.[8] The FFP Code of Conduct goes beyond labor-law compliance and requires that workers on participating farms be educated about their rights and mandates health-and-safety committees on each farm that include worker representatives to monitor compliance with the FFP. The FFP code requires the use of technology to record hours worked, with workers checking in and out so that their hours of work are recorded accurately.

Growers rather than contractors are considered to be the employers of all workers on their farms, including workers brought to farms by intermediaries. Pay stubs issued by FFP farms must have information required by law plus a line for the FFP premium pay and a telephone number for workers to call with complaints.

---

[5] Mature green tomatoes are picked green and ripened with ethylene. They are often purchased by fast-food chains.

[6] Six tomato pickers began a hunger strike December 20, 1997, to pressure nine tomato growers to raise piece rates; the hunger strike ended a month later when ex-President Carter offered to mediate talks between workers and growers. However, there was no mediation, as growers refused to meet with workers. One said, "Why should the growers talk to these people when they have all the labor they need to get the tomatoes picked?...There are more pickers than there are jobs and the people keep on coming...It's a hundred times better than where they came from...Picking tomatoes has always been a job for people with no skills. It's a stepping stone to climb the economic ladder." https://migration.ucdavis.edu/rmn/more.php?id=267.

[7] The FFP requires tomato buyers to pay growers an extra 1.5 cents a pound for the Florida mature green tomatoes they buy, and growers to keep 0.2 cents or 13 percent of the premium to cover grower costs and to pass 1.3 cents or 87 percent of the extra funds to tomato pickers. A worker picking 120 32-pound buckets a day picks 3,840 pounds, and the extra $0.013 cents a pound is $49.92 a day.

[8] See http://www.fairfoodstandards.org/resources/fair-food-code-of-conduct/.

There are two entities involved in the FFP. The Immokalee-based CIW makes agreements with major tomato buyers, including Mcdonald's, Subway, and Burger King. Under these CIW-buyer agreements, tomato growers such as Ag-Mart, DiMare, Gargiulo, and Lipman receive the extra 1.5 cents a pound for the tomatoes they sell to participating buyers, and pay an extra cent per pound to workers as a line item on worker paychecks.[9] CIW staff negotiate agreements with tomato buyers, and three-person teams educate workers on participating farms about their rights.[10] CIW staff are paid from foundation grants,[11] a funding system that the CIW hopes to change when tomato growers and buyers pay fees because they value CIW education efforts and the ability to use the FFP label on their tomatoes.[12]

The Sarasota-based Fair Food Standards Council audits farms to ensure compliance with the FFP labor protocols. The FFSC monitors the complaint hotline, responds to worker complaints, and audits participating farms by interviewing workers in every crew and sometimes over half of the workers employed on a farm. Most complaints deal with supervisors who allegedly violate FFP standards; the FFSC can order growers to fire supervisors who commit major violations, such as sexual harassment. Worker complaints are investigated within two or three days, and the usual remedy for a valid complaint is grower agreement to fix the problem and develop a plan of action to prevent recurrence.[13]

The CIW believes that the FFP has increased worker earnings and productivity and reduced worker turnover, but there have been no analyses of payroll records that compare worker earnings and turnover on participating and non-participating farms. The CIW says that the average piece rate wage under the FFP was $0.82 per 32-pound bucket in 2012, up from less than $0.50 a bucket in the 1990s.[14] The major benefits of the FFP to workers are less unpaid waiting time for workers as

---

[9] The list of participating buyers and growers is at http://www.fairfoodprogram.org/partners/.

[10] During worker training, CIW staff distribute "Know your rights and responsibilities" booklets to workers.

[11] The CIW's IRS Form 990 for 2017, the most recent available, listed $2.9 million in grants and contributions and expenses of $1.5 million to hold meetings to discuss human rights and community issues, to conduct media outreach, and "to raise awareness of farm worker issues and campaign for protecting their human rights and creating humane working conditions." The CIW had assets of $6.1 million in 2017.

[12] There were several slavery cases linked to Florida tomatoes, but none since the FFP was unveiled in 2011.

[13] The CIW reported receiving over 1,000 complaints since 2011. Two-thirds are considered valid in the sense that they deal with a potential violation of an FFP standard at an FFP farm—usually a complaint about a supervisor breaking FFP standards. Supervisors can be put on probation or suspended and required to undergo FFP education before returning to regular work. Many of the other complaints deal with issues at non-FFP farms or issues not covered by the FFP.

[14] Kent Shoemaker, CEO of Lipman, the largest US field-tomato grower, in December 2014 said Lipman paid $0.55 a bucket to pick field tomatoes, plus a $0.10 per bucket bonus or a total of $0.65 a bucket, and that the average Lipman harvester earned $12.83 an hour in 2014, suggesting almost 20 buckets per hour. http://www.andnowuknow.com/headlines/lipman-ceo-kent-shoemaker-challenges-eva-longorias-food-chains-documentary/robert-lambert/43834#.VNtw90bF9IF.

farmers tighten scheduling and higher earnings due to the higher piece rate and because pickers no longer have to overfill buckets.

H-2A job orders suggest that the prevailing piece rate for picking Florida mature green tomatoes was $0.65 per 32-pound bucket in 2015, below the $0.70 rate desired by the CIW. In order to earn at least the AEWR of $10.26 an hour, workers would have to pick at least 16 buckets per hour in 2015. Del Monte's H-2A tomato job order specifies a minimum productivity standard of 20 buckets an hour or 120 buckets in a six-hour day, a total of 3,840 pounds of tomatoes or almost 2 tons a day.[15] At $0.65 a bucket, this productivity standard generates $13 an hour or $78 for a six-hour day.

The CIW reported $5.1 million in extra payments for tomato pickers in 2010–11, reflecting funds that had been held in escrow from previous years, and an average $3.2 million a year between 2011–12 and 2013–14 (Fair Food Program, 2014, 39). During these years, Florida growers shipped an average 35 million 25-pound cartons of tomatoes (Florida Tomato Committee, 2014, 1), or about 700 million pounds of tomatoes. Not all of the tomatoes picked by workers are packed into cartons, and some tomatoes generate higher per-pound premiums for workers, such as cherry and grape tomatoes, but these data suggest that FFP premiums were paid on 20–25 percent of the Florida tomato crop.

CIW staff report that some growers participating in the FFP are issuing fewer W-2 statements with stable production, suggesting less worker turnover. They also report that fewer workers are leaving tomato harvesting temporarily to work in strawberries, where piece-rate earnings can be higher. In short, anecdotal evidence suggests improved worker earnings and satisfaction under the FFP, but there are limited data and few analyses of the effects of the FFP on workers and production (Brudney, 2016).

The production of mature green tomatoes in Florida is shrinking, suggesting that the FFP will become less important unless it expands to other commodities and areas. The US consumes about 6.5 billion pounds of fresh tomatoes a year, or 20 pounds per person. Over half of these tomatoes are imported, most from Mexico and fewer from Canada. California and Florida dominate the production of field or mature green tomatoes, with each producing a third of the US total; the other third of US field-tomato production is from Tennessee, Ohio, and North and South Carolina, and other states.

Florida tomatoes are worth more than California tomatoes because they are produced during the winter months when prices are highest, with grower prices usually topping $1 a pound in February and March.[16] Food service outlets such as

---

[15] The UFW, in announcing its renewed three-year contract with Pacific Triple E in California, said that workers could pick 200 buckets in 6.5 hours, or almost 31 buckets an hour.

[16] In some years including 2012 there was no winter spike in grower prices, which remained below $0.40 a pound.

fast food restaurants buy half of the mature green or slicing tomatoes grown in California and Florida, but mature green tomatoes are only a seventh of the fresh tomatoes sold by retailers.

Tomatoes are sold in 25-pound cartons, and Florida growers say that they should receive at least $8.75 a carton or $0.35 a pound to cover their growing and harvesting costs. Grower prices in recent years have ranged from $5 to $25 a carton. The demand for mature green or slicing tomatoes is falling, and many growers are switching to grape, cherry, Roma, and heirloom tomatoes, which are worth more per pound but are more expensive to produce.

Florida growers estimate that 200 hours are required to plant and harvest an acre of mature green tomatoes, and that a peak 30,000 workers were employed to harvest 33,000 acres (35,000 acres were planted in 2014, and 33,000 acres were harvested).[17] QCEW data suggest far fewer workers. Between 2008 and 2018, the number of vegetable and melon establishments in Collier County, Florida, where most of the tomato growers are based, was stable at twenty, but average employment in NAICS 11121 that covers all vegetables and melons fell from 3,600 to 2,100. Average weekly wages rose from $325 to $510 over the 2008 to 2018 decade, up 57 percent or slightly faster than the rise in weekly wages for all workers employed in Florida agriculture, which increased 51 percent from $415 to $625 a week.

The CIW faces challenges and opportunities. The challenges include reduced US field-tomato production as consumers purchase more tomatoes that are ripened on the vine and grown under protected culture structures such as greenhouses and plastic-covered hoop houses. A second challenge is the growing number of H-2A workers, which means that the FFP could wind up setting standards for guest workers rather than US workers.[18] The FFP has not reduced exits from the farm workforce enough to prevent tomato growers from hiring more guest workers.

Financial sustainability is another challenge. There may be opportunities to expand the FFP from tomatoes to other commodities and in other states, especially if buyers and growers are convinced that the FFP benefits them. The CIW eventually needs to collect fees from growers and buyers to cover its costs.

The CIW is frequently lauded by reporters and researchers who praise its efforts to expose worker trafficking and slavery in Florida tomato fields (Estabrook, 2011). Most research praises the CIW, including one book that called the FFP "the only bright light" to help prevent abuses of farm workers (Marquis, 2017, 172) rather than providing critical analysis.

---

[17] These acreage totals exclude cherry, grape, and greenhouse tomatoes.
[18] Del Monte's job order seeking H-2A certification for 2015 includes productivity standards, viz., workers should pick at least 120 buckets of round tomatoes in a 6-hour day (20 per hour), 100 buckets of Romas (16.7 per hour), and 20 buckets of grape and cherry tomatoes (3.3 per hour). Workers are guaranteed $10.26 an hour; the job order does not specify a piece rate, but it should be at least $0.51 per bucket.

The CIW won the 2010 Hero Acting to End Modern-Day Slavery Award and the 2015 Presidential Medal for Extraordinary Efforts to Combat Human Trafficking in Persons. The CIW's mobile Florida Modern-Day Slavery Museum recounts its efforts to detect and help to prosecute traffickers, but may leave the impression that trafficking is common. One trafficked worker is one too many, but exaggerating the scale of the trafficking problem may do more to raise money than to improve compliance with labor laws in agriculture.

Equitable Food Initiative

The second major private farm-labor compliance program is the Equitable Food Initiative launched by Oxfam America in 2012 with the support of Costco and other stakeholders. Unlike the FFP's focus on tomatoes grown in southwest Florida, the EFI is an international program that covers farms and workers in all commodities and in Canada, Mexico, and the US. Like the FFP, the EFI aims to ensure that participating growers comply with all applicable labor laws, but EFI stresses the need to educate workers about food safety, and uses "farmworker assured" on its label to suggest that consumers will be buying safer food if a farm has been certified by EFI.

The first US farming operation certified by EFI was an Andrew & Williamson (A&W) strawberry farm in California in July 2014. Workers pick berries for piece-rate wages, but were guaranteed at least $9.05 an hour in 2015, when the state's minimum wage was $9 an hour, after completing EFI training that makes them more aware of food-safety issues such as personal hygiene and animal droppings and undergoing training in labor-management collaboration. Costco encouraged growers to join EFI, and paid a premium price for certified produce, some $3.9 million in 2018–19, of which $3.4 million was payments to workers.[19] The EFI emphasizes that hundreds of pickers can monitor food-safety protocols better than a one-time third-party auditor.[20]

EFI has 326 performance indicators grouped into four categories: cross-sectional, labor, food safety, and environmental.[21] Each category includes three to ten items labeled as critical, major, and minor, and all critical indicators are audited once a year. For example, cross-sectional standards include compliance with federal, state, and local labor laws (major), labor-management cooperation to develop a leadership team on the farm (critical), and non-retaliation against workers who participate in EFI or report violations of EFI

[19] Costco paid $3.9 million in premiums for EFI-certified produce between 2014 and 2017; 85 to 90 percent goes to workers.
[20] Media reports stress the food-safety aspects of having farm workers monitor fresh produce to ensure that it is safe. See http://www.nytimes.com/2013/05/25/business/a-program-to-combat-food-contamination.html?searchResultPosition=1.
[21] See https://equitablefood.org/efi-standards/.

standards (critical). Labor standards range from compliance with worker health-and-safety regulations to fair compensation. Workers are to be informed of the terms and conditions of employment and "an accurate definition of the piece rate system" (minor). EFI certification requires compliance with all indicators.

EFI develops leadership teams on each participating farm that involve supervisors and workers who are trained to maintain compliance with labor and food-safety standards. Trained supervisors and workers, the multi-stakeholder teams at the heart of EFI, extend their knowledge to the farm's entire workforce to make compliance a joint responsibility of both supervisors and workers. Each farm's teams meet regularly to ensure continued compliance with EFI standards, which reportedly builds and improves relationships between labor and management (Scully-Russ and Boyle, 2018).

Once a farm is in compliance with EFI standards, a third-party auditor issues a certificate of compliance that allows the farm to put the EFI label—Responsibly Grown, Farmworker Assured—alongside its own label on its produce. EFI staff are funded by foundation and corporate grants to publicize the program, train leadership teams on farms, and work with growers and buyers.

By mid-2020, EFI had certified forty two farms, including twenty five in Mexico. Certified farms produce a range of fresh fruits and vegetables, from blueberries and strawberries to vegetables and melons.

The effects of EFI on productivity and worker turnover have not been evaluated. Worker–management collaboration should lead to more compliance with labor laws and increased worker satisfaction, but EFI has not underaken before and after studies of measurable indicators such as worker earnings and labor costs per box. Impact evaluations report that workers feel freer to voice concerns and better understand management goals, which should reduce turnover and perhaps reduce labor costs.[22] Some growers believe that workers who are invested in both labor and food-safety compliance, and who understand their firm's business goals, will contribute to less shrinkage, the 5–10 percent of produce that is shipped to retailers and rejected because of problems that range from too much inferior fruit to not cooling harvested produce quickly enough.[23]

US growers who participate in the EFI hope that preferred access to buyers who may pay higher prices and reject less produce justifies the slightly higher wages paid to workers and the cost of training workers and responding to complaints. If workers are more satisfied and productive, the result could be win-win, with workers achieving higher earnings without raising labor costs per unit produced (Gordon, 2016).

---

[22] https://equitablefood.org/our-impact.
[23] Quality issues are usually the purview of management rather than workers. For example, harvested produce must be cooled quickly to maximize its shelf life: one rule of thumb is that each hour berries are harvested and waiting in the field to be cooled reduces their shelf life by one day, and another holds that "cut to cool" time for leafy green vegetables should be a maximum four hours.

Fair Trade USA and Others

There are several definitions of fair trade. Politicians often define fair trade in terms of protecting local producers, arguing that countries that artificially depress the value of their currency gain an advantage in exporting and thus threaten local producers of competing commodities. Another definition of fair trade is concern for the welfare of producers and their employees, so that eating a fair-trade banana gives additional satisfaction knowing it was produced under "fair" conditions for farmers and workers. Most fair-trade programs are based on this altruistic or feel-good consumer model (Ehrlich, 2018, 16).

Oakland-based Fair Trade USA (previously TransFair USA) certifies fair-trade products to enable sustainable development and to empower communities that produce food and other commodities. Fair Trade USA "audits and certifies transactions between US companies and their suppliers to guarantee that the farmers and workers producing Fair Trade Certified goods are paid fair prices and wages, work in safe conditions, protect the environment and receive community development funds to empower and uplift their communities."[24] This triple win for people, the planet, and profit is supported by supermarkets such as Kroger and Walmart that pay a premium for Fair Trade USA-certified products.[25]

Manufacturers, importers, and retailers paid about $9 million in "net service fees" to use the Fair Trade Certified label in 2014 on coffee, cocoa, fresh produce, and consumer packaged goods (one firm provides almost a quarter of these service fees). In addition, Fair Trade USA reported $2 million in grants and contributions, and received a $10 million matching challenge grant in November 2014; that is, Fair Trade USA could receive the $10 million grant if it received $10 million in matching contributions.

Fair Trade premiums are added to the cost of the product and paid to brands that pass them on to growers and workers. Small farms with fewer than five permanent and twenty-five temporary workers can use premiums to cover the cost of compliance, while larger producers must invest the premiums in the Community Development Projects selected by workers. Over $600 million in premiums was returned to farmers and workers between 1998 and 2019.[26] Fair Trade USA audits its brands to ensure that premiums are returned to farmers and workers.

The Fair Trade USA agricultural production standard includes six modules dealing with worker empowerment, fundamental rights at work, wages and working conditions, environmental sustainability, traceability, and internal

---

[24] http://www.fairtradecertified.org.
[25] Fair-trade coffee and cacao may be bought at a minimum price, providing a price floor for growers.
[26] https://www.fairtradecertified.org/.

management. Some of these standards are subjective, such as "fair wages" or employer plans to improve health and safety, and some standards vary by size of farm.[27] To be certified, a farm must earn at least 40 percent of the progress points in the initial certification, maintain at least 40 percent of possible progress points in years two through five, and achieve 100 percent by year six.[28] Participating farms are audited annually to monitor compliance and track improvements. Commodities that satisfy the agricultural production standard can include the fair-trade label.

In 2011 Fair Trade USA bought Good World Solutions, which has Fair Wage Guides "to assess the impact of Fair Trade certification on farmers and workers." Labor Link allows farm employers to select from among several surveys that ask employees questions about their satisfaction with their jobs. The workers can call a number and answer questions anonymously, and the results of the worker surveys are provided to farm employers (Brown and Getz, 2015, 185). Each fair-trade farm has three worker committees: a Fair Trade Committee to manage the spending of premiums, a Social Engagement Team to improve worker–management dialogue, and a Health and Safety Committee.

At the end of 2019, Fair Trade USA had certified ten times more farms in Mexico, seventy-one, than in the US, seven (and one in Canada), suggesting that growers abroad see certification as a means to obtain access to preferred buyers.

There is a competing Fairtrade International organization based in Bonn, Germany, with similar goals that certifies coffee, tea, cocoa, and other commodities produced in developing countries and exported to industrial countries. Like Fair Trade USA, Fairtrade International returns the premiums it collects from buyers to farmers, who collectively decide how to spend them to improve the community. Fair Trade USA, which is two syllables, resigned from the Fairtrade (one word) Labelling Organization (FLO) in 2011, and paid almost $1.1 million to the FLO in 2014.

Raynolds (2018) reviewed Fairtrade International's activities in developing countries, and concluded that they are more likely to inform hired workers of their rights than to empower them. Fairtrade International was founded by NGOs in 1997 to empower producers by setting standards, auditing and certifying producers, and promoting fair-trade certified products. Many producers certified by Fairtrade International rely on hired workers, raising concerns from those in the fair-trade movement who envision fair-trade premiums helping cooperatives of small farmers.

---

[27] Small farms are defined as those with five or fewer permanent workers and less than a peak 25 workers, mid-sized as six to 25 permanent workers and up to 100 peak workers, and large as more than 25 permanent workers and more than 100 peak workers.

[28] https://www.fairtradecertified.org/sites/default/files/filemanager/documents/APS/Dairy/DRAFT_FTUSA_STD_APSDairyAmendment_EN_1.0.0.pdf

Fairtrade International established a Workers' Rights Advisory Committee in 2010 to deal with worker participation in certification, wages, and unionization, and released a 57-page document of standards for hired farm workers in 2015. Worker participation is encouraged by sharing audit results with workers. The worker standards specify maximum 48-hour work weeks and only voluntary overtime, and the living-wage provision calls for workers to be paid the higher of minimum or prevailing wages. Certified farms must commit to gradually increasing wages until they reach living wage levels established by Fairtrade International, albeit without a timeline. Raynolds (2018, 201) noted that living-wage levels have been established for workers employed in South African grapes, Dominican Republic bananas, and Kenyan flowers. Fair-trade-certified firms must allow union representatives to meet with workers on the farm prior to certification, and certified farms are to "seek" to establish a collective bargaining agreement within a year of certification.

A third global organization that may expand from developing to industrial countries is the Swiss-based IMO Group's Fair for Life Social & Fair Trade Certification Program, which aims "to ensure fair and positive relations between producers and their cooperatives or contracting companies, between workers and their employer, between sellers and buyers on the world market while at the same time ensuring performance of standards."[29] The ECOCERT Group bought the Fair for Life program in 2014, and in 2016 two certifications were announced, one for Corporate Social Responsibility and another for Fair Trade and Responsible Supply-Chains.[30] Fair for Life certifies both products and firms, including farm commodities as well as cosmetics and apparel products. Fair for Life recognizes Fair Trade USA as having similar standards.

Other private certifying organizations include the Agricultural Justice Project (AJP), a Gainesville, Florida-based effort to develop standards for farm employers and FLCs.[31] The AJP charges growers 0.5 percent of their gross sales for inspection and certification as well as the right to use AJP's "food justice certified" label, meaning that a farm with $1 million in sales would pay $5,000. Retailers pay 0.75 percent of their gross sales of food-justice-certified produce.

The AJP's emphasis is on organic produce and sustainability. The AJP lays out standards in five areas, including farmers' rights in negotiations with buyers for prices that "cover the cost of production of the farm products plus a fair return on the farmer's investment and a living wage for the farmer." The farm-worker and food-system-worker rights include living wages, fair conflict resolution procedures, and health-and-safety protections. Buyers' rights include transparency to

[29] http://www.fairforlife.org
[30] http://www.fairforlife.org/pmws/indexDOM.php?client_id=fairforlife&page_id=materials&lang_iso639=en.
[31] http://www.agriculturaljusticeproject.org.

know farmers' costs of production, and farm-intern rights include written contracts and a "fair stipend to cover living expenses." The AJP website listed five certified US farms and one retailer in fall 2019.[32] Farms and retailers are certified by Quality Certification Services (QCS), which forwards the fees it collects to AJP. QCS, in turn, certifies farms that satisfy a variety of standards, from organic to bird-friendly to Global GAP.[33] The AJP also certifies workers organizations, and listed six in fall 2019, including the Agricultural Workers Alliance in Canada.

The Portland-based Fair World Project (FWP) has since 2010 aimed to protect the use of the term fair trade, to expand markets for "authentic fair trade," to educate consumers, and to advocate for a "just economy." Its farm-worker justice campaigns include efforts to support farm workers at Washington's Sakuma Farms and opposition to the Trans-Pacific Partnership.[34] The FWP has been critical of Fair Trade USA, especially its plans to develop a fair-trade dairy standard with Chobani on farms in New York State and Idaho.[35]

Fair World released a report in 2016 that found only two of seven labor-certification programs met its criteria, the CIW's FFP and the AJP's Food Justice Certified; it offered qualified support for EFI and Fairtrade International programs (Lindgren, 2016). The report praised the FFP and FJC programs for conducting frequent audits and interviewing many of the workers employed on the audited farms, and criticized labor-certification programs that use professional auditors to interview workers without having worker representatives present during the interviews.

Fair World wants growers to hire workers directly rather than via contractors, but fails to understand that contractors can bring workers to farms even though the workers are considered to be employees of the farm. Simply making the farm operator responsible for all employees working on the farm may eliminate contractors in name but not in practice, since most large farms rely on supervisors who may be akin to contractors to recruit and supervise crews of workers.

---

[32] http://www.agriculturaljusticeproject.org/en/learn-more/?pane=purchase.

[33] http://www.qcsinfo.org.

[34] Sakuma Brothers negotiated a two-year collective bargaining agreement with Familias Unidas por las Justicia in June 2017 covering 600 workers on its 700-acre berry farm. The contract requires workers to join the union or pay agency fees within thirty days of employment. Agitation for the contract began in 2013, after Sakuma fired a worker who complained about low piece rates and poor housing. Many of his Mixtec and Triqui co-workers walked out in protest. Sakuma pays piece-rate wages to its berry harvesters, and aims to have blueberry and strawberry workers earn at least $15 an hour. Under the contract, three test pickers named by the union test-pick a field, and their average pounds picked per hour are used to determine the piece rate per pound to achieve an average $15 an hour. If the entire crew earns less than $15, the piece rate is raised; if the crew averages more than $17, the piece rate cam be reduced. Strawberry fields are picked two or three times a season, blueberry fields two to five times, and blackberries up to twenty times. See https://migration.ucdavis.edu/rmn/more.php?id=2077. Fair World called for a boycott of Sakuma: https://fairworldproject.org/news/press-releases/driscoll-berry-boycott-and-labor-dispute-intensifies/.

[35] https://fairworldproject.org/theres-nothing-fair-about-fair-trade-usas-fair-trade-dairy/

Most fair-trade programs deal with commodities produced in developing countries and exported to industrial countries, such as coffee and cocoa. There have been relatively few rigorous studies of the effects of fair-trade programs on farmers, farm workers, and communities. However, most suggest that farm workers rarely benefit from the fair-trade premiums that are returned to farmers.

Meemken et al., (2019) examined the effects of fair-trade programs on two types of workers employed in the Ivory Coast cocoa sector. Workers employed directly by cocoa cooperatives benefitted because fair-trade auditors monitored their wages and working conditions regularly. However, workers employed by the small cocoa farmers who belonged to the cooperative did not benefit from the fair-trade certification of the cooperative's cocoa, in part because there was no monitoring of conditions for hired workers on coop member farms.

Nunn (2019) reinforced skepticism about fair trade's benefits for hired farm workers. There are 1,400 Fair Trade-certified producer organizations worldwide aiming to help 1.6 million Fair Trade-certified farmers and workers in 73 countries across 19 product categories. Over a third (580,000) of fair-trade-represented farmers and workers are involved in coffee production, followed by 258,000 in tea production and 142,000 in cocoa production.

Fair-trade coffee normally promises farmers a minimum price that aims to cover production costs and include a premium for satisfying labor, environmental, and other standards. Nunn's study of coffee cooperatives in Costa Rica found that they sought fair-trade certification when they had trouble selling their coffee; that is, the cooperatives with the best labor and environmental conditions did not necessarily seek fair-trade certification because they could sell their coffee without the need for fair-trade certification. Cooperatives that had trouble selling their coffee, on the other hand, sought fair-trade certification for marketing purposes. Even after becoming fair-trade certified, much of the coffee sold by fair-trade certified cooperatives did not always receive fair-trade premium prices.

Analysis of the benefits of fair-trade premiums found that coffee farmers, who were a third of those in the Costa Rica coffee sector, benefitted as their average incomes of $2,400 rose by 2 percent. Coffee brokers, who were about 6 percent of people in the coffee sector, lost almost 3 percent of their average $4,000 annual incomes. Hired farm workers, who were over 60 percent of the workers in the sector, saw no change in their $1,600 average incomes. These findings led Nunn to conclude that fair trade raises the overall revenue from coffee and benefits primarily coffee growers, not their hired workers.

A review of efforts to "bring fair trade home" noted the difficulty of translating broad policy goals into concrete objectives on participating farms. For example, the Domestic Fair Trade Association, an umbrella organization for groups focused on issues that range from organic to family farming, has been unable to agree on definitions or methodologies to determine "fair prices and wages" and "fair labor practices" on US farms (Brown and Getz, 2015, 181–2). Fair trade is an appealing concept, creating consumer demand for fair-trade-labeled products, but such products may be too small a share of the market and offer too small a premium price to transform the lives of hired workers involved in the production of fair-trade commodities.

After a half-century of union activities in US agriculture, fewer than 25,000 workers are covered by union contracts, mostly those negotiated by the UFW in California and the FLOC in North Carolina. After several decades of private labor-compliance programs in the US, fewer than 25,000 workers are employed on farms that have been certified by one of the labor certifiers. Some 2.5 million workers are employed for wages each year on US farms, suggesting that less than 2 percent have been affected by union contracts or private labor-certification programs.[36]

The gap between all farm workers and farm workers covered by union agreements or certification is similar abroad. Raynolds (2018, 206) put the number of workers covered by labor-certification programs at less than 13 million of the 400 million workers that the ILO estimates are employed for wages in agriculture each year. The largest programs, the Ethical Trading Initiative that covers 9.8 million workers and the Social Accountability Initiative that covers 2.1 million, operate in both agriculture and industry. The Rainforest Alliance certifies coffee, cocoa, tea and fruit and flower farms with over a million farm workers, but has one of the weakest worker protection programs, since its focus is on protecting ecosystems and promoting sustainability.

Unions want to have a persisting role in the workplace, but the goal of private labor-compliance labeling programs should be to work themselves into irrelevance. When all farmers produce safe food, there is no need for private firms to set food-safety standards and to audit and certify compliant farms. Similarly, when all farms comply with labor laws that protect farm workers, there is no need for private firms to set labor standards and to audit and certify compliant farms.

Farms can always go beyond minimum requirements in food safety and labor protections, and many do so to gain a competitive advantage or because of union or other pressure. If labor-compliance programs succeed in gaining enough participation so that some of their standards become norms for particular commodities and areas, these norms can be incorporated into labor laws, with enforcement by government labor inspectors replacing private audits and certificates.

---

[36] Voltaire quoted an Italian proverb in his *Dictionnaire philosophique* that translates as "the best is the enemy of the good." The basic idea is that achieving absolute perfection may be impossible, so that expending ever more effort can result in diminishing returns.

Food Buyers and Farm Workers

Governments have trouble enforcing labor laws in agriculture because few farm workers complain of violations, making monitoring and enforcement costly. Unions have trouble sustaining bottom-up pressure on wages and working conditions for farm workers because of the revolving-door nature of the labor market. More capable farm workers leave for nonfarm jobs and new entrants to farm work are often vulnerable guest workers who are afraid to antagonize their employer and lose the opportunity to work abroad at higher wages than they could earn at home.

Consumer pressure—directly in the form of boycotts that aim to persuade food buyers and supermarkets to require their farmer-suppliers to abide by labor protocols such as those developed by the CIW, or in the form of fair-trade purchases that create a demand for the products of suppliers who are certified as in compliance with labor and other protocols—affect a very small share of farm commodities, with the possible exception of coffee and cocoa.

Given the limitations surrounding government enforcement, union pressure, and consumer pressure via fair trade, what could improve protections for hired farm workers? The best protection for all workers at all times is full employment, which gives workers the power to say no to jobs that offer substandard wages and working conditions because workers have alternatives. The ILO has long called on governments to assure decent work, meaning jobs for all who want to work that pay a living wage and allow for personal development.[37] However, decent work is an aspirational goal, leaving the question of what to do until all countries are able to offer all of their residents good jobs.

After full employment that empowers workers to say no to bad jobs, the second strongest protection for low-skilled workers is an easy-to-understand minimum wage. Almost all low-skilled workers know whether the minimum wage is $10 an hour or $15 an hour, and most refuse to work for less than the minimum wage. Workers sometimes set their own minimum wage, as when the day laborers who gather outside home-improvement stores agree among themselves that none will work for less than $15 an hour. Some employers do not pay low-skilled workers at least the minimum wage, and some refuse to pay for work performed (wage theft), but most labor-law violations involving farm workers deal with failure to pay overtime wages, improper record-keeping, or violating sometimes complex regulations governing housing, transportation, and work-related benefits.

The PMA–UF Ethical Charter

If full employment and easy-to-understand minimum wages are two good protections that governments can offer to protect farm workers, what more can food

---

[37] http://www.ilo.org/global/topics/decent-work/lang—en/index.htm.

buyers do to ensure labor-law compliance on the farms that supply them with labor-intensive commodities? The Produce Marketing Association (PMA) and the United Fresh Produce Association (United Fresh, UF) in 2018 released an Ethical Charter on Responsible Labor Practices to improve grower compliance with labor laws in the fresh-produce supply chain.[38] The charter asserts that "responsible labor practices are the right thing to do and our success as an industry depends on it."

The charter's goals are grouped in three areas—Respect for Laws at Work, Respect for Professional Conduct, and Respect for Human Rights. Respect for Laws at Work means that "employers shall adhere to the law and regulations as established by the applicable jurisdiction" and provide a "safe, hygienic and sanitary environment at both work-related sites, and at any housing mandated or provided by the employer." Respect includes paying workers for all hours worked and making pay calculations "transparent to workers." The charter notes that "agricultural labor needs vary by season, crop and task, and workers are sometimes needed for shorter or longer time periods than a standard workweek." It calls on employers to "inform workers about their expectations regarding hours of work and gain their [worker] agreement at time of hiring."

The Respect for Professional Conduct goal asserts that "direct communication between management and their employees is the most effective way of resolving workplace issues and concerns." The charter calls on employers to encourage workers to "timely disclose concerns, and [employers] shall prohibit retaliation against anyone who, in good faith, reports concerns." Many firms with "open-door" policies are nonetheless found to have not acted on some employee complaints or allowed retaliation against complaining workers.

Employers are asked to recruit workers ethically, and to "bear the costs of recruitment and placement." However, the charter does not call on governments to require all contractors to be registered, nor for farmers to deal only with registered contractors. California's SB 477 prohibits foreign labor contractors from charging workers recruitment fees after January 1, 2016; requires contractors to fully disclose wages and employment conditions to workers during recruitment; and requires contractors who recruit workers abroad for work in the state to register with the California Labor Commissioner. SB 477 also prohibits employers from using unregistered contractors to obtain workers for their operations.

California has gone further with contractors who bring workers to farms.[39] For example, California in 2003 amended Labor Code (Section 2810) to require that

---

[38] http://www.ethicalcharter.com.

[39] The charter makes farmers who use labor contractors responsible for their activities, but does not distinguish between labor contractors who bring only workers to a farm and custom harvesters who bring workers and equipment to a farm. Under California's Agricultural Labor Relations Act, labor contractors who bring only workers to a farm cannot be employers, so that if a contractor's workers vote to unionize, the contract is with the farm where the workers are employed. However, custom harvesters that bring both workers and equipment to a farm are employers in their own right, and if their workers vote to unionize, the contract is with the custom harvester, not the farm where the

contracts "with a construction, farm labor, garment, janitorial, security guard, or warehouse contractor" to "include funds sufficient to allow the contractor to comply with all applicable local, state, and federal laws or regulations governing the labor or services to be provided." The purpose of the 2003 amendment is to improve labor-law compliance among contractors who often hire immigrant and low-skilled workers to perform work for another entity.[40] Farms that use contractors can protect themselves from charges that they aided contractor non-compliance with labor laws via written contracts that include ten elements, including the name and license number of the contractor, proof that the contractor has workers' compensation insurance, vehicle IDs if contractors transport workers, the number of contractor workers and the wages paid to each contractor employee, and the commission the farmer paid to the contractor.

California's AB 1897, effective January 1, 2015, made it easier to hold farm employers jointly liable for the labor-law violations of contractors who bring workers to their farms. California employers with twenty-five or more workers, including at least six provided by contractors, are by law jointly liable with their contractors to ensure that all workers employed on their farm receive the wages due them and are covered by workers' compensation insurance. Workers who do not receive wages or workers' compensation protections can sue their contractor employer *and* the client employer individually or on a class-action basis. Farmers and other "client employers" can require contractors to verify their compliance with wage and workers' compensation laws, and can require contractors to indemnify them for any fines assessed because of contractor violations.[41]

The ethical charter calls on buyers of produce to "mitigate the impact of their planning and purchasing practices on the commitment" of farm employers to the charter's labor-protection goals. This suggests that buyers should be aware of how the prices they pay for commodities affect the ability of farm employers to satisfy labor laws.[42] Fresh produce is sometimes sold at less than the total cost of production due to oversupply and other factors. However, since farmers may harvest when the market price covers the variable cost of harvesting and packing, but not the fixed or sunk costs already incurred for land and planting, it can be hard to develop and implement "fair prices" for fresh produce.

The Respect for Human Rights goal calls for "freely chosen" work that is "not performed under threat, coercion, force or menace of penalty," that is, there

---

workers happen to be working. Cesar Chavez insisted that labor contractors could not be employers for union purposes, but he failed to anticipate that many of the contractors could buy equipment and become custom harvesters, one reason why it has proven difficult to organize California farm workers (Martin, 2003, ch. 5).

[40] http://law.onecle.com/california/labor/2810.html.
[41] https://migration.ucdavis.edu/rmn/more.php?id=1887.
[42] For example, if a buyer requires extra commodities on short notice, should the buyer pay more to cover the cost of overtime work on the farm?

should be no debt peonage, forced labor, slavery, or other involuntary labor. Employers are to abide by laws governing union organizing and bargaining, including the right of workers to refrain from union activity, and should treat all workers with "dignity and respect." The ILO and the US National Labor Relations Act encourage and promote collective bargaining as the preferred method of determining wages and work-related benefits, although the NLRA also allows employers to campaign against union efforts to organize their workers. Many farm employers lawfully hire labor consultants during union-organizing drives to persuade workers that they are better off without a union.

There should be no discrimination in hiring, promotion, and layoffs, and employers are asked not to hire anyone "below the legal age of employment or younger than 15 where no minimum employment age exists." The authors of the charter emphasized that they wanted to balance the right of children to work legally against the need to protect their mental and physical health and their right to education. In some developing countries, schooling is not readily available to children 14 and older, which creates a dilemma when parent employees want farmers to hire their out-of-school children.

The PMA–UF charter essentially asks employers to comply with applicable labor laws, including to pay all recruitment and placement costs of migrant workers and to monitor the activities of third-party labor contractors who recruit on behalf of the employer. The link between the prices offered by buyers and the ability of farmers to comply with labor laws is vague. The charter does not add any new audits or database of compliant and noncompliant farms, and explicitly asserts that "the charter does not mandate or control how companies make their own business decisions."

The PMA–UF charter sets a low bar in the sense that it calls on farmers and buyers to abide by applicable labor laws, which they should do even without the charter. The charter, prepared by a twenty-person committee of growers and buyers and endorsed by over seventy growers and buyers,[43] did not include labor-law enforcement personnel with experience enforcing labor laws in agriculture, researchers, or members of the public. In this sense, the PMA–UF charter may presage the food-safety pattern, viz., creating an industry-led voluntary compliance program that eventually proved inadequate, followed by a federal law that strengthened the industry's voluntary effort.

If the charter sets a low bar by calling on employers to obey labor laws, many of the labor certification systems set high bars and certify relatively few farmers, so that few farm workers are covered. A fundamental union principle is to "take wages out of competition," meaning that industrial unions such as the United Auto Workers want to organize all auto firms and have them pay the same or similar wages so that no firm has the advantage of lower labor costs.

---

[43] https://www.ethicalcharter.com/endorsers.

The CIW was able to take wages out of competition in the Florida tomato industry on the subset of farms that participate in its FFP, but has been unable to persuade enough buyers to join the program to ensure that the majority of Florida tomatoes are picked under the FFP. The other farm-labor certification programs in the fresh-produce industry have even more limited impacts, confined to particular farms rather than covering entire commodities or areas.

From Food Safety to Labor Compliance

The best hope for monitoring and improving the farm-labor market in the ever-richer countries that increasingly rely on vulnerable hired farm workers may lie with the buyers of fruits and vegetables. Produce buyers and grower associations have developed and enforced a culture of food safety that makes adherence to safety protocols an integral and ongoing priority of farm operators. Buyer pressure may represent the best hope to create a similar culture of respect for farm workers and farm-labor laws.

Fresh fruits and vegetables are perishable, so farmers must "sell or smell" their commodities. A buyer threat not to purchase from farms that fail to comply with labor laws would provide a powerful incentive for farm employers to develop systems to monitor their adherence with labor laws in the same way that farms check the water used to irrigate commodities and the temperatures of those commodities to monitor food safety.

Monitoring adherence to labor laws is more difficult than monitoring compliance with food safety protocols for several reasons. First, payroll records may provide the most efficient monitor of compliance with labor laws, but they may not be accurate. A persisting problem is measuring hours worked, especially if crew supervisors keep records on paper that are entered into computers at the end of work days. Portable electronic record-keeping systems are available to measure the start and stop times of workers as well as their units of work accomplished. Encouraging or requiring their use would make it easier to monitor compliance with minimum wage and similar laws.

Second, fruits and vegetables cannot speak or complain about their safety in the same way that employees can inform labor law agencies of violations, potentially making the detection of labor law violations easier. However, vulnerable workers rarely complain of violations, which can range from harassment to forced labor, and workers may be reluctant to speak to investigators who visit them because they are unsure of the consequences.

There are not enough farm labor investigators, which suggests that the optimal strategy is for enforcement agencies to use statistical and violation data to target commodities, employers, and areas most likely to violate labor laws, and impose penalties on violators that are sufficient to change their behavior and induce adherence among other farm employers. Governments in several countries have mounted enforcement sweeps targeting particular commodities and areas after egregious violations. However, without sustained enforcement, worker turnover and cost-saving pressures may encourage a return to a culture of violations.

The third suggestion acknowledges the realities of farm labor and aims for incremental improvements. Workers should be educated so they know their labor law rights, but worker turnover means that education must be an ongoing rather than a one-time event. The closest analogy to the food safety model to improve labor law compliance would be to require egregious labor law violators to submit certified payroll data for a year or two after significant violations were found so that enforcement agencies have a low-cost way to monitor employer compliance. The submission of certified payroll data is required of US government contractors and, while such data do not ensure compliance, they do provide indicators of non-compliance.

The fourth challenge is responding to worker complaints or charges of labor law violations. Commodities are perishable, and not all complaints and charges are valid. The goal of enforcement is compliance and restitution, and the question for buyers is whether to stop buying from farms that have worker complaints or investigator charges pending. Private labor certification programs normally take a mend-rather-than end approach to remedying labor law violations, such as requiring the employer to discipline or re-educate a supervisor who is not report-ing all hours worked or harassing workers. If buyers refuse to buy from employers with pending complaints, perverse incentives could be created, as with com-plaints that are made in support of demands for wage increases. Similarly, com-petitors may file complaints to reduce supply and put upward pressure on prices.

These considerations suggest that buyers should continue to purchase from farms with complaints and charges until violations are confirmed in judicial pro-ceedings. However, such an approach allows employers to stay in business with-out remedying violations, and could let them resume the same business under a new name, as sometimes happens with labor contractors.

Farmers need workers, and workers need jobs, so refusing to buy produce from farms that violate labor laws penalizes both the employer and the employees who may have endured poor conditions, since they may lose their jobs. For this rea-son, labor laws include penalties for violations that also provide incentives for compliance, such as higher fines for repeat offernders.

This economic reality leads to an mend-rather-than-end policy toward labor law violators; enforcement agencies normally require farmers to remedy viola-tions and pay back wages owed to workers rather than stop production and elim-inate jobs. The optimal strategy for improving compliance is to empower workers by ensuring that they have other job options, so that employers who fail to com-ply cannot find or retain workers. However, enforcement agencies can use data to target enforcement efforts and make investigators more efficient. Food safety investigators confronting a cluster of illnesses among consumers look for one item consumed by all. Similarly, labor violations that could go unchecked in the absence of complaints and investigations may be detected if agencies have a database of violations by commodity, employer, and area to detect patterns and launch investigations.

The alternative to negative pressure on violating employers such as refusal-to-buy is positive encouragement, such as offering certified producers preferential treatment or premium prices. This is the approach of most fair-trade organizations. Growers are willing to pay for certification if the cost of coming into compliance is low and certification gives them preferred access to particular buyers or higher prices.

Compliance with labor laws means knowing employer obligations, developing policies to implement these obligations, and ensuring that managers and supervisors abide by employer obligations on a day-to-day basis. The best way to ensure day-to-day compliance is bottom-up pressure from workers who refuse to work on non-compliant farms, forcing all farms to comply in order to obtain workers. The fact that there may be more workers available to fill seasonal jobs than can be hired, and that most workers have no other job options, means that workers can rarely exert such bottom-up pressure.

Top-down pressure from produce buyers may offer more promise, but it is important to be realistic. Produce buyers know production costs and grower prices, and often send inspectors into fields to check yields, quality, and harvesting practices. Buyers may not want to take the extra responsibility to ensure labor-law compliance, but they are often the best positioned actors in the supply chain to do so.

One last issue is whether labor laws need to be strengthened; that is, are violations of labor laws that protect farm workers isolated or systemic, and what changes to them could induce a culture of compliance? Most farm employers make three points, viz., worker complaints and charges suggest that violations are relatively rare, there is already too much government regulation of agricultural production practices, and seasonal workers who return every year are voting with their feet to accept the wages and working conditions offered. Migrant advocates are convinced that labor-law violations and exploitation are systemic, and that new laws, tougher penalties, and more enforcement are priorities.

There are no data to prove whether farmers or advocates are correct. One violation is one too many. The food safety trajectory may help to clarify the issue. When spinach sickened and killed consumers in September 2006 despite the voluntary food safety standards in place, there was widespread recognition that the entire industry would have to adopt improved food-safety standards to avoid more outbreaks. Growers had an incentive to improve food safety so that they collectively do not suffer when one farmer ships contaminated produce.

Labor-law violations are different in the sense that they affect workers on one farm rather than workers on all farms. It is only when violations become so commonplace that buyers or consumers associate particular commodities with exploited workers that the entire industry can be motivated to act. There were fears of such an industry-wide impact on Mexican produce exports after the *Los Angeles Times* articles in December 2014, which promoted responses that included the PMA–UF ethical charter. There have not been recent similar sector-wide *Harvest of Shame* (1960)-type exposés in US agriculture.

A careful analysis of two decades of data on federal labor law enforcement in agriculture highlights the challenges and opportunities.[44] The US Department of Labor's Wage and Hour Division (WHD), the major federal agency that protects the rights of US farm workers and H-2A guest workers. conducted over 31,000 investigations in US agriculture between FY00 and FY19. Investigators ordered $66 million to be paid in back wages to 154,000 farmworkers, and assessed $56 million in civil money penalties for labor law violations. The number of WHD agricultural investigations fell from over 2,000 a year in the early 2000s to 1,100 a year or about 100 a month in 2020. WHD investigators normally work in teams of two and conduct five to 10 investigations during two-weeks stints visiting farms.

The data show that violations of H-2A regulations are the major source of back wages owed to farm workers and dominate the civil money penalty (CMP) assessments that are levied for labor law violations in agriculture. In FY2000, violations of the Migrant and Seasonal Worker Protection Act generated about $1 million in back wages and CMPs, compared with $100,000 for H-2A violations. In FY19, violations of MSPA led to $4 million in back wages and CMPs, compared with $5 million for H-2A violations.

Second, farm labor contractors (FLCs) account for a disproportionately high share of labor law violations. FLCs employ a seventh of US farm workers, but account for a quarter of all agricultural labor law violations. FLCs are expanding their share of all farm worker employment, and their share of H-2A guest worker employment, suggesting more farm labor law violations.

Third, within a particular commodity or NAICS code, the five percent of investigations that find the most violations account for 50 to 75 percent of all violations in that commodity. For example, the five percent of US crop farms with the most violations accounted for two-thirds of all violations found on all US crop farms, and a similar five-percent of worst violators accounted for two thirds of all violations among FLCs. Inducing compliance among bad apples, or putting them out of business, could decrease the total number of violations by two thirds or more.

The farm labor market is analogous to a room whose size and shape are unclear. There are bad actor employers who violate labor laws and are not detected because

---

[44] The data analysis is included in blogs at: https://migration.ucdavis.edu/rmn/blog/

their vulnerable workers do not complain. When these employers are detected or exposed, it may seem that farm labor law violations are widespread and systemic, and that major changes are required to farm labor laws and their enforcement. However, a third of farm employers who were investigated in the US over the past 15 years were found to be in full compliance with federal labor laws. The worst violators, fewer than five percent of all employers investigated, account for most of the violations found. If the buyers of farm commodities can act as first line of defense against bad apple labor law violators, as they do to ensure food safety, they can help to build a food system that protects and respects farm workers.

Epilogue

Much of the world's extreme poverty is in rural and agricultural areas. Many young people living on farms in developing countries realize that they will never be able to climb the economic ladder and escape poverty if they farm as their parents and grandparents did. The bright lights of cities attract rural youth to urban areas at home and abroad, meaning that millions of people change both their residence from rural to urban and their occupation from farm to nonfarm each year. The United Nations Development Programme (UNDP) estimated that there were four internal migrants who moved from agricultural to urban areas within their countries for each international migrant who left her country of birth and remained abroad a year or more (UNDP, 2009).

Many countries that are richer than their neighbors rely on workers from poorer countries to fill especially seasonal farm jobs, so that agriculture often serves as a port of entry into richer countries for rural migrants from poorer countries. Some of these migrants settle abroad, risking the transfer of rural poverty from one country to another if migrant farm workers are unable to climb the job and economic ladder of destination countries.

The farm-labor prosperity paradox highlights the fact that the smaller share of all workers employed in the agricultural sector of richer countries includes hired workers who do more of the country's farm work. The fewer and larger farms that dominate farm production depend on hired workers who are increasingly vulnerable. Most are domestic workers unable to find nonfarm jobs and foreigners with often restricted work and residence rights.

Economist Lloyd Fisher, examining California's farm-labor market in the early 1950s, was pessimistic that public policy could improve conditions for seasonal farm workers. He concluded that "the brightest hope for the welfare of seasonal agricultural workers lies in the elimination of the jobs upon which they now depend, and the development of programs for the transfer of workers from agricultural to industrial labor markets" (Fisher, 1953, 148). Fisher believed that hastening the movement of people out of agriculture would spur mechanization to maintain food production, while improved health care and education for migrant farm-worker children would break the cycle of poverty.

The plight of farm workers has attracted private and public attention for decades, but few durable solutions. Unions find it difficult to organize farm workers and negotiate wage increases even with favorable legislation, while the NGOs that develop fair-trade agreements with produce buyers and engage in top-down

The Prosperity Paradox: Fewer and More Vulnerable Farm Workers. Philip Martin, Oxford University Press (2021).
© Philip Martin.
DOI: 10.1093/oso/9780198867845.001.0001

efforts to help farm workers generally require foundation or other outside support to sustain their limited footprint.

Government policies are often contradictory. Most governments in rich countries have policies that aim to preserve family farms, in part by exempting them from labor laws in the belief that such farms cannot cope with complex farm-labor laws. But the desire to preserve family farms obscures the fact that most farm workers are employed on large farms, many of which are just as prepared as nonfarm employers to comply with labor laws. Governments sometimes try to mitigate the low incomes of farm workers by supporting special programs that provide education and other services for farm worker children and training for youth and adults who want to achieve higher nonfarm incomes. The labor-law exemptions do not do much to preserve family farms, and special farm-worker assistance programs reach only a small share of farm workers.

US farmers became accustomed to the arrival of newcomers from rural Mexico over the past three decades. The Mexico–US migration hump that began in the mid-1980s, peaked in 2000, and ended with the 2008–9 recession may usher in a new era in farm labor. Rising farm labor costs are forcing employers to adjust to an aging and settled but still largely unauthorized Mexican-born farm workforce.

Employer adjustments to rising wages can be grouped into the 4-S strategies of satisfying current workers to reduce turnover, stretching workers with productivity-improving changes such as conveyor belts in fields to reduce walking and carrying, substituting machines for workers where possible, and supplementing the current workforce with guest workers. Some growers and produce buyers have the import option, producing abroad or buying labor-intensive commodities from lower-wage countries.

After three decades of farm workers being readily available at half of average US nonfarm wages, farm-labor costs are rising faster than labor costs in nonfarm industries due to fewer unauthorized newcomers, rising state minimum wages, requirements to pay overtime to farm workers on the same basis as nonfarm employers, and health-insurance mandates that do not exempt agriculture. Rising labor costs are encouraging farmers to consider new investments to cope with more costly farm labor.

The question is where to invest. Satisfying and stretching workers are short-term strategies that delay rather than solve labor availability issues, since workers tend to drift out of the most difficult hand-harvesting jobs in their forties. Longer term, the choices for farmers who operate only in rich countries center on substitution versus supplement, that is, investing in labor-saving mechanization versus building housing for guest workers. Many growers are investing in machines *and* building housing for guest workers, while some are expanding production abroad and shrinking the production of labor-intensive commodities at home.

The production of farm commodities in all rich countries is concentrating on fewer and larger farms that depend on hired workers. The question is whether these hired workers will be better-educated local workers who operate machines and are paid high wages or local workers with little education and similar low-skilled workers from abroad. The farm labor prosperity paradox raises questions. Will a more mechanized agriculture reverse the adage that the best way to help seasonal farm workers to achieve higher incomes is to help them to escape from agriculture? Will the fewer and better educated workers who operate machines in a more mechanized agriculture become career farm workers? Alternatively, will agriculture continue to offer entry-level jobs to workers who have few other job options, encouraging experienced farm workers to change occupations for upward mobility rather than climbing the farming job ladder?

References

Abella, Manolo. 1999. *Sending Workers Abroad*. International Labor Office, Geneva. http://www.ilo.org/global/publications/ilo-bookstore/order-online/books/WCMS_PUBL_9221085252_EN/lang—en/index.htm.

Andrews, James. 2013. "Jack in the Box and the Decline of E. coli." Food Safety News. http://www.foodsafetynews.com/2013/02/jack-in-the-box-and-the-decline-of-e-coli/.

Basok, Tanya. 2007. "Canada's Temporary Migration Program: A Model Despite Flaws." Migration Policy Institute. http://www.justicia4migrantworkers.org/bc/pdf/SAWP-A_Model_Despite_Flaws.pdf.

Baum, Herbert. 2005. "Quest for the Perfect Strawberry; A Case Study of the California Strawberry Commission and the Strawberry Industry: A Descriptive Model for Marketing Order Evaluation." iUniverse. http://www.strawberries-for-strawberry-lovers.com/quest-for-the-perfect-strawberry-book-review.html.

Beckman, Jayson 2017. "The Global Landscape of Agricultural Trade, 1995–2014." USDA-ERS. EIB-181 http://www.ers.usda.gov/webdocs/publications/85626/eib-181.pdf?v=0.

Böhning, Roger. 1996. "Employing Foreign Workers. A manual on policies and procedures of special interest to middle- and low-income countries." International Labor Office. http://www.ilo.org/global/publications/ilo-bookstore/order-online/books/WCMS_PUBL_9221094537_EN/lang--en/index.htm.

Bonatti, Luigi. 2019. "Is Immigration Necessary for Italy? Is it Desirable?" EconPol Policy Report 17. http://www.econpol.eu/publications/policy_report_17?econNL201912.

Bovay, John, Peyton Ferrier, and Chen Zhen. 2018. "Estimated Costs for Fruit and Vegetable Producers To Comply With the Food Safety Modernization Act's Produce Rule." USDA ERS EIB 195. https://ageconsearch.umn.edu/record/276220/.

Brown, Sandy and Christy Getz. 2015. *Domestic fair trade in the US. Chapter 10 in Laura Reynolds and Elizabeth Bennett. Handbook of Research on Fair Trade*. Elgar. http://www.elgaronline.com/view/9781783474608.xml.

Brudney, James. 2016. "Decent Labor Standards in Corporate Supply Chains, the Immokalee Workers Model," pp. 351–76, in Joanna Howe, Rosemary Owens, eds., *Temporary Labour Migration in the Global Era: The Regulatory Challenges*. Hart. http://www.bloomsbury.com/au/temporary-labour-migration-in-the-global-era-9781509906291/.

Burton, Alvin W., and Irwin B. Telpov, eds. 2003. *Farm Labor: 21st Century Issues and Challenges* Nova. http://www.novapublishers.org/catalog/product_info.php?products_id=6198.

CAHRC. 2009. "Labour market information on recruitment and retention in primary agriculture."https://cahrc-ccrha.ca/sites/default/files/files/publications/LMI-Recruitment-Retention/LMI%20Executive%20Summary.pdf.

Calvin, Linda. 2007. "Outbreak Linked to Spinach Forces Reassessment of Food Safety Practices." Amber Waves. June, 2007. http://www.ers.usda.gov/amber-waves/2007-june/outbreak-linked-to-spinach-forces-reassessment-of-food-safety-practices.aspx.

Calvin, L., Jensen, H., Klonsky, K., and Cook, R. 2017. "Food Safety Practices and Costs Under the California Leafy Greens Marketing Agreement." Washington DC: U.S. Department of Agriculture, Economic Research Service, Economic Information Bulletin No. 173, June. Retrieved from http://www.ers.usda.gov/webdocs/publications/83771/eib-173. pdf?v=42893.

Calvin, Linda, and Philip Martin. 2010. "The US Produce Industry and Labor: Facing the Future in a Global Economy." USDA. Economic Research Report No. (ERR-106). November. http://www.ers.usda.gov/Publications/ERR106/.

Canada Agriculture and Agrifood. 2016. "An Overview of the Canadian Agriculture and Agri-Food System 2016." https://foodsecurecanada.org/sites/foodsecurecanada.org/files/aafcaac-an_overview_of_the_canadian_agriculture_and_agri-food_system_2016.pdf.

Catholic Relief Services. 2016. "Farmworker Protections and Labor Conditions in Brazil's Coffee Sector." http://www.crs.org/our-work-overseas/research-publications/farmworker-protections-and-labor-conditions-brazil's-coffee.

Cavanna, Paola. 2020. "Forced Labour and Other Forms of Labour Exploitation in the Italian Agri-Food Sector: Strong Laws, Weak Protection for Migrant Workers: Exploitation and Legal Protection of Migrant Workers." https://link.springer.com/chapter/10.1007%2F978-3-319-93979-7_4.

CAW (Commission on Agricultural Workers). 1992. "Report of the Commission on Agricultural Workers." http://onlinebooks.library.upenn.edu/webbin/book/lookupname?key=United%20States.%20Commission%20on%20Agricultural%20Workers

Charlton, Diane J. Edward Taylor, Stavros Vougioukas, and Zachariah Rutledge. 2019. "Innovations for a Shrinking Agricultural Workforce." Choices. http://www.choices-magazine.org/choices-magazine/submitted-articles/innovations-for-a-shrinking-agricultural-workforce.

Choudry, Aziz and Adrian Smith, eds. 2016. *Unfree Labor? Struggles of Migrant and Immigrant Workers in Canada*. PM Press. https://books.google.com/books?hl=en&lr=&id=O9enDAAAQBAJ&oi=fnd&pg=PT8&dq=hired+workers+in+canada+agriculture&ots=cYEDdqCgag&sig=X3t7kJ2qwqcA3i4sTBGhG3FnovI#v=onepage&q&f=false.

Collart, A. J. 2016. "The Food Safety Modernization Act and the Marketing of Fresh Produce. Choices. Quarter 1." http://www.choicesmagazine.org/choices-magazine/theme-articles/producer-impacts-of-the-food-safety-modernization-act/the-food-safety-modernization-act-and-the-marketing-of-fresh-produce.

Conrad, Alfred, and John Meyer. 1958. "The economics of slavery in the ante bellum South." *Journal of Political Economy*. Vol 66. No 2, 95–130. http://www.j-bradford delong.net/Teaching_Folder/Econ_210a_f99/Readings/Conrad_Meyer.pdf.

Consterdine, Erica, and Sahizer Samuk. 2015. "Closing the seasonal agricultural workers scheme: a triple loss." Sussex Centre for Migration Research Working Paper. http://sro.sussex.ac.uk/id/eprint/58525/.

Cook, Roberta. 2011. "Fundamental Forces Affecting the US Fresh Berry and Lettuce/Leafy Green Subsectors." *Choices*. Vol 26. No 4. http://ageconsearch.umn.edu/record/120009.

Cook, Roberta. 2017. "Global Fresh Berry Trends." November 16. Amsterdam Produce Show.

Cook, Roberta, and Linda Calvin. 2005. "Greenhouse Tomatoes Change the Dynamics of the North American Fresh Tomato Industry." USDA ERS Report 2. April. ucce.ucdavis.edu/files/datastore/234-447.pdf.

Corrado, Alessandra, Francesco Saverio Caruso, Martina Lo Cascio, Michele Nori, Letizia Palumbo, and Anna Triandafyllidou. 2018. "Is Italian agriculture a 'pull factor' for irregular migration—and, if so, why?" EUI. http://cadmus.eui.eu/handle/1814/60950.

Corrado, Alessandra, Carlos de Castro, and Domenico Perrotta, eds. 2016. *Migration and Agriculture Mobility and change in the Mediterranean area.* Routledge. http://www.routledge.com/Migration-and-Agriculture-Mobility-and-change-in-the-Mediterranean-area/Corrado-de-Castro-Perrotta/p/book/9781138962231.

Correa-Cabrera, Guadalupe, and Arthur Sanders Montandon. 2018. "Arguments to Reform Mexico's Anti-Trafficking Legislation." Wilson Center. March 23. http://www.wilsoncenter.org/publication/arguments-to-reform-mexicos-anti-trafficking-legislation-0.

Crandall, Philip, Corliss O'Bryan, Jay Neal, and John Delery. 2015. "Best Practices for Making Long-Term Changes in Behavior". *Food Safety Magazine.* June–July, 2015. http://www.foodsafetymagazine.com/magazine-archive1/junejuly-2015/best-practices-for-making-long-term-changes-in-behavior/.

Crespi, John, and Stéphan Marette. 2001. How Should Food Safety Certification be Financed? American Journal of Agricultural Economics." Vol. 83, issue 4, 852–61. https://econpapers.repec.org/article/oupajagec/v_3a83_3ay_3a2001_3ai_3a4_3ap_3a852-861.htm.

Crowe, Samuel, Barbara Mahon, Antonio Vieira, and Hannah Gould. 2015. "Vital Signs: Multistate Foodborne Outbreaks—United States, 2010–2014." *Morbidity and Mortality Weekly Report (MMWR).* Vol 64. No. 43. 1221–5. November 6, 2015. http://www.cdc.gov/mmwr/preview/mmwrhtml/mm6443a4.htm?s_cid=mm6443a4_w.

CRS. 2019. "Foodborne Illnesses and Outbreaks from Fresh Produce." February 4, 2019. https://fas.org/sgp/crs/misc/IF11092.pdf.

Curtain, Richard, Matthew Dornan, Stephen Howes, and Henry Sherrell. 2018. "Pacific seasonal workers: Learning from the contrasting temporary migration outcomes in Australian and New Zealand horticulture." *Asia & the Pacific Policy Studies* Volume 5, Issue 3. https://onlinelibrary.wiley.com/doi/full/10.1002/app5.261.

Daglia Calil, Yuri Clements, and Luis Ribera. 2019. "Brazil's Agricultural Production and Its Potential as Global Food Supplier". Choices. http://www.choicesmagazine.org/choices-magazine/theme-articles/the-agricultural-production-potential-of-latin-american-implications-for-global-food-supply-and-trade/brazils-agricultural-production-and-its-potential-as-global-food-supplier.

de Grammont, Hubert, and Sara Lara. 2004. *Encuesta a hogares de jornaleros migrantes en regiones hortícolas de México: Sinaloa, Sonora, Baja California Sur y Jalisco.* Universidad Nacional Autónoma de México. https://books.google.com/books/about/Encuesta_a_hogares_de_jornaleros_migrant.html?id=8fR0lywWHdQC.

de Grammont, Hubert, and Sara Lara. 2010. "Productive Restructuring and 'Standardization' in Mexican Horticulture. Consequences for Labour." Journal of Agrarian Change. Vol 10. No 2. April, 2010, 228–50. http://onlinelibrary.wiley.com/doi/10.1111/j.1471-0366.2009.00246.x/abstract.

Diagnóstico Del Programa de Atención a Jornaleros Agrícolas. 2010. Secretaría De Desarrollo Social (SEDESOL). May, 2010. http://www.inapam.gob.mx/work/models/SEDESOL/Resource/1778/3/images/Diagnostico_PAJA.pdf.

Dias-Abey, Manoj. 2018. "Justice on Our Fields: Can Alt-Labor Organizations Improve Migrant Farm Workers' Conditions." Harvard. https://heinonline.org/HOL/LandingPage?handle=hein.journals/hcrcl53&div=8&id=&page=.

Dufty, Niki, Peter Martin, and Shiji Zhao. 2019. "Demand for farm workers. ABARES farm survey results 2018." ABARES Report 19.10. https://apo.org.au/sites/default/files/resource-files/2019/10/apo-nid261741-1390166.pdf.

Ehrlich, Sean. 2018. *The Politics of Fair Trade: Moving Beyond Free Trade and Protection*. Oxford. https://global.oup.com/academic/product/the-politics-of-fair-trade-9780199337644?cc=us&lang=en&.

Escobar, Agustin, Philip Martin, and Omar Starbridis. 2019. "Farm Labor and Mexico's Export Produce Industry." Wilson Center. http://www.wilsoncenter.org/publication/farm-labor-and-mexicos-export-produce-industry.

Estabrook, Barry. 2011. *Tomatoland: How Modern Industrial Agriculture Destroyed Our Most Alluring Fruit*. Andrews McMeel. https://publishing.andrewsmcmeel.com/catalog/detail?sku=9781449401092.

EU. 2017. "CAP Explained." https://publications.europa.eu/en/publication-detail/-/publication/541f0184-759e-11e7-b2f2-01aa75ed71a1.

Eurostat. 2013. "How many people work in agriculture in the European Union." https://ec.europa.eu/agriculture/sites/agriculture/files/rural-area-economics/briefs/pdf/08_en.pdf

Eurostat. 2019. "European Union: agriculture statistical factsheet." https://ec.europa.eu/info/food-farming-fisheries/farming/facts-and-figures/markets/production/production-country/statistical-factsheets.

Fair Food Program. 2014. "Annual Report." http://fairfoodstandards.org/reports.html.

Feingold, David. 2010. "Trafficking in Numbers. The Social Construction of Human Trafficking Data." In Peter Andreas and Kelly M. Greenhill, eds. *Sex, Drugs, and Body Counts: The Politics of Numbers in Global Crime and Conflict*. Ithaca, NY: Cornell University Press.

Findeis, J., A. Vandeman, J. Larson, and J. Runyon, eds. 2002. "The Dynamics of Hired Farm Labor: Constraints and Community Responses." CABI. https://www.cabi.org/bookshop/book/9780851996035.

Fine, Janice, and Gregory Lyon. 2017. "Segmentation and the Role of Labor Standards Enforcement in Immigration Reform." *Journal on Migration and Human Security*. https://journals.sagepub.com/doi/pdf/10.1177/233150241700500211.

Fisher, Lloyd. 1953. *The Harvest Labor Market in California*. Harvard. https://books.google.com/books?id=mUAKYAAACAAJ&dq=The+Harvest+Labor+Market+in+California&hl=en&newbks=1&newbks_redir=0&sa=X&ved=2ahUKEwjl1dLpj_TlAhUJnZ4KHTE7BqcQ6AEwAXoECAEQAg.

Florida Tomato Committee. 2014. Annual Report. https://www.floridatomatoes.org/grower-resources/.

FPAA. Fresh Produce Association of the Americas. 2015–16 Annual Report. http://www.freshfrommexico.com/pdf/FPAA_Annual_Report_2015-2016_CORRECTED.compressed.pdf.

Friedland, William. 1994. "The Global Fresh Fruit and Vegetable System," in McMichael, Philip., ed. *The Global Restructuring of Agro-food Systems*. Cornell. https://www.cornellpress.cornell.edu/book-listing/?q=The+Global+Restructuring+of+Agro-food+Systems.

Fuller, Varden. 1991. "Hired Hands in California's Fields." Special Report no. 91-1. Giannini Foundation. https://giannini.ucop.edu/publications/historic/special-reports/.

Gabriel, Christina, and Laura Macdonald. 2017. "After the International Organization for Migration: recruitment of Guatemalan temporary agricultural workers to Canada." *International Migration*. Vol 44. No 10. http://www.tandfonline.com/doi/abs/10.1080/1369183X.2017.1354062.

Gale, Jr., H. Frederick, Linda Foreman, and Thomas Capehart. 2000. "Tobacco and the Economy: Farms, Jobs, and Communities." USDA-ERS-ARE 789. https://www.ers.usda.gov/webdocs/publications/41156/14942_aer789a_1_.pdf?v=0.

Galindo, Jose. 2019. "Some aspects on the failure of agrarian reforms in Mexico and other Latin American countries." *Forum for Development Studies*. Vol 46. No 1. http://www. tandfonline.com/doi/abs/10.1080/08039410.2018.1519516.

Gallegos, Zorayda. 2018. "Campo Mexicano." El Pais. https://elpais.com/especiales/2018/campo-mexicano/.

Gantz, David. 2019. "The US-Mexico Trade Relationship under AMLO. Challenges and Opportunities." Baker Institute. https://papers.ssrn.com/sol3/papers.cfm?abstract_id= 3377591.

GAO (Government Accountability Office). 2017. "A National Strategy Is Needed to Address Fragmentation in Federal Oversight." January 13, 2017. http://www.gao.gov/products/GAO-17-74.

Garcia, Junior, and Maia, Alexandre. 2019. "Employment and forms of occupation in rural Brazil: from minifundio-latifundio to regulated rural labour market," in Antonio M. Buainain, Rodrigo Lanna, Zander Navarro, eds. 2019. *Agricultural Development in Brazil The Rise of a Global Agro-food Power*. Routledge. http://www. routledge.com/Agricultural-Development-in-Brazil-The-Rise-of-a-Global-Agro-food-Power/Buainain-Lanna-Navarro/p/book/9781138492776.

Gibson, John, and David McKenzie. 2014. "Development through Seasonal Worker Programs. The Case of New Zealand's RSE Program." Policy Research Working Paper No. 6762. World Bank. https://openknowledge.worldbank.org/handle/10986/18356.

Gibson, John, David McKenzie, and Halahingano Rohorua,. 2008. "How pro-poor is the selection of seasonal migrant workers from Tonga under New Zealand's recognized seasonal employer program?" Policy Research Working Paper Series 4698. World Bank. https://ideas.repec.org/p/wbk/wbrwps/4698.html.

Gollin, Douglas. 2014. "The Lewis model: A 60-year retrospective." *Journal of Economic Perspectives*. Vol. 28, No. 3. https://www.aeaweb.org/articles?id=10.1257/jep.28.3.71.

Gonzalez, Humberto. 2019. "What socioeconomic impacts did 35 years of export agriculture have in Mexico?" *Journal of Agrarian Change*. Volume 20, Issue 1. https://onlinelibrary.wiley.com/doi/full/10.1111/joac.12343.

Gonzalez, Humberto, and Alejandro Macias. 2017. "Agrifood Vulnerability and Neoliberal Economic Policies in Mexico." *Review of Agrarian Studies*. Vol. 7, no. 1, January–June, 2017. https://ideas.repec.org/a/fas/journl/v7y2017i1p72-106.html.

Gordon, Jennifer. 2016. "Roles for Workers and Unions in Regulating Labor Recruitment in Mexico," pp 329–50 in Joanna Howe, Rosemary Owens, eds. *Temporary Labour Migration in the Global Era: The Regulatory Challenges*. Hart. http://www.bloomsbury. com/au/temporary-labour-migration-in-the-global-era-9781509906291/.

Guthman, Julie. 2019. *Pathogens, Chemicals, and the Fragile Future of the Strawberry Industry*. University of California Press. https://www.ucpress.edu/book/9780520305281/wilted.

Hansen-Kuhn, Karen. 2019. "Bold farm plans in Mexico offer a ray of hope in 2019." ITAP. https://www.iatp.org/blog/201903/bold-farm-plans-mexico-offer-ray-hope-2019.

Haque, Tobias, and Truman Packard. 2014. "Well-being from work in the Pacific island countries." World Bank. WP 87894. http://documents.worldbank.org/curated/en/2014/01/19485962/well-being-work-pacific-island-countries.

Helfer, Laurence R. 2019. "The ILO at 100: Institutional Innovation in an Era of Populism." Duke Law School Public Law & Legal Theory Series No. 2019-57. SSRN. https://ssrn. com/abstract=3433820.

Hennebry, Jenna. 2012. "Permanently Temporary? Agricultural Migrant Workers and Their Integration in Canada." IRPP. No. 26. http://irpp.org/research-studies/study-no26/.

Hennebry, Jenna, and Kerry Preibisch. 2012. "A model for managed migration? Re-examining best practices in Canada's seasonal agricultural worker program." *International Migration*. Vol 50, S319–40. February,2012. http://onlinelibrary.wiley.com/ doi/10.1111/j.1468–2435.2009.00598.x/abstract;jsessionid=EAC124BEAB8CFC5F2E4C EF6DC8E76CE1.f02t04?userIsAuthenticated=false&deniedAccessCustomisedMessage.

Hertz, Tom, and Steven Zahniser. 2013. "Is There A Farm Labor Shortage?" *American Journal of Agricultural Economics*, Volume 95, Issue 2, 476–81. https://academic.oup. com/ajae/article/95/2/476/71148.

Hufbauer, Gary and Jeffrey Schott. 2005. *NAFTA Revisited: Achievements and Challenges.* Peterson Institute. https://www.piie.com/bookstore/nafta-revisited-achievements-and-challenges.

ILO. 2012. "International Labour Organization Global Estimate of Forced Labor. Results and Methodology." http://www.ilo.org/global/topics/forced-labour/publications/ WCMS_182004/lang--en/index.htm.

ILO. 2015. "Submission 31 to the Australian Federal Parliament Joint Standing Committee on Migration." http://www.aph.gov.au/Parliamentary_Business/Committees/Joint/ Migration/Seasonal_Worker_Programme/Submissions.

ILO. 2018a. "Social protection for migrant workers in ASEAN: Developments, challenges, and prospects." http://www.ilo.org/asia/media-centre/news/WCMS_655163/lang--en/ index.htm.

ILO. 2018b. "Note on Public Employment Services in Mexico." http://www.ilo.org/ emppolicy/units/country-employment-policy-unit-empcepol/WCMS_618066/lang— en/index.htm.

ILO. 2019a. "World Employment and Social Outlook.". http://www.ilo.org/wcmsp5/groups/ public/---dgreports/---dcomm/---publ/documents/publication/wcms_670542.pdf.

ILO. 2019b. Global Commission on the Future of Work. "Work for a brighter future." http://www.ilo.org/global/topics/future-of-work/lang—en/index.htm.

IMF. 2018. "Formality and Equity—Labor Market Challenges in Mexico." IMF Report 18/308. http://www.imf.org/en/Publications/CR/Issues/2018/11/07/Mexico-Selected-Issues-46344.

INEGI. 2016. "Estadisticas del Dia del Trabajador Agricola." May 15, 2016. http://www. inegi.org.mx/saladeprensa/aproposito/2016/agricola2016_0.pdf.

International Justice Mission and Issara Institute. 2017. "Labor Trafficking in the Thai fishing industry." Summary Report. https://www.ijm.org/.

Kitroeff, Natalie, and Geoffrey Mohan. 2017. "Wages rise on California farms. Americans still don't want the job." *Los Angeles Times.* March 17, 2017. http://www.latimes.com/ projects/la-fi-farms-immigration/.

Levy, Santiago. 2018. "Under-Rewarded Efforts: The Elusive Quest for Prosperity in Mexico." IADB. https://publications.iadb.org/handle/11319/8971.

Lewis, W. Arthur. 1954. "Economic Development with Unlimited Supplies of Labour." *The Manchester School.* Vol. 22, Issue 2: 139–91. https://onlinelibrary.wiley.com/doi/ abs/10.1111/j.1467–9957.1954.tb00021.x.

Lindgren, Kerstin, 2016. "Justice in the Fields: A report on the Role of Farmworker Justice." https://fairworldproject.org/wp-content/uploads/2016/10/Justice-In-The-Fields-Report.pdf.

Lurtz, Casey Marina. 2019. *From the Grounds Up: Building an Export Economy in Southern Mexico.* Stanford. https://www.sup.org/books/title/?id=27693.

Luthria, Manjula. 2008. "Seasonal migration for development? Evaluating New Zealand's RSE Program." *Pacific Economic Bulletin* 23(3): 165–70. http://siteresources.worldbank. org/INTPACIFICISLANDS/Resources/SeasonalMigrationManjula.pdf.

MacDonald, James, Robert Hoppe, and Doris Newton. 2018. "Three Decades of Consolidation in US Agriculture." USDA, ERS, EIB-189. https://www.ers.usda.gov/publications/pub-details/?pubid=88056.

Mahdavi, Pardis. 2018. "Human Trafficking or Voluntary Migration?" In Gracia Liu-Farrer and Brenda Yeoh, eds. *Routledge Handbook of Asian Migrations*. London: Routledge.

Mann, Nicola-Anne. 2014. "Intensive Berry Production Using Greenhouses, Substrates and Hydroponics. Is this the Way Forward?" Nuffield International. http://nuffieldinternational.org/live/Reports.

Markon, Jerry. 2007. "Human Trafficking Evokes Outrage, Little Evidence." *Washington Post*, September 23, 2007. http://www.washingtonpost.com/wp-dyn/content/article/2007/09/22/AR2007092201401_pf.html.

Marosi, Richard. 2014. "Hardship on Mexico's farms, a bounty for U.S. tables." *Los Angeles Times*, December 7–14, 2014. http://graphics.latimes.com/product-of-mexico-camps/.

Marosi, Richard. 2016. "A year after a violent and costly strike, Baja farm laborers see uneven gains." *Los Angeles Times*. May 21, 2016. https://www.latimes.com/world/mexico-americas/la-me-baja-farm-labor-snap-story.html.

Marquis, Susan. 2017. *I Am Not a Tractor! How Florida Farmworkers Took on the Fast Food Giants and Won*. Cornell. http://www.cornellpress.cornell.edu/book/9781501713088/i-am-not-a-tractor/.

Martin, Philip. 1994. "Good intentions gone awry: IRCA and US agriculture." *The Annals of the Academy of Political and Social Science*, Vol 534: 44–57. July 1994. http://www.jstor.org/stable/1048497.

Martin, Philip. 2003. *Promise Unfulfilled: Unions, Immigration, and Farm Workers*. Ithaca. Cornell University Press. www.cornellpress.cornell.edu/book/?GCOI=80140100792940&CFID=9652803&CFTOKEN=f1155d49f162eed5-5AABB7F9-C29B-B0E5-30D66D992EBABD0B&jsessionid=84301cb0683d5770849b171b6b4e272f564cTR

Martin, Philip. 2009. *Importing Poverty? Immigration and the Changing Face of Rural America*. Yale University Press. https://yalebooks.yale.edu/book/9780300209761/importing-poverty.

Martin, Philip, 2014. "The H-2A Program; Evolution, Impacts, and Outlook," in David Griffith, ed. *(Mis)managing Migration. Guestworkers' Experiences with North American Labor Market*, ch. 2, pp. 33–62. SAR Press. https://sarweb.org/mismanaging-migration/.

Martin, Philip. 2016. "Labor Compliance in Fresh Produce: Lessons from Food Safety." *Choices*, Quarter 3. http://www.choicesmagazine.org/choices-magazine/submitted-articles/labor-compliance-in-fresh-produce--lessons-from-food-safety.

Martin, Philip. 2017a. *Merchants of Labor: Recruiters and International Labor Migration*. Oxford University Press. https://global.oup.com/academic/product/merchants-of-labor-9780198808022?cc=us&lang=en&.

Martin, Philip. 2017b. "Immigration and Farm Labor. Challenges and Issues." Giannini Foundation. https://s.giannini.ucop.edu/uploads/giannini_public/dd/d9/ddd90bf0-2bf0-41ea-bc29-28c5e4e9b049/immigration_and_farm_labor_-_philip_martin.pdf?.

Martin, Philip. 2019. "The Role of the H-2A Program in California Agriculture." *Choices*. Quarter 1. http://www.choicesmagazine.org/choices-magazine/theme-articles/the-role-of-guest-workers-in-us-agriculture/the-role-of-the-h-2a-program-in-california-agriculture.

Martin, Philip, Brandon Hooker, and Marc Stockton. 2018. "Employment and earnings of California farm workers in 2015." *California Agriculture*. Vol 72. No 2. http://calag.ucanr.edu/archive/?article=ca.2017a0043.

Martin, Philip, and David Martin. 1994. *The Endless Quest: Helping America's Farm Workers*. Westview Press. http://www.amazon.com/The-Endless-Quest-Helping-Americas/dp/0813317681.

Meemkem, Eva-Marie, Jorge Sellare, Christophe N. Kouame, and Matin Qaim. 2019. "Effects of Fairtrade on the livelihoods of poor rural workers." *Nature Sustainability* 2, 635–42. https://www.nature.com/articles/s41893-019-0311-.

Mendoza, Cristobal. no date. "Immigrant Employment in Spanish Farming: The Case of the Girona Fruit Sector." Changing Face. https://migration.ucdavis.edu/cf/more. php?id=40.

Migration News. 1995. "Pros and Cons of Guest Workers." Vol 2. No 7. https://migration. ucdavis.edu/mn/more.php?id=686.

Minor, Travis, Gerard Hawkes, Edward W. Mclaughlin, Kristen Park, and Linda Calvin. 2019. "Food Safety Requirements for Produce Growers: Retailer Demands and the Food Safety Modernization Act." USDA-ERS-EIB 206. http://www.ers.usda.gov/publications/ pub-details/?pubid=92760.

Mize, Ronald. 2019. "The State Management of Guest Workers: The Decline of the Bracero Program, the Rise of Temporary Worker Visas," in Marinari, Maddalena, Madeline Hsu, and María Cristina García, eds. *A Nation of Immigrants Reconsidered: US Society in an Age of Restriction, 1924–1965*, 123–43. University of Illinois Press. http://www.jstor.org/ stable/10.5406/j.ctv9b2wjb.

Mohan, Geoffrey. 2017. "As California's labor shortage grows, farmers race to replace workers with robots." *Los Angeles Times*. July 21, 2017. https://www.latimes.com/projects/ la-fi-farm-mechanization/.

Mortimore, Sara, William Sperber, and Carol Anne Wallace. 2019. *Food Safety for the 21st Century: Managing HACCP and Food Safety throughout the Global Supply Chain*. Wiley. https://onlinelibrary.wiley.com/doi/book/10.1002/9781444328653.

Nattrass, Nicoli, and Jeremy Seekings. 2019. *Inclusive Dualism: Labour-Intensive Development, Decent Work, and Surplus Labour in Southern Africa*. Oxford. https:// global.oup.com/academic/product/inclusive-dualism-9780198841463?cc= us&lang=en&.

New Zealand Government Submission. 2015. Submission 10 to the Australian Federal Parliament Joint Standing Committee on Migration. July 2015. www.aph.gov.au/ Parliamentary_Business/Committees/Joint/Migration/Seasonal_Worker_Programme/ Submissions.

Nori, Michele. 2017. "The shades of green: migrants' contribution to EU agriculture: context, trends, opportunities, challenges." EUI Policy Brief 21/2017. https://cadmus.eui.eu/ handle/1814/49004.

Nunn, Nathan. 2019. "The Economics of Fair Trade." *NBER Reporter*, 2019:2. http://www. nber.org/reporter/2019number2/nunn.html.

Pabrua, Frances, and John Williams, Jr. 2003–4. "Challenges, Progress and Solutions in Produce Safety." *Food Safety magazine*, Dec. 2003/Jan. 2004. http://www.foodsafetymagazine.com/magazine-archive1/december-2003january-2004/challenges-progress-and-solutions-in-produce-safety/.

Parr, Broderick, Jennifer Bond, and Travis Minor. 2017. "Vegetables and Pulses Outlook." Economic Research Service VGS 359. October 17, 2017. https://www.ers.usda.gov/publications/pub-details/?pubid=85539.

Pawel, Miriam. 2009. *The Union of Their Dreams: Power, Hope, and Struggle in Cesar Chavez's Farm Worker Movement*. Bloomsbury. http://miriampawel.com/https:// miriampawel.com/the-union-of-their-dreams/.

Pawel, Miriam. 2014. *The Crusades of Cesar Chavez*. Bloomsbury. https://miriampawel. com/the-crusades-of-cesar-chavez/.

Pigot, Mami. 2003. "Decent Work in Agriculture." Prepared for ILO Symposium, April 30, 2003. http://www.ilo.org/wcmsp5/groups/public/---ed_dialogue/---actrav/documents/publication/wcms_111457.pdf.

Pratt, Lawrence, and Juan Manuel Ortega. 2019. "Protected Agriculture in Mexico: Building the Methodology for the First Certified Agricultural Green Bond." IADB. https://publications.iadb.org/en/protected-agriculture-mexico-building-methodology-first-certified-agricultural-green-bond.

President's National Advisory Committee on Rural Poverty. 1967. "The People Left Behind." https://files.eric.ed.gov/fulltext/ED016543.pdf.

President's National Advisory Committee on Rural Poverty. 1968. "Rural Poverty in the United States." https://catalog.hathitrust.org/Record/001325329.

Raynolds, Laura. 2018. "Fairtrade Certification, Labor Standards, and Labor Rights." *Sociology of Development*. Vol 4. No 2. https://online.ucpress.edu/socdev/article/4/2/191/83264/Fairtrade-Certification-Labor-Standards-and-Labor.

Ruhs, Martin. 2017. "Rethinking International Legal Standards for the Protection of Migrant Workers: The Case for a "Core Rights" Approach." *AJIL Unbound*, Vol. 111. http://www.cambridge.org/core/journals/american-journal-of-international-law/article/rethinking-international-legal-standards-for-the-protection-of-migrant-workers-the-case-for-a-core-rights-approach/6B32574F803A37598B7697069168C937.

Rural Migration News. 1999. "Guest Workers: Advocates Change." Vol 5. No 3. https://migration.ucdavis.edu/rmn/more.php?id=392.

Rural Migration News. 2018a. "California: Travel, Housing." Vol 24. No 4. https://migration.ucdavis.edu/rmn/more.php?id=2208.

Rural Migration News. 2018b. "Goodlatte H-2C; H-2B." https://migration.ucdavis.edu/rmn/more.php?id=2146.

Russo, Robert. 2018. "Collective Struggles: A Comparative Analysis of Unionizing Temporary Foreign Farm Workers in the United States and Canada." *Houston Journal of International Law*. https://commons.allard.ubc.ca/fac_pubs/492/.

Rye, Johan Fredrik, and Sam Scott. 2018. "International Labour Migration and Food Production in Rural Europe: A Review of the Evidence." *Sociologia Ruralis*: 58 (4) https://onlinelibrary.wiley.com/doi/full/10.1111/soru.12208.

Sarig, Yoav, James F. Thompson, and Galen K. Brown. 2000. "Alternatives to Immigrant Labor." CIS. https://cis.org/Report/Alternatives-Immigrant-Labor.

Schmitt, Guenther. 1991. "Why is the Agriculture of Advanced Western Economies still organized by family farms? Will this continue to be so in the future?" *European Review of Agricultural Economics*, Vol 18. No 4. https://academic.oup.com/erae/article-abstract/18/3–4/443/553546.

Scully-Russ, Ellen, and Kevin Boyle. 2018. "Sowing the Seeds of Change: Equitable Food Initiative Through the Lens of Vygotsky's Cultural–Historical Development Theory." *New Directions for Adult and Continuing Education*. 159: 37–52 https://onlinelibrary.wiley.com/doi/10.1002/ace.20286.

Seifert, Stefan, and Marica Valente. 2018. "An Offer that You Can't Refuse? Agri-mafias and Migrant Labor on Vineyards in Southern Italy." DIW Berlin Discussion Paper No. 1735. https://papers.ssrn.com/sol3/papers.cfm?abstract_id=3180586.

SIAP. 2017. "Atlas Agroalimentario 2017." http://www.gob.mx/siap/articulos/publicaciones-siap-generando-panoramas-claros-para-la-mejor-toma-de-decisiones?idiom=es.

Siudek, Tomasz, and Aldona Zawojska. 2016. "Foreign labour in agricultural sectors of some EU countries." AgEcon. https://ageconsearch.umn.edu/record/249797/.

Strom, Stephanie, and Steven Greenhouse. 2013. "On the Front Lines of Food Safety." *New York Times*, May 25, 2013. http://www.nytimes.com/2013/05/25/business/a-program-to-combat-food-contamination.html.

Strong, Jennifer, and Daniela Hernandez. 2018. "Robots Head for the Fields." *Wall Street Journal*. October 2, 2018. https://www.wsj.com/articles/robots-head-for-the-fields1538426976?mod=hp_jr_pos1.

Stupková, L. Crespo. 2016. "Global Value Chain in Agro-export Production and Its Socio-economic Impact in Michoacán, Mexico." *Agris on-line Papers in Economics and Informatics*. Vol 8. No 1. https://ageconsearch.umn.edu/bitstream/233962/2/agris_on-line_2016_1_crespo-stupkova.pdf.

Taylor, Edward, and Diane Charlton. 2018. *The Farm Labor Problem: A Global Perspective.* Academic Press. http://www.elsevier.com/books/the-farm-labor-problem/taylor/978-0-12-816409-9.

Todaro, Michael. 1969. "A Model of Labor Migration and Urban Unemployment in less Developed Countries." *American Economic Review*, Vol. 59, No. 1, 138–48. https://www.jstor.org/stable/1811100?seq=1#page_scan_tab_contents.

UNDP. 2009. "Human Development Report 2009 Overcoming barriers: Human mobility and development." http://hdr.undp.org/en/content/human-development-report-2009.

US Department of State. 2019. "Trafficking in Persons 2019." http://www.state.gov/bureaus-offices/under-secretary-for-civilian-security-democracy-and-human-rights/office-to-monitor-and-combat-trafficking-in-persons/.

US Senate. Subcommittee on Migratory Labor of the Committee on Labor and Public Welfare. 1960. "The Migrant Farm Worker in America." https://catalog.hathitrust.org/Record/001428765.

Verma, Veena. 2002. "The Mexican and Caribbean SAWP." http://www.nsi-ins.ca/wp-content/uploads/2012/11/2002-The-Mexican-and-Caribbean-Seasonal-Agricultural-Workers-Program-Regulatory-and-Policy-Framework-Executive-Summary.pdf.

Vietor, Richard and Haviland Sheldahl-Thomason. 2017. "Mexico: A Mosaic of Different Realities." Harvard Business School, Case 717–051. https://www.hbs.edu/faculty/Pages/item.aspx?num=52490.

Vosko, Leah F. 2016. "Blacklisting as a modality of deportability: Mexico's response to cir-cular migrant agricultural workers' pursuit of collective bargaining rights in British Columbia, Canada." *Journal of Ethnic and Migration Studies*, Vol. 42. http://www.tand-fonline.com/doi/abs/10.1080/1369183X.2015.1111134.

Vosko, Leah F. 2018. "Legal but Deportable: Institutionalized Deportability and the Limits of Collective Bargaining among Participants in Canada's Seasonal Agricultural Workers Program." *ILR Review*. Vol. 71. No 4. https://journals.sagepub.com/doi/full/10.1177/0019793918756055.

Vosko, Leah F., Eric Tucker, and Rebecca Casey. 2019. "Enforcing Employment Standards for Temporary Migrant Agricultural Workers in Ontario, Canada: Exposing Underexplored Layers of Vulnerability." *International Journal of Comparative Labour Law and Industrial Relations*. Vol. 35/2, 227–54 http://www.kluwerlawonline.com/abstract.php?area=Journals&id=IJCL2019011.

Whitener, Leslie, and Robert Coltrane. 1981 "Hired Farmworkers: Background and Trends for the Eighties." USDA ERS. https://files.eric.ed.gov/fulltext/ED211306.pdf.

Wood, Duncan, ed. 2017. "Charting a New Course: Policy Options for the Next Stage in U.S.-Mexico Relations." Wilson Center. https://www.wilsoncenter.org/article/charting-new-course-policy-options-for-the-next-stage-us-mexico-relations.

World Bank Data. 2008. "World Development Report 2008: Agriculture for Development." http://web.worldbank.org/WBSITE/EXTERNAL/EXTDEC/EXTRESEARCH/EXTWDR S/0,,contentMDK:23062293~pagePK:478093~piPK:477627~theSitePK:477624,00.html.

World Bank Data. 2017. "World Development Indicators." http://wdi.worldbank.org/tables.

Zahniser, Steven, Sahar Angadjivand, Thomas Hertz, Lindsay Kuberka, and Alexandra Santos. 2015. "NAFTA at 20: North America's Free-Trade Area and Its Impact on Agriculture." USDA WRS-15-01. February. http://www.ers.usda.gov/publications/pub-details/?pubid=40486.

Zahniser, Steven, Ed Taylor, Thomas Hertz, and Diane Charlton. 2018. "Farm Labor Markets in the United States and Mexico Pose Challenges for U.S. Agriculture." USDA EIB-201. November, 2018. http://www.ers.usda.gov/publications/pub-details/?pubid=90831.

Zhang, Zhao, Paul H. Heinemann, Jude Liu, Tara A. Baugher, and James R. Schupp. 2016. "The development of mechanical apple harvesting technology: A review." Transactions of the ASABE. 59(5): 1165–80. https://elibrary.asabe.org/abstract.asp?aid=47485.

Zlolniski, Christian. 2019. *Made in Baja The Lives of Farmworkers and Growers behind Mexico's Transnational Agricultural Boom.* UC Press. http://www.ucpress.edu/book/9780520300637/made-in-baja.

Index